VALUE AND UNEQUAL EXCHANGE
IN INTERNATIONAL TRADE

Contrary to the claims made by neoliberal governments and mainstream academics, this book argues that the huge increase in trade in recent decades has not made the world a fairer place: instead, the age of globalization has become a time of mass migration caused by increasing global inequality.

The theory of unequal exchange challenges the free trade doctrine, claiming that transfers of value from poorer to richer countries are hidden behind apparently equivalent market transactions. Following a critical review of the existing approaches, the book proposes a general theory of unequal exchange in the light of an innovative reconstruction of Marx's international law of value, in which money and exchange rates play a crucial role in decoupling value captured from value produced by different countries, even in perfectly competitive world markets. On this theoretical basis, the book provides an empirical analysis of the international transfers of value in both traditional trade and global value chains. The resulting world mapping of unequal exchange shows the geographical hierarchy of capital global exploitation by revealing a world divided into two quite separate camps of donor and receiving countries, the former being the poorer countries and the latter the richer countries.

This book is addressed to scholars and students of economics and social sciences, as well as activists of the North and the South, interested in a better understanding of the asymmetric power relations implied in global trade. It makes a significant contribution to the literature on political economy, trade, Marxism, international relations, and economic geography.

Andrea Ricci is tenured Assistant Professor in Economics at the University of Urbino, Italy. He obtained a MA in International Economics from the Graduate Institute of International and Development Studies of Geneva (Switzerland) and a PhD in Political Economy from the Università Politecnica delle Marche (Italy).

ROUTLEDGE FRONTIERS OF POLITICAL ECONOMY

For more information about this series, please visit: www.routledge.com/books/series/SE0345

VALUE AND UNEQUAL EXCHANGE IN INTERNATIONAL TRADE

The Geography of Global Capitalist Exploitation

Andrea Ricci

Routledge
Taylor & Francis Group

LONDON AND NEW YORK

First published 2021
by Routledge
2 Park Square, Milton Park, Abingdon, Oxon OX14 4RN

and by Routledge
605 Third Avenue, New York, NY 10158

Routledge is an imprint of the Taylor & Francis Group, an informa business

British Library Cataloguing-in-Publication Data
A catalogue record for this book is available from the British Library

Library of Congress Cataloging-in-Publication Data
Names: Ricci, Andrea, author.
Title: Value and unequal exchange in international trade: the geography of global capitalist exploitation/Andrea Ricci.
Description: Abingdon, Oxon; New York, NY: Routledge, 2021. |
Series: Routledge frontiers of political economy | Includes bibliographical references and index.
Identifiers: LCCN 2020053542 (print) | LCCN 2020053543 (ebook)
Subjects: LCSH: International trade. | Income distribution. |
Economics. | Capitalism.
Classification: LCC HF1379 .R526 2021 (print) | LCC HF1379 (ebook) |
DDC 382–dc23
LC record available at https://lccn.loc.gov/2020053542
LC ebook record available at https://lccn.loc.gov/2020053543

ISBN: 978-0-367-51397-9 (hbk)
ISBN: 978-0-367-51399-3 (pbk)
ISBN: 978-1-003-05366-8 (ebk)

Typeset in Times New Roman
by Deanta Global Publishing Services, Chennai, India

CONTENTS

FIGURES

TABLES

ABBREVIATIONS OF MARX'S WORKS CITED IN THE TEXT

MCGP: Marx, K., *Critique of the Gotha Programme.* Written: 1875. Source: *Marx/Engels Selected Works, Volume Three.* 1970. Moscow: Progress Publishers. Available at: www.marxists.org/arc hive/marx/works/1875/gotha/index.htm.

MEC: *Marx-Engels Correspondence.* Available at: www.marxists.org/ archive/marx/letters/index.htm

MECW: Marx, K., Engels, F., *Marx & Engels Collected Works, 50 volumes.* 1975–2004. London: Lawrence and Wishart.

MEOC: Marx, K., Engels, F., *Opere di Marx e Engels. Volume XXXI, due tomi.* 2011. Napoli: La Città del Sole.

MEW: Marx. K. *Economic Works of Karl Marx 1861–1864 The Process of Production of Capital. Draft Chapter 6 of Capital. Results of the Direct Production Process.* Available at: www.marxists.org/ archive/marx/works/1864/economic/index.htm.

MG: Marx, K., *Grundrisse. Foundations of the Critique of Political Economy (Rough Draft),* Written: 1857–1861. Source: *Grundrisse.* 1973. London: Penguin Books in association with New Left Review. Translated by Martin Nicolaus. Available at: www.marxis ts.org/archive/marx/works/1857/grundrisse/index.htm

MK1:   Marx, K. *Capital. A Critique of Political Economy. Volume I: The Process of Production of Capital.* First English edition of 1887. Translated: Samuel Moore and Edward Aveling, edited by Frederick Engels. Moscow: Progress Publisher. Online Version: Marx.org 1996, Marxists.org 1999. Available at: www.marxists.or g/archive/marx/works/1867-c1/index.htm

MK1FGE: Marx, K. *Das Kapital:Kritik der politischen Oekonomie. Erster Band. Buch I: Der Produktionsprocess des Kapitals.* 1867. Hamburg: Verlag von Otto Meissner.

MK2:   Marx, K. *Capital. A Critique of Political Economy. Volume II: The Process of Circulation of Capital.* Written: 1863-1878, edited for publication by Engels in 1885. Source: First English edition (1907). Moscow: Progress Publishers, 1956. Available at: www.m arxists.org/archive/marx/works/1885-c2/index.htm

MK3:   Marx, K., *Capital. A Critique of Political Economy. Volume III: The Process of Capitalist Production as a Whole*. Written: 1863–1883. First Published: 1894. Edited by Frederick Engels. Source: Institute of Marxism-Leninism, USSR, 1959. New York: International Publishers. Online Version: Marx.org 1996, Marxists .org 1999. Available at: www.marxists.org/archive/marx/works /1894-c3/index.htm

MKFGE: Marx, K. *Capital. A Critique of Political Economy. Volume I: The Process of Production of Capital. First Chapter*. First German edition of 1867. English translation by Albert Dragstedt. Source: Dragstedt, A. (1976). *Value: Studies by Karl Marx*. London: New Park Publications, pp. 7–40. Available at: www.marxists.org/arc hive/marx/works/1867-c1/commodity.htm

MMMs: Marx, K., *Mathematical Manuscripts*. Written: 1881. Edited by S. A. Yanovskaya. Translated: Pradip Bapsi. 1994. Calcutta: Viswakos Parisad.

MNW: Marx, K., *Notes on Adolph Wagner's "Lehrbuch der politischen Ökonomie"*. Written: 1881. Available at: www.marxists.org/arc hive/marx/works/1881/01/wagner.htm

MTSV: Marx, K., *Theories of Surplus-Value [Volume IV of Capital]*, Written: 1863. Source: Theories of Surplus Value. Moscow: Progress Publishers. Available at: www.marxists.org/archive/ marx/works/1863/theories-surplus-value/index.htm

MVPP: Marx, K., *Value, Price and Profit*. Written between the end of May and June 27, 1865. First published: 1898. Edited by Eleanor Marx Aveling. New York: International Co., Inc, 1969. Available at: www.marxists.org/archive/marx/works/1865/value-price-profit/ index.htm

PREFACE

This book, the result of long years of reflection and research, was written during turbulent months for both the individual and the collective life of each of us, wherever we are in the world. And it was written in Italy, the country that first experienced the devastating consequences of the Sars-CoV-2 virus on the bodies and minds of many people, even more than where it appeared for the first time. The images of the endless chain of military vehicles travelling into Bergamo at night, one of the richest cities in Europe, and loading hundreds of corpses for incineration, or those of an elderly, white-dressed Pope Francis walking alone in the rain of a ghostly and deserted Rome, will remain forever etched in my memory, as will the continuous ringing of sirens in the darkest days of the pandemic. The place where I work and teach, Urbino, the Ideal City of the Renaissance, has paid a high price in terms of infected and victims. As I hand over the manuscript to the publisher, the plague rages even more than before in Europe, after a short summer break, and we still do not know the final outcome of this story for each of us.

In these months, we lived in a continuous swing of worries and hopes. Our daily habits have been upset, especially in the most pleasant aspects of existence, those of affectivity, conviviality, and enjoyment. We have still learned little about the biology of the virus, but a great deal about the social effects of the pandemic in the world of global capitalism. All the injustices, contradictions, and inequalities of the social system have been amplified. Despite the heavy troubles suffered, I live in a small part of the world that is rich and well equipped. In other parts, less rich and less fortunate, the pain suffered by people is much greater. All of this is alarming and calls for urgent practical action for a radical transformation of the current social system before other even more devastating crises break out, starting with the climate and environmental emergency.

The virus put an end to a whole historical phase, that of neoliberal capitalist globalization, which began just 30 years ago with the fall of the Berlin Wall. The post-pandemic world of tomorrow will be very different from that of before. We do not know whether it will be better or worse. It is up to the individual and collective engagement and struggle of each of us, wherever we are, to make it better. This book deals with a salient aspect of the world of before, exploring on a theoretical and empirical level the phenomenon of unequal exchange in international trade, and its role in the enlarged reproduction of the gap in economic development between rich and poor countries. Although with varying degrees of intensity, the topics covered will remain relevant in the world to come, as long as the capitalist mode of production continues to exist.

A few limited parts of the book are revised and modified versions of my following papers: "The mathematics of Marx", *Lettera Matematica*, 2018, *6*(4), 221–5, for paragraph 3.3.1; "Unequal exchange in the age of globalization", *Review of Radical Political Economics*, 2019, *51*(2), 225–45, for paragraph 5.4.2; and "Unequal exchange and Global Value Chains", forthcoming in *Research in Political Economy*, vol. 36, for paragraphs 6.1 and 6.2. The vast majority of the arguments are, therefore, presented for the first time.

I spent the forced social isolation imposed by the rigid lockdown writing this book. It cost me effort, but it also gave me intellectual satisfaction. The same cannot be said for the people closest and dearest to me, as my voluntary self-isolation in studying and writing added to the discomfort of the pandemic emergency. Therefore, I would like to thank Loredana for the patience, love, and material and moral support she has given me during this difficult period.

November 23, 2020

1

INTRODUCTION

Theoretical foundations and measurement of unequal exchange

Andrea Ricci

1.1 The cultural hegemony of free trade neoliberalism

The Covid-19 pandemic in 2020 most likely marked the end of a long histori-cal phase of the world economy, known as capitalist globalization, which began exactly three decades earlier with the fall of the Berlin Wall and the close of the Cold War. During this period, the emergence and widespread diffusion of new information and communication technologies, which at that time were taking their first timid steps, transformed private, social, and economic life, thus supporting the expansion of the capitalist global market. The world economic geography has been profoundly restructured both in the localization of industrial activities, especially manufacturing, and in the size and composition of the international flows of goods, services, and financial assets, as never before in the history of capitalism. The hallmark of this phase has been the liberalization of domestic and international markets for goods, capital, and labour, pursued through a broad spectrum of neoliberal economic policies by almost all governments worldwide. The removal of all political, social, and environmental obstacles to the free play of market forces was promoted as the only instrument able to provide economic efficiency and distributive equity, ensuring economic growth and social welfare to all countries in the world regardless of their initial stage of development.

After 30 years, the shining promises of the neoliberal new world order have dissolved in the dramatic social impact of the pandemic emergency, which has revealed all the fragilities, inequalities, and injustices of capitalist globaliza-tion. The medical effects of the disease caused by the biological virus reinforce the economic effects of the crisis caused by the social virus of neoliberalism. Fundamental primary needs, such as the safeguarding of health and the pres-ervation of basic economic conditions of individuals and communities, have proved to be luxuries, reserved for a minority of privileged people in the world. The global birth inequalities of national citizenship add to the domestic class inequalities in determining the many drowned and the few saved in the post-pandemic world.

At other times, neoliberal globalization has appeared to be about to die. For the first time at the turn of the new millennium, when a powerful no-global popular movement inflamed the streets of the world in protest against neoliberal policies, bringing together farmers and students, workers and intellectuals, and churches and trade unions. There was a second time at the end of the first decade of the new century when the bursting of the Wall Street bubble and the bankruptcy of some big financial corporations produced a world economic crisis on a scale comparable to the Great Depression preceding the Second World War. On both occasions, after a short period of turmoil, the neoliberal order regained strength as the only possible option to govern the complex world of today. The neoliberal model showed a great capacity for adaptation, abandoning economic policy guidelines previously considered inviolable, such as monetary tightening and a balanced state budget, without ever sacrificing its fundamental tenets of the supremacy of private enterprise and capitalist competition.

The cultural hegemony of neoliberalism has been an essential element of its endurance to the adverse events provoked by itself, preserving a passive mass consensus despite the practical failure of its policies. The success of the neoliberal model has, however, resulted more from the weakness, both practical and theoretical, of possible alternatives than from its internal coherence. One of its fundamental political and ideological pillars is the doctrine of free trade, which advocates that international trade is mutually beneficial for all countries and ensures a fair distribution of the gains, provided that it is not hampered by public intervention. This view is as old as economic science itself, having been formulated since Adam Smith and David Ricardo, and subsequently retained by the neoclassical and marginalist schools as the main legacy of classical political economy. The neoliberal belief in the free market is stronger at the international level than it is at the national level. In fact, the possibility of *super partes* state intervention in domestic markets is contemplated to guarantee equal opportunities for competing firms. This is not the case in the international arena where sovereign states rather than private firms are the players, because the absence of an impartial world sovereign authority precludes this option. Hence, the market should be the only ruler of the global economy. The birth in 1995 of an international institution, the World Trade Organization, exclusively dedicated to sanctioning every minimum infraction of the rule of free trade, marked the crowning of the neoliberal vision of the world.

The political and theoretical critique of the ideology of free trade has been mainly focused on the unrealism of hypotheses rather than on the internal fallacy of doctrine. The huge gulf separating the ideal world of perfect competition between firms and equal power between states, from the real world of monopolies and imperialism, has been the privileged target of the political and cultural challenge to neoliberalism. The dominant ideology, however, had an easy time replying to this criticism by providing two types of reactions. On the one hand, neoliberalist fundamentalism reiterated with even greater firmness the need for market liberalization to counteract private and state monopolies, in an attempt to bring the real world closer to the ideal. On the other hand, reformist neoliberalism attempts to bring the ideal world closer to the real one by relaxing the hypotheses of the original model, with the introduction of market imperfections that can justify second-best exceptions of specific and limited government market regulations. Paradoxically, social and political anti-liberalist movements have often simultaneously supported both internal tendencies of the dominant ideology, endorsing both the enhancement of market competition to fight monopolies and partial redistributive measures, without being able to propose a consistent alternative system.

The lack of a coherent theoretical critique of the principle of free trade, not just in the real world but also in the imaginary world of perfect competition, has contributed to the neoliberal cultural hegemony. In fact, only a few have contended that a situation of perfectly competitive free trade, besides being far removed from reality, does not represent an ideal world at all, because it would be marked by horizontal exploitative relations between peoples and nations in addition to the vertical exploitation between social classes. This is certainly a politically slippery ground because it risks fuelling anti-democratic nationalist and revanchist movements, thereby concealing the class oppression of capital on labour both nationally and globally. In reality, the opposite is true. The refusal to investigate reality for fear of the consequences that knowledge can bring means hiding one's head in the sand, thus leaving the field free for authoritarian national and ethnic fundamentalism.

1.2 The "practical circumstances" of unequal exchange in heterodox and Marxist economics

However, there is also a strictly theoretical reason behind the lack of a radical critique of free trade, which brings together various heterodox economic approaches. It lies in the idea that the general equilibrium of perfect competition in all markets of goods and productive resources, within and between countries, represents a neutral situation between trade partners. Neutral in the sense that the exchange would be equivalent because the equilibrium market price would conform to the natural or ideal price or, for Marxists, to the value in its pure or modified form of the price of production. In other words, when all markets, including that of capital and labour, are perfectly competitive, both nationally and internationally, free trade would ensure equivalent international exchange between countries. Equivalent does not mean fair, but that the reasons for unfairness in the international distribution of wealth lie elsewhere than in the sphere of commodity exchange. They were identified from time to time in some "practical circumstances" of historical, political, or social nature such as the different economic starting conditions, the legacy of colonialism, or the over-exploitation of the workers of the Periphery. In any case, in a world of perfect competition, the commodity exchange would not play any autonomous role in determining the social and geographical distribution of the economic surplus, limiting itself to passively recording the underlying extra-market unequal conditions.

With regard to non-Marxist heterodox approaches, this statement is somehow tautological since the ideal or natural price, denoting a situation of equivalent exchange, is defined just as the equilibrium market price of a general perfect competition economy. In such a view, therefore, the inequality of international exchange can only arise from the violation of perfect competition in any one of the domestic or international markets. Non-Marxist approaches differ among themselves on the question of whether or not real capitalism can approach the ideal model by means of appropriate corrective measures and reforms. Those who consider it possible adopt a moderate and reformist attitude, while those who consider real capitalism irreformable adopt a more radical stance of moral revolt against the system, often lacerated by a sentiment of impotence faced with the gap between the rational and the real. The question stands out differently for Marxists.

In Marxist economic theory, the price is the monetary expression of an underlying economic category, the value, deriving from the abstract labour socially necessary for the production of the commodities exchanged on the market and consumed by society. Beyond the major differences between the various approaches on what value and abstract labour are, which will be discussed extensively in the book, in Marxist economics, the exchange is defined as equivalent when there is correspondence between the equilibrium price and value, or more precisely, when the market price fluctuates around a long-term regulating price determined by the value of the commodity. The automatic mechanism that ensures this result in capitalism is referred to as the law of value. Price, therefore, represents in the sphere of commodity circulation the realization in money form of the value created in the sphere of production. In the economic works that Marx left us, the correspondence between regulating market price and value does not occur in two cases. The first exception derives from extra economic factors resulting from natural or artificial monopolies in the production or exchange of commodities. They somehow represent concrete historical deviations of the pure capitalist mode of production, which undermine its internal coherence except in one case. The virtuous exception providing dynamism to the capitalist system is the temporary technological monopolistic advantage that an innovative firm has over the average of the sector, which allows it to sell its production at a price higher than its individual value. In the long run, however, this advantage is going to disappear because of capitalist competition. The second exception to the perfect equivalence of market exchange is instead a structural feature of a mature competitive capitalist system resulting from the equalization of profit rates between industries.

Marx's theoretical intention was to show that capitalism is a contradictory system based on exploitative relations even in its pure form of perfect competition when the law of value can operate without any obstacles whatsoever. In a general static equilibrium of perfect competition, the capitalist profit derives exclusively from the equivalent exchange of a very special commodity, the labour power, which, unique among all other commodities, is able to create a value greater than its own value when used productively. The monopoly of the conditions of production by capital, resulting from the private ownership of the means of production, is what allows the appearance of the capitalist surplus. This latter represents the specific capitalist social form taken by the economic surplus, resulting from the difference between the resources employed and the product obtained from the economic activity of the whole society.

The analysis of the formation of the capitalist social surplus is the subject of the first book of Marx's *Capital*. In this theoretical framework, Marx exposes the functioning of the law of value in its purest form, considering only the competition between individual capitals operating within a given sector of production, i.e. producing a commodity of the same type. At a high level of abstraction, this can be formally described as the competition in a self-replacing system between firms producing a composite commodity, the net product, which is the sum of the quantity of products remaining after subtracting the quantity of each product used as an intermediate good in the social process of production. Traditionally, in Marxist economics, this situation is described as the competition between capitals of identical organic composition equal to the social average, where the organic composition of capital refers to the ratio between means of production, or constant capital, and labour, or variable capital. The distribution of the capitalist social surplus among the many individual capitals composing the total social capital occurs through the law of value. Or, looking at the thing from another point of view more in line with reality, the competition between individual capitalist profit-seeking firms spontaneously generates an objective regulatory mechanism of distribution of the capitalist social surplus represented by the law of value. In static equilibrium, the distribution of capitalist social surplus arises through the determination of the regulating market price resulting from the functioning of the law of value. Under perfect competition and an identical organic composition of capital, the regulating price corresponds to the value produced in each firm, and consequently, all market exchanges are equivalent exchanges.

In the third book of *Capital*, Marx removes the hypothesis of an identical organic composition of capital, used to pinpoint in its essence the formation of the capitalist surplus resulting from the social exchange between total capital and labour power of the whole society, in order to address the more concrete case of capitalist competition between firms producing different commodities. In this situation, if commodities were exchanged as before at their value, the firms operating in sectors with a lower-than-average organic composition of capital would obtain a higher rate of profit than those in the opposite situation, since they would extract more surplus value per unit of capital. Inter-industry competition, therefore, leads to a modification of the law of value assuring the equalization of profit rates for all capitals. The market regulating price this time no longer fluctuates around value but around the price of production, determined by the sum of the average industry cost of production and the general average rate of profit. This modification of the law of value implies transfers of value in equilibrium from sectors with a lower organic composition of capital to those with a higher one. In a pure capitalist economy, therefore, exchanges normally are non-equivalent because the commodities are not sold at their value, but at a value modified by the equalization of profit rates forced by capitalist competition.

The formation of prices of production is the only essential modification of the law of value that Marx has fully analyzed, although not the only one he suggested in referring to the international market. It is also the only one admitted by the subsequent Marxist economic theory, in which the divergence between regulating market price and price of production can derive exclusively from extra economic impediments to the complete implementation of the capitalist law of value. According to the prevailing Marxist economics, which generally ignored Marx's suggestions on the international dimension, in an equilibrium of perfect competition on all markets, commodities are exchanged at prices of production, and the only transfers of value operating in trade derive from the formation of the general rate of profit. The price of production is the Marxist transposition of the classical natural or ideal price into the concrete capitalist economy. The exchanges that take place on its basis, therefore, should not be considered as unequal in the strict sense, rather as mere non-equivalent exchanges, because they occur in full compliance with capitalist social rationality. In this sense, non-equivalent exchange would represent the specific capitalist form of equivalent market exchange. The unequal exchange in international trade would, therefore, constitute a deviation from the law of value, resulting from concrete historical circumstances extraneous to pure capitalist logic, imposed by direct or indirect coercive methods by imperialist powers or large transnational monopolistic corporations. Such a view has sometimes led Marxist economists to look favourably on economic globalization and trade liberalization as long as it is accompanied by the fight against monopolies.

Chapter 2 of this book presents a review of the main arguments brought against the doctrine of free trade by the various economic schools that have supported the thesis of unequal exchange in international trade. Starting from ancient mercantilism to subsequent neomercantilism, economic structuralism, and dependency theory of more recent times, non-Marxist heterodox approaches have highlighted a series of typical exceptions to perfect competition in domestic and international markets of goods and production factors that determine an unequal distribution of the trade gains between countries at different levels of development. Marxist approaches have in turn outlined, in addition to value transfers resulting from different organic compositions of national capitals, the impediments to the full enforcement of the law of value that arise from monopolistic conditions on the side of capital, with the theory of monopoly capitalism, and labour, with Emmanuel's thesis on the bargaining power of Western trade unions.

The literature review reveals that the thesis of unequal exchange has not yet found its own independent theoretical foundation, as a structural element inherent in the normal functioning of the capitalist economy at world level, but rather derives from the imperfect operation of the competitive laws governing capitalism, be they the law of supply and demand or the law of value. This does not mean that unequal exchange theories do not attach considerable importance to the phenomenon, as one of the main causes of differences in economic development between rich and poor countries. On the contrary, they all consider unequal exchange as a concrete historical way of reproducing huge inequalities on a global scale. However, the lack of an independent theoretical foundation makes unequal exchange a political, historical, or sociological phenomenon more than economic in the strict sense, placing it at a more concrete level of analysis than the fundamental laws of the global capitalist mode of production. In other words, by removing the specific practical circumstances, it would be possible to envisage a capitalist world economy without unequal exchange, where international trade between different states takes place on the basis of equivalent exchange relations. In this way, however, it becomes hard to understand why capitalist globalization is to be opposed, rather than promoted to its extreme consequences by pursuing full liberalization of all domestic and international markets, as the neoliberal utopia demands. The lack of an independent theoretical foundation of the unequal exchange thus facilitates the popularity of the doctrine of free trade.

1.3 The theoretical foundations of unequal exchange

An independent theoretical foundation requires that unequal exchange in international trade arises as a natural product of the capitalist mode of production on a global scale, in its purest form of a perfectly competitive world economy. The thesis presented in this book is that this independent theoretical foundation can be found in Marx's value theory. A consistent formulation of the international law of value, following Marx's suggestions, can reveal the exploitative relations between developed and backward countries hidden behind the appearance of one price of commodities in the world market, resulting from the free and unconditional play of perfectly competitive market forces.

In addition to the formation of prices of production, in some isolated passages of his work, Marx mentions a further essential modification of the law of value at the international level compared with the pure version outlined in the first book of *Capital*. Marx's intentions were to conclude the critique of political economy with two books on the state and international trade. According to the original plan, the examination of the world market should have been the culmination of the investigation on the capitalist mode of production. Unfortunately, Marx did not manage to complete his project and the last books of *Capital* were never written. Afterwards, Marxist economics did not follow Marx's suggestions on the topic, and so the international law of value was not the focus of systematic research able to clarify its essential difference with the national case. On the rare occasions when a few Marxist economists have ventured into the subject, the limits of the prevailing general interpretations of Marx's value theory have prevented meaningful theoretical conclusions to be reached. In fact, the specificity of the international law of value can be grasped only through a reconstruction of the fundamental categories of Marxian theory, from the concept of value to its determinations of substance, form, and measure, which goes beyond the prevailing interpretations.

Chapter 3, after reviewing the salient points of the Marxist debate on abstract labour as the substance of value, outlines the concept of value as a social algorithm. This concept of value differs from the prevailing interpretations because of its processual and relational rather than substantial character. In the substantialist view, value is conceived as a qualitative property of the commodity deriving from a social substance objectified in it, the abstract labour. This property is alternatively intended as the quality common to all commodities to be the product of human labour in the productivist approach or to have market exchangeability in the circulationist approach. In any case, the value is understood as something static, objective, "dead", as a social quality or substance of the commodity that is added to its natural qualities such as weight, length, hardness, etc. In reality, abstract labour, the value-creating substance, is living labour, labour in motion, a pure activity considered at the very moment in which it is performed, but not as concrete action of the individual worker, rather as social labour of the whole society. The substance of value is potentiality in becoming rather than actuality already become. Objectified abstract labour is expressed by the determination of exchange value as the form of value, not by the substance of value, which is processuality, subjectivity in movement. Value is just the mechanism, procedure, or code that transforms the living social subjectivity of abstract labour into the dead social objectivity of exchange value. In this sense, value is a social algorithm, a real abstraction.

The processual concept of value allows for a coherent reading of the intricate development of value determinations in Marx's theory. The private character of production in capitalism determines the splitting of the general category of social labour, defined as the set of human activities required for the production of goods necessary for the satisfaction of social needs, into abstract labour necessary for social production and abstract labour necessary for social consumption. Abstract labour, with its dualistic determination, is the historically specific social form assumed in capitalism by social labour in general. The code of value, which originates from the spontaneous and uncoordinated activity of individual market players as a generative structure of social order, restores to unity the dualism of abstract labour. It thus ensures in an impersonal and unconscious way the division of social labour among members of the community, which in pre-capitalist societies was the conscious and planned outcome of social practices inherited from tradition or dictated by political and religious constraints. We will see how the modern mathematical notion of algorithms was anticipated by Marx in the study of differential calculus included in the mathematical manuscripts written in the last years of his life. The dual nature of the social substance of value as abstract labour is reflected in the dualism of its social form of expression of exchange value, as value in production and value in circulation. Given the dual nature of the exchange value, its magnitude can be conveyed in the two distinct measures of market exchange ratio of commodities, or extrinsic measure, and quantity of objectified socially necessary abstract labour, or intrinsic measure. The social algorithm of value acts as an operator of market equivalence between these two expressions of exchange value, thus achieving the consistent division of social labour and the continuous renewal of the cycle of material and social reproduction of capitalist society.

In a capitalist economy, the exchange of commodities takes place through the general intermediation of money. Capitalism is by its nature a monetary economy of private production and circulation of commodities where money is the only visible manifestation of the dual measure of exchange value. Therefore, Chapter 4 is devoted to money and how it can simultaneously express both intrinsic and extrinsic measures of exchange value in the form of market price. The nature of money is the object of a long Marxist debate, which has given rise to conflicting approaches, both deriving from a substantialist concept of value that leads to one-sided notions of abstract labour and exchange value. These different interpretations can be schematically divided into productivist and circulationist, including the traditional and more recent versions of both. The former argues that socially necessary labour time spent in production is the only measure of value and money merely represents the phenomenal reflection of it, thus determining the collapse of the social form into the social substance of value. The latter, on the other hand, claims that abstract labour arises exclusively in the act of commodity circulation where money is the only possible measure of value, thus determining the collapse of the social substance into the social form of value.

Marxist debate has focused on the commodity nature of money, and in particular on whether Marx's assumption of gold as money-commodity is essential to the labour theory of value. If so, the definitive demonetization of gold in the 1970s would make Marx's original formulation obsolete. The thesis argued in Chapter 4 is that money is by its very nature a commodity in general, which in capitalism can take different specific forms without changing its functions as the general intermediary of exchange and measure of value. Marx, in the first book of *Capital*, assumes that gold is the money-commodity for "the sake of simplicity", and not for a logical or theoretical necessity. Both in the form of a capitalist commodity such as gold and in the form of a non-capitalist commodity such as inconvertible fiat money, money in capitalism always expresses visibly both the intrinsic and extrinsic measures of the exchange value of commodities. The only difference between the two forms of money-commodity is in the mode of expression of the intrinsic measure of value, which in the case of gold is immediate as the abstract labour time socially necessary to produce one unit of it, while in the case of fiat money it is mediated by the monetary expression of labour time or MELT. The MELT as the real measure of value expresses the equivalent conversion ratio that exists at a given time between the intrinsic unit of measurement in labour time and the extrinsic unit of measurement in money. The proposed definition of MELT here is not subject to problems of circular reasoning that it encounters in other interpretations of Marx's value theory, such as in the *New Interpretation*, because the equivalent conversion of the extrinsic and intrinsic measures of exchange value is ensured by their common reference to the same set of material objects, tangible and intangible, which constitutes the social product of a given period. The bare physical objectuality of the commodity, its merely bodily form, acts as the common mediating element within the dualistic social determinations of substance, form and measure of value.

The substantialist notions of value, whether productivist or circulationist, consider only the social form of the process of production and circulation, neglecting the material form. In this way, value loses its conceptual unity as the prime mover of the capitalist economy and takes on a dual nature expressed in the opposition between substance and form of value, socially necessary labour and money, both considered as internally unitary determinations without any possible common denominator between them. In the processual notion, on the contrary, value as a social algorithm, real abstraction, is a primary and as such unitary concept, which is articulated in the internally dualistic determinations of substance and form of value. Within both, the dualistic determinations of substance and form of value there is a common element consisting of the material, bodily, form of commodity. The capitalist social process of production and circulation is aimed at the valorization of capital, but it must always simultaneously ensure the material reproduction of society, as a subordinate but essential result for its existence. Periodically, economic crises break the coherence between material and social reproduction, but they represent transitory periods that are overcome by the re-establishment of the necessary social and material conditions of capital reproduction; otherwise, the system could not survive its crises. In capitalism, the abstraction of social labour in general concretely materializes in the direct, effective labour time performed by all the workers employed in the production of all the commodities exchanged in the market. At the level of the whole society, the quantity of abstract labour, in both of its determinations of labour necessary for social production and social consumption, necessarily coincides with the total direct labour supplied in a given period for the production of the exchanged commodities. Abstract labour, in turn, produces exchange values that are necessarily objectified in physical material objects, whether tangible or intangible. The social form of exchange value, in both of its determinations of value in production and value in circulation, is always inevitably coupled with the material form of commodity, where use value, the product of concrete labour, and exchange value find their common bearer. The circulation of commodities, therefore, is not only the circulation of exchange values in monetary form but simultaneously circulation of exchanges values in the bodily form of material objects. The social algorithm of value establishes the fundamental equivalence between the expression in objectified abstract labour time and the monetary expression of exchange value, placing both as equivalents of the physical quantity of goods produced and exchanged in a given period. As it will be shown, the physical quantity of the social product acts as a common denominator allowing, on the one hand, the simultaneously visible manifestation in money form of both intrinsic and extrinsic measures of value, and, on the other hand, their mutual equivalent conversion into MELT.

The dualism of the determinations of substance, form, and measure of value, which the social algorithm of value restores to unity, opens the possibility of non-equivalence in market exchange. The equivalence in fact is valid only at the general level of society as a whole, where value created in production is necessarily equal to value in circulation. This is not the case at the level of individual exchanges, which are normally never equivalent since general equivalence is the result of a statistical average, as Marx states. The non-equivalence of individual exchanges implies that the exchange value created in production is quantitatively different from the exchange value realized in circulation. In this situation, a universal labour unit converts into a different amount of money units for the two trading partners, resulting in individual MELTs different from the average social MELT. When exchanges are non-equivalent, value transfers between the elementary units of the system occurs in the process of the circulation of commodities. In *Capital*, Marx deals with two forms of non-equivalent exchange, each of them deriving from the action of capitalist competition in perfectly competitive markets, within the same industry and between different industries, respectively. Value transfers take place in the first book within the same industry between individual firms with labour productivity different from the social average, and then in the third book between individual industries with the organic composition of capital different from the average of total social capital. In the first case, they are temporary because capitalist competition acts for their elimination, while in the second case, they are permanent, and involve a modification of the law of value resulting from the formation of prices of production that ensure the equalization of profit rates in all industries.

In addition to inter-industry and intra-industry competition between capitals, there is a third form of capitalist competition, occurring on the world market between different national capitals. Marx proposed to deal with the effects of this third form of capitalist competition on the law of value in the planned book on international trade and the world market, which he never wrote. However, he left some important indications in several passages of his published and unpublished work, expressly referring to a further essential modification that the law of value undergoes at the international level when considering the competition between national capitals on the world market. Moreover, he also expressly mentioned the exploitation of rich countries over poor ones resulting from value transfers operating in international trade, even in perfect competition. These suggestions show how Marx regarded unequal exchange at the international level as a structural and not accidental feature of the global capitalist mode of production. However, they have been largely ignored or neglected by subsequent Marxist literature.

The reconstruction of the category of value and its dualistic determinations of substance, form, and measure allows us, in Chapter 5, to identify which are the essential modifications of the law of value at an international level, and why they give rise to unequal exchange as a structural phenomenon of the global capitalist economy regardless of its degree of competitiveness. In the world market, the elementary units are individual countries, rather than firms as in the domestic market. After having determined, following Marx's suggestions, the universal labour unit resulting from the average of different national labour intensities, we will see how the essential modification of the law of value is the consequence of international differences in labour productivity, which lead to different monetary expressions of the international value per unit of universal labour between countries. This modification is directly reflected in the different value of money between countries according to their level of economic development, which manifests itself in a systematically higher price level in more developed than in less developed economies.

This phenomenon, already noted by Ricardo and subsequently proven by a large amount of empirical work up to the present day, is known in literature as the "Penn effect". It shows that the long-term equilibrium real exchange rate is systematically overvalued for richer countries, and vice versa undervalued for poorer ones, compared with the level that would guarantee the international purchasing power parity of different national currencies. The "Penn effect" represents an embarrassing unresolved enigma for neoclassical economics because it contradicts the theoretical foundations of the standard theory of international trade that underlies the doctrine of free trade. In fact, if the long-term equilibrium real exchange rate is different from the purchasing power parity rate, the terms of trade, indicating the relative price of imported and exported goods of equal value, are systematically different from unity, and would make international trade not equivalent. Countries with an overvalued real exchange rate would gain from international trade to the detriment of countries with an undervalued real exchange rate, obtaining in exchange for a given volume of exported goods a number of imported goods of higher value. Since the overvaluation of the real exchange rate affects richer countries, international trade favours them at the expense of poorer countries. Despite the vast amount of research, no convincing explanation has succeeded in reconciling the consolidated empirical evidence of the "Penn effect" with the neoclassical theory of free trade. Similarly, the rare attempts to formulate a heterodox theory of international trade failed in this regard.

In the international law of value presented in Chapter 5, the "Penn effect" finds a consistent theoretical justification. It is the empirical manifestation of the difference between exchange value in production and exchange value in circulation of the commodities in the world market, which results in unequal exchange in international trade and involves a systematic transfer of value from less developed to more developed countries. The international law of value ensures that a commodity from whatever country produced is sold at the same identical price on the perfectly competitive world market, and yet this equilibrium international price implies international transfers of value. These value transfers between countries on the international market have a similar nature to value transfers between firms of the same industry with different labour productivities on the domestic market. However, there is a fundamental difference between the two situations because on the international market the differences between individual value and social value of commodities tend to persist and reproduce continuously, while on the domestic market they are eliminated by firms' competition. The crucial factor that differentiates the international law of value from the domestic version is the simultaneous presence of different national currencies, each expression of a specific national unit of social labour, having a different international purchasing power as a result of the international competition of capitals.

Unlike neoclassical general economic equilibrium, and also many Marxist interpretations of labour value theory, in Marx, the thesis of the long-term neutrality of money is not valid. The existence of different currencies, in which national prices are expressed, prevents the competitive mechanism from eliminating long-term differences between individual and social value in the world market, as it happens instead at domestic level between firms with different labour productivity. Real exchange rate adjustments, both under fixed and flexible exchange rates, crystallize this difference and thus allow labour productivity to act in the same way as labour intensity in defining the international value of commodities, in contrast to what happens domestically. In the last paragraph of Chapter 5, a formal disaggregated general model of unequal exchange is presented in accordance with the theoretical lines previously devised, which is able to encompass as special cases all the various forms of unequal exchange and inter and intra-industry value transfers identified in the literature reviewed in Chapter 2.

1.4 Mapping unequal exchange in the actual global economy

The empirical measurement of unequal exchange in the actual world economy is addressed in Chapter 6. The process of economic globalization in the last 30 years has not been confined to the sphere of commodity circulation with the boom in trade flows between countries; it has also affected the sphere of production. The liberalization of goods, labour, and capital markets, the reduction of transport costs and shipping times, and the spread of new information and communication technologies have all contributed to the emergence of a new model of organization of production on a global scale. This new industrial paradigm has replaced the old vertical and spatial integration of production with a new horizontal integration under the control of large multinational corporations based on the dispersion of the manufacturing cycle between firms and countries around the globe aimed at minimizing costs. It has thus given rise to what in the specialist literature are called global value chains (GVC), focusing on the delocalization of stages of production through the practices of outsourcing and offshoring, in which the value realized on the final market is produced to varying degrees by each stage of production in a multitude of factories scattered all over the world. The resulting new international division of labour is characterized by the concentration of the intermediate stages of processing and material assembly in peripheral countries, where labour costs are lower, and the initial and final stages of conception, design, engineering, and marketing are in central countries, where the major part of the distributed value added is gathered. All this has led to the dependent industrialization of several enclaves in some peripheral countries, once specialized in agricultural products and raw materials, and extensive deindustrialization in central countries. It has resulted everywhere in the strengthening of the power of the global capital to exploit labour and appropriate the economic surplus.

The new organization of world production has also had consequences on the structure of international trade. The flows of intermediate and semi-finished goods have strongly increased their share in total imports and exports of each country, so that they account for a large part of world trade. This category of goods crosses the border several times to be processed in a number of different countries before reaching the final consumer market. The traditional method of recording imports and exports based on gross value, used in official balance of payments accounting, has therefore become less and less indicative of the countries' real trade position, as it is subject to repeated double counting. A more accurate picture of net trade flows, on the other hand, is given by exports and imports measured in terms of value added, the statistics of which are available in various databases compiled by international institutions and research centres. The empirical measurement of value transfers presented in Chapter 6 uses the UNCTAD-EORA annual data on value-added trade, along with data from other official international economic institutions for the other variables of the model and considers 175 countries aggregated in 16 regions of the world economy for the period 1990–2019. The empirical analysis is based on an aggregate model developed in line with the theoretical foundations established in previous chapters, which can identify international intra-industry value transfers representing unequal exchange in the strict sense, divided into transfers within GVC, and embedded in traditional domestic final exports.

The picture that emerges from the empirical analysis is that of a world divided into two rigidly separated parts, with, on the one hand, the richer countries of the Centre, which continuously benefited from an unequal exchange over the entire period, and on the other hand, the poorer countries of the world's Periphery, which constantly suffered an outflow of domestically produced value through trade. These latter countries, in turn, are divided into two groups of countries, those of the emerging Periphery, affected by a rapid process of industrialization that has brought their per capita income closer to the world average, and those of the poor Periphery, where more than half of the world's population lives, with very low per capita income levels. Both the aggregated and detailed analysis by regions shows that in the period of globalization, although with alternating phases of expansion and contraction and with a geographical restructuring of flows, the dimension of unequal exchange has continued to grow, especially within GVC.

The value transfers resulting from international trade are a substantial cause of the huge inequalities in economic and social development in the global capitalist economy. They configure a mechanism of global exploitation by the capital of central countries towards peripheral workers, alongside the one suffered by them at a domestic level, involving the drainage of value achieved through the channel of international trade. The concrete manifestation of this mechanism is the structural misalignment in real exchange rates, which determine long-run terms of trade permanently unfavourable to the less developed countries. The resulting international monetary hierarchy leads to the emergence of a "currency rent" for the richer countries resulting from their monopoly of hard currencies in the financial and foreign exchange markets. The presence of monopolistic conditions on the goods market only exacerbates the unequal exchange spontaneously generated by the operation of the international law of value in perfectly competitive markets. Contrary to the doctrine of free trade, the liberalization of international trade, rather than granting a fair benefit to all the countries involved, consolidates the world's economic and political hierarchy by reproducing on an enlarged scale the predominance of the capitalistically more developed Centre and the dependence and subordination of the Periphery, both in its emerging regions and in the poorest and marginalized ones. The theoretical and analytical framework proposed in this book aims to provide appropriate conceptual and operational tools to investigate the phenomenon of unequal exchange in the world economy, in order to contribute to practical actions promoting a more just and rational international economic and social order.

2

THE HERESY OF UNEQUAL EXCHANGE

Andrea Ricci

2.1 The antecedent: The dispute between mercantilism and free trade

The sharing of costs and benefits of international trade between countries is a long-standing issue in economic and political debate. It precedes the emergence of classical political economy as an independent academic discipline distinct from moral and political philosophy. This new field of study arose during the second half of the 18th century in France with the works of the physiocrats, like Turgot and Quesnay, and notably in Britain with the publication of the Adam Smith (2010) magnum opus, *An Inquiry into the Nature and Causes of the Wealth of Nations*, in 1776. In that period, classical political economy developed in response to the mercantilist trade and economic policies pursued by the Absolutist states, dominant in continental Europe up to the French Revolution, and the young British parliamentary monarchy, still strongly influenced by the interests of feudal landlords.

2.1.1 Mercantilism

Mercantilism was not a coherent and systematic doctrine but rather a collection of concrete practices and behaviours, adopted by European states from the 16th to the 18th centuries, with regard to economic policy and trade regulation.[1] It was intellectually supported by a large crowd of advisers to the prince of varying talent, including some very bright minds like Thomas Mun (1571–1641) and Sir James Steuart (1713–1780) among others, manly through writing pamphlets and popular essays designed to persuade the nascent public opinion of the effectiveness of government policies. The ultimate goal of mercantilist practices was the strengthening of the power of the Crown at both domestic and international level. For this purpose, the growth of the Treasury's spending ability was the fundamental intermediate objective of the entire economic policy required for financing the expansionistic ambitions of the Royal House. The best way of ensuring the success of such a strategy was the influx of gold achieved by any means necessary, be it trade, colonial pillaging, or piracy. In this contest, the hunger of gold was not an end in itself, as implied by the "fear of goods" reproached by the Swedish economic historian Eli Heckscher (2013) in his massive and influential work on *Mercantilism* published in 1931. It was rather motivated by the potential availability of material resources at the disposal of the State assured by the hoarding of precious metals in the public purse. In this sense, the mercantilists always considered money as the representative of use value, quite the opposite of the bourgeois primacy of the exchange value and capital valorization.

The typical mercantilist economic policy was a mix of domestic market liberalization and foreign market regulation. The promotion of domestic trade during the mercantilist era can be explained by the government intention of assuring that a part of private commercial gains flowed back into the public finances as gold receipts, by means of taxes, duties, and other levies of all kinds on domestic incomes and transactions. To this end, the mercantilist policy promoted the unification of the internal market by removing the feudal constraints that previously restricted the free movements of goods, capital, and people inside national boundaries. However, one of the most effective ways to ensure the increase in public finances was the attainment of a regular inflow of gold from abroad to be partly converted into higher state revenues through the exercise of seigniorage rights in the coinage of money. This goal was pursued through the achievement of a permanent imbalance between purchases and sales of commodities from and to other countries to ensure a positive trade balance. Unlike domestic trade, international trade was, therefore, subject to strict state regulation. Government interventions in international transactions, mainly in the form of import duties and export subsidies, were the distinctive protectionist policies of the mercantilist State, seeking to ensure a permanent manipulation of the terms of trade[2] to its own advantage. On the ideological level, the typical mercantilist point of view on a commercial transaction is an arm-wrestling match where there is necessarily a winner and a loser, and the very idea of a mutual and common advantage deriving from this kind of exchange is ruled out in advance. In this view, considering the country as a whole, domestic trade is neutral with respect to national net benefits because the gain of some is the loss of others, but this is not the case in international trade that ends up resembling a struggle rather than a mutual economic relationship.

It is possible to distinguish at least three different conceptions of the mercantilist gains from trade.[3] In an early version, the winner is always the seller, the one who receives cash payment, because the hoarding of precious metals is considered as the ultimate end of trade activity. This rough and primitive idea was soon overtaken in favour of another more elaborate conception whereby trade gain always takes the form of relative profit, or "profit upon alienation", originating from the sale of the commodity above its real value, or vice versa the purchase below its real cost. Since in mercantilist economic thought the real value of a commodity is ultimately defined by the gold or silver received in exchange for it,[4] at the aggregate national level, trade with foreign countries is favourable when there is a surplus in the balance of trade, that is when the total real value of

17

exports exceeds that of imports. In both notions, trade benefits are static since the exchange is regarded as a non-repeatable zero-sum game, where the given value of the whole transaction is split once and for all in two asymmetrical parts, and total gains and loss equalize.

The third mercantilist view on the gains from trade is far more modern and sophisticated because the exchange is not seen as an isolated act, but it is framed into a dynamic series of economic actions. Trade is advantageous if it makes full use of all the productive capacity of the player involved. This occurs for the seller when the good has absorbed all the possible labour needed for its production, or further labour can be added to the purchased items for the buyer. In this way, it is convenient to export finished goods and import raw materials and intermediate products for a country, because that maximizes the real returns of trade by stimulating the generation of additional national income and full employment. Hence, the recommendation to specialize in producing and exporting labour-intensive commodities, such as manufactured and luxury goods, and importing matter-intensive commodities, such as agricultural and primary products. However, also in this dynamic version, focused on the commodity composition of the trade balance, the fact remains that in commercial relations there is always a winner and a loser, and therefore, trade is by its own nature an unequal exchange.

In recent times, economic historiography has stressed the variety and complexity of the mercantile system by highlighting how the most brilliant thinkers of the period were unquestionably aware of the link between a favourable balance of trade and the expanding domestic production and increasing productivity.[5] In the light of what already stated by Marx and Keynes,[6] the contribution made by mercantilism to the transition from a natural to a money economy is now widely recognized by supporting a process of primitive accumulation of capital and allowing low domestic interest rates and the steady growth of aggregate demand.

In the mercantilist era, primitive accumulation of capital was in fact the result of a twofold process of spoliation of the national peasantry and foreign territories through the enclosures of common fields and international transfers of value and wealth, respectively, in what has been described as an "accumulation by dispossession" attained by both coercive and consensual means.[7] According to several Marxist scholars, the unequal exchange pursued by means of mercantilist trade played an important role in the capitalist modernization of Western European countries, particularly Britain, France, and Holland, along with colonial exploitation, chattel slavery, and filibustering expeditions.[8] A prominent Japanese historian of economic thought, Noboru Kobayashi, concluded his lifelong research on the subject by claiming that the proper definition of mercantilism is just the economic theory of primitive capital accumulation.[9] In turn, on the macroeconomic conditions of capitalist development, Keynesian authors underlined how the influx of gold, resulting from the success of mercantilist trade policies, contributed to increase the internal money circulation and to keep down the domestic interest rate, thus promoting investment and full employment.[10] For this reason, Post-Keynesian economists locate in mercantilism the roots of the demand-orientated theory of economic development, in which the balance of payments represents the ultimate constraint on the long-run equilibrium rate of growth.[11]

According to these modern interpretations, therefore, the mercantilist mixture of domestic market liberalization and trade protectionism boosted the development of capitalism. But that was not the idea of the founders of the classical political economy.

2.1.2 The dogma of free trade and neo-mercantilist exceptions

Classical political economy was originally part of the grand design of Illuminism, where the general cultural and philosophical project aimed at subverting the spiritual foundations of the ancient regimes by undermining their religious, moral, political, and even economic legitimacy. At the social level, this hegemonic plan was rooted in the surging rise of a new class, the Third Estate, a variegated social group consisting of entrepreneurs, merchants, artisans, moneylenders, freelancers, and adventurers of various kinds, grown in the folds of the struggle between absolutism and feudalism. The common secular faith of these new social circles was trade and economic freedom, which provided an excellent ideological platform able to meld the nascent system of beliefs and moral principles with the material interests of the bourgeoisie.

In this new and revolutionary view, the social order is no more the result of a system of rules sanctioned by a higher power as a direct offshoot of a divine plan, but rather the spontaneous outcome of a myriad of individual and uncoordinated actions, all of which motivated by selfish interests displayed in the working of the market. Unlike the apologetic ignorance of the history of the vulgar bourgeois economists repeatedly ridiculed by Marx, in the founders of classical political economy,[12] the natural order of the market was a yet unwitting intuition of the principles of self-organization of non-living and living matter creating order from chaos, later on evidenced by the physical and biological sciences during the next centuries. The aim of Marx's critique was just to make conscious the "ideological unconscious"[13] of the classical political economy by revealing how these constituent processes apply to the social and economic capitalist system, albeit in a contradictory and oppressive form. In him, this theoretical critique was accompanied by the practical critique of communism, as the real movement supposed to make conscious the real unconscious of the capitalist social self-organization.

In the political and economic sphere, the new bourgeois spirit of the age advocated by classical political economy recognized mercantilism as the main enemy because of its ambivalent view regarding the freedom to trade, only granted within the limits of the state's interest and tightly confined within national borders. It may even be said that the core political message of classical economists was precisely to support and demonstrate that free market exchange is always and every case, by its very nature, advantageous for all the participants, be they buyers or sellers. This win–win situation would also apply to international trade, which would foster economic development, thus enhancing the wealth of nations, on the sole condition that it be free from restrictions of any kind, like state, feudal, or monopolistic constraints.

The classical rational argument in favour of free trade was established first by Adam Smith (2010) in 1776 with the principle of absolute advantages, according to which a country should specialize in producing and exporting goods requiring a lower labour cost of production than its foreign competitors, and vice versa, it should import goods with a higher domestic labour cost of production. Forty years later, this argument was further extended and perfected by David Ricardo (2004), who first formulated the concept of comparative advantages by which it is the ratio of home sectoral labour productivities that should determine the production and trade specialization of a country. In this case, the trade advantage in export-ing or importing a particular good is given by its lower or higher domestic cost of production relative to goods of different kinds, that is, by the domestic oppor-tunity cost rather than the absolute cost in the international market. The princi-ple of comparative advantages provided the conclusive rationale to the free trade doctrine by stating that international trade is always mutually beneficial even in the presence of higher labour productivity in all industries for a country, as was the case of Britain during the first Industrial Revolution. In static terms, industrial specialization deriving from free trade would assure an optimal allocation of pro-ductive resources within and between countries. Meanwhile, in dynamic terms, free trade would have a positive impact on the growth of home labour productiv-ity by the enlargement of the market, intensification of the division of labour, and exploitation of economies of scale. Therefore, trade liberalization would be the optimal policy for every country at all times regardless of the level of economic development because international trade enriches, and never impoverishes, the country under all possible circumstances by maximizing the static and dynamic allocative efficiency.[14]

Since its formulation, the principle of comparative advantages has always remained at the core of mainstream economics, even when the neoclassical and marginalist schools replaced classical political economy as the dominant orthodox approach, and the Ricardian model of international trade, with labour as the only factor of production, was superseded by the Heckscher–Ohlin model, formulated in terms of multiple factors of production. In modern times, the principle of *lais-sez-faire*, both within and outside national economic borders, has performed the mythological function of ideological legitimization of the new bourgeois social order, replacing the traditional pillars of the Ancient Regime based on the princi-ple of authority, with that of freedom and autonomy. Consequently, the free trade doctrine has become much more than an economic policy stance, turning into an indisputable dogma of faith, so much that these words of Keynes still define the attitude of a large part of the ruling intellectual circles today:

> I was brought up, like most Englishmen, to respect free trade not only as
> an economic doctrine which a rational and instructed person could not

doubt but almost as a part of the moral law. I regarded departures from it
as being at the same time an imbecility and an outrage.

(Keynes, 1933, p. 755)

Despite its cultural hegemony, *laissez-faire* has rather been the exception than
the norm of trade policies concretely pursued by states. There is a widespread
consensus among economic historians in the view that the free trade attitude actually only guided the economic government decisions during a 50-year period,
between the second and third quarter of 19th century in England, reaching its
zenith with the abolition of the Corn Laws in 1846 and the Navigation Acts in
1849.[15] After this short break, even in Britain, the trade policy returned to the old
practices of protection, albeit in new forms defined as neo-mercantilism. There
is, however, a substantive difference between the mercantilist policies at the time
of primitive capitalist accumulation until the 18th century, and the subsequent
neo-mercantilist measures at the time of industrial capitalism.[16] In the era of commercial capitalism, mercantilism was an offensive political and economic strategy
adopted by the emerging powers, notably Britain, France, and the Netherlands,
to undermine the dominion of the old colonial empires of Spain and Portugal.
In the era of industrial capitalism, instead, protectionism was more a defensive
strategy attempted by backward countries in order to prevent the widening of the
economic and technological gap with the most advanced nations, or vice versa by
the dominant countries to preserve the competitive advantages accumulated by
their early development.

In this modern contest, free trade was called into question by some heterodox
political and economic theories as economic nationalism of the 19th century and
Keynesianism during the Great Depression of the 1930s. These neo-mercantilist
approaches did not contest the moral and rational basis of the free trade doctrine, but they disputed the overall effectiveness of trade liberalization under all
conditions, without taking into account the specific stage of national economic
development or the actual macroeconomic conjuncture. Their objections were
thus directed towards the practical feasibility of the free trade policy. In the presence of special and exceptional historical circumstances, political realism could
require some derogation of liberal principles on behalf of supreme national interests related to the state's power and the maintaining of the social order, as in the
case of international antagonisms or mass unemployment.

For example, the German economist Friedrich List (2016), one of the most
influential figures of economic nationalism, in his *The National System of
Political Economy* published in the German language in 1841, envisaged free
trade as an ultimate goal for all developed nations. However, he believed that
the removal of trade barriers should be gradual, selective, and less than full in
the presence of different national levels of economic development, otherwise
it would impede the industrialization of developing countries, the so-called
"infant industry argument" for protection. The methodological bases of List's

theory differ from the individualism of neoclassical political economy because it considers the national interest as an autonomous entity expressed in terms of state power and not coinciding with the pure and simple summing-up of the individual interests of citizens. In this conceptual framework, the pursuit of national interest may necessitate the departure from the standard criterion of microeconomic efficiency and the introduction of protectionist measures, even though free trade would assure the optimal allocation of resources among individual subjects. The instrumental, and imperialistic, character of List's refusal of free trade is proved by the fact that the need for trade protection was not considered as a general rule, but on the contrary, it was strictly limited to European countries. According to him, indeed, the economic relations between the mother country and its colonies should be based on free trade, because the "savage states" in the "torrid" zone have to specialize in producing and exchanging their primary agricultural products with the manufactured goods of the European "temperate" states, in full accordance with the Ricardian theory of comparative advantages.[17]

Likewise, Keynes's position on the advisability of trade protection was subject to a repeated shift of opinion, from the full adherence to free trade doctrine of his early works to the policy recommendation in favour of tariffs in the 1930s, and again to the restoration of a system of multilateral trade after the Second World War. These apparently contradictory views can be explained by the fact that Keynes, while considering free trade as a situation of optimal allocative efficiency, recognized particular institutional circumstances preventing the maintenance of full employment, principally related to the international monetary system and wage flexibility, as a ground for adopting temporary measures of trade protection.[18] In particular, the imposition of tariffs was admitted in the case of an asymmetrical mechanism of adjustment of trade imbalances, where the burden is entirely on deficit countries forced to adopt contractionary economic policies resulting in mass unemployment. In Keynes's thought, therefore, in the presence of institutional market imperfections, the adoption of second-best policies, including trade protection, is justified by the possible trade-off existing between allocative efficiency and distributive justice, in order to reach the right balance between conflicting economic, political, and social goals.

In neo-mercantilist approaches, the claims made towards liberal trade policy are of a pragmatic nature and they do not undermine the theoretical validity of the classical model. In fact, the desired departure from free trade policy does not depend on the fallacy of the market mechanism to generate an optimal economic outcome, but on some extra-economic factors, such as institutional, technological, and political impediments, preventing the normal functioning of competitive market forces and resulting in an asymmetric distribution of the trade advantages between different partners. Therefore, free trade remains the Creed towards which some sins, more or less venial, can be tolerated. For a more radical challenge, we must turn our gaze to unequal exchange theories.

2.2 Structuralist unequal exchange

The aim of this chapter is not to provide a complete and detailed account of the extensive debate on the topic,[19] but rather to pinpoint the main typologies of unequal exchange that can be derived from the major original contributions in order to define a taxonomy of the different forms and sources of unequal exchange existing in the relevant literature. For this purpose, the main contributions are grouped into three theoretical and methodological lines of investigation that will be examined in the following order: (1) structuralist approach; (2) Marxist and neo-Marxist approaches; and finally, (3) Emmanuel's theory of unequal exchange.

The concept of unequal exchange is shared by several approaches to international trade and economic development which are very different from each other in terms of ideological and political attitude. What is common to all of them are two characteristic features that enable a distinctive, albeit varied, analytical framework representing a radical departure from the classical and neoclassical paradigm. First, the view that the uneven distribution of trade gains and losses represents the historical result of a capitalist world economy in which countries at different levels of economic development trade among themselves. Second, the idea that free trade contributes to the persistence of economic and social disparities between nations, giving rise to the continuous reproduction of development on the Centre and underdevelopment on the Periphery of the world capitalist system as aspects of a single global process. Unlike mercantilist and neo-mercantilist theories, therefore, unequal exchange is no more a limited exception to an otherwise optimal free trade situation. On the contrary, it is a typical element of the capitalist world economy, as it has historically evolved in the wake of persistent and diverging paths of national development. In doing so, the unequal exchange argument is much more than a venial sin against the free trade orthodoxy. It is a veritable heresy that contests both the rational and ethical basis of the myth of *laissez-faire* along with its practical feasibility and concrete achievements. Despite this ambition, however, existing theories have so far failed to provide a consistent general theoretical demonstration of the existence of unequal exchange in the presence of universal conditions of perfect competition. Indeed, as we shall see, they have in one way or another, implicitly or explicitly, resorted to some form of imperfect competition in national or international markets for goods or productive factors. This is perhaps the main reason for the limited consideration they have aroused in mainstream economics, which has thus been able to consider unequal exchange as an eccentric case that confirms the general validity of the free trade rule.

In reference to economic analysis, the term "structuralism" came into use over the third quarter of the previous century in Latin America, where it became the prevalent approach to macroeconomics and development studies. The structuralist approach had a major influence on the economic policy of the whole subcontinent through the Economic Commission for Latin America and the Caribbean (ECLAC), a United Nations regional commission devoted to promoting economic and social development through regional cooperation.[20] The historical roots of economic structuralism, however, can be traced back in the British debate on economic planning and market failures of the 1930s and 1940s, according to which the free play of market forces may not achieve a socially optimal allocation of resources.[21] In this debate, the reasons that may differentiate the ideal neoclassical model from the concrete historical reality of actual capitalist economies were identified in three different aspects: wrong signals conveyed by prices due to monopoly or other extra-market influences; improper or even a perverse response to price signals by the factors of production, particularly labour; and, finally, partial or total immobility of factors of production. As a result of these distortions, some form of state intervention, like national economic planning, was required to improve the efficiency and the balanced distribution of economic resources, both in static and dynamic terms.

The application of this analytical framework to the particular condition of less developed countries is at the origin of the structural approach to development policy. According to structuralist economists, the failure of the equilibrating mechanism of the price system to reach a steady economic growth and an equitable income distribution is accentuated by historical features of the peripheral backward economies.[22] Whereas in other social sciences, such as linguistics and anthropology from which it comes, the term "structuralism" denotes a synchronic analytical procedure, in development economics, it corresponds to a diachronic, historical, and comparative process of investigation. The methodology of structural development analysis comprises the following key tenets: a holistic approach to economic behaviour, the principle of circular and cumulative causation, and the concept of a dualistic world economic system.

The first point concerns the refusal of neoclassical methodological individualism that states that all economic phenomena can be derived from the behaviour of individual agents so that the macrodynamic of the system can be reduced to the simple aggregation of a multitude of independent micro-actions grouped under a few stylized figures of representative agents.[23] Conversely, in the structuralist methodology, the economic system is more than the sum of its constitutive elements, since it represents an integrated arrangement of relations among individual parts deriving their meaning only in mutual connection, such as in the case of developed and underdeveloped economies or Centre and Periphery. The orderly patterns of these relations constitute the social, institutional, and technological structures shaping the behaviour of the individual units. The dynamic of the system, in fact, arises from the process of structural change that provides the whole with independent and autonomous properties not present in its isolated parts. The link between the macro and micro dimensions, however, is not unidirectional since the structures are in turn formed and modified by the conscious and unconscious individual social actions, thus giving a historical dimension to the process of structural change.

As a result, in structuralist economic analysis, the mechanisms of interdependence and feedback play an important role. Interdependence refers to the necessary internal relation existing among parts belonging to an integrated system, and feedback denotes the process of mutual action and reaction among parts and between parts and the whole. These concepts are particularly emphasized in the principle of circular and cumulative causation, the use of which in development economics is mainly related to the Swedish economist Gunnar Myrdal.[24] This principle describes a process of mutual, self-reinforcing causal interrelationships between variables, resulting in a dynamic path of growing divergence from the initial equilibrium, in such a way that the original cause of a phenomenon becomes its own effect. In Myrdal's development model, this mechanism is triggered by the free play of market forces acting in compliance with the profit motive. It implies that the economic backwardness of a region is ultimately explained by its initial backwardness, and the same goes for the accelerating growth of an already developed area.

Due to the operation of the circular and cumulative causation, therefore, a free market economy is typically characterized by a dualistic structure that continuously reproduces itself. This self-reinforcing process gives rise to poverty traps, from which it is very difficult to escape without an active state intervention of economic planning and income redistribution. The notion of economic dualism, both at the domestic and international level, lies at the heart of the structuralist model of unequal exchange developed by the British African-Caribbean economist Sir Arthur Lewis, winner of the Nobel Prize in Economic Sciences in 1979.

2.2.1 Lewis's dualistic model

The starting point of Lewis's model[25] is the observation that in backward economies the labour market is segmented in two distinct and separate sectors. On the one hand, the traditional or informal sector consists of all the peasant, craft, and self-employment subsistence activities devoted to maintaining family consumption and carried out in rural villages and suburbs by means of a pre-modern, stagnant technology inherited from past centuries. On the other hand, the modern or formal sector comprises manufacturing, mining, plantations, and commercial farming activities located in urban areas, managed by a class of entrepreneurs and capitalists for profit, and performed by wage workers using modern industrial production techniques. While traditional production is almost entirely absorbed by self-consumption and domestic demand, the production of the modern sector is manly addressed to meet foreign demand in compliance with a typical export-led pattern of growth. In terms of the labour market, the traditional sector is marked by a chronic and persistent excess of the unskilled workforce, the so-called "labour surplus", that keeps labour productivity at a very low level, thus determining an unlimited supply of labour and a subsistence real wage. On the contrary, in the modern sector, wages are higher to encourage migration from "country" to "town" and to promote the urbanization and expansion of the monetary market economy.

The modern sector wage rate, however, remains lower than labour productivity because the latent competition of informal workers undermines the individual and collective contractual capacity of the industrial workforce. Hence, the modern sector real wage is exogenously fixed just over the traditional subsistence level. Furthermore, the level of employment is determined by the labour demand deriving from the stock of capital available in the short run, in accordance with a classical political economy view. This implies that the major constraint to the economic growth of a dual backward economy is given by the amount of saving necessary for financing the capital investment. As Lewis (1954, p. 416) emphasizes, indeed, "the central fact of economic development is rapid capital accumulation... We cannot explain any 'industrial' revolution... until we can explain why saving increased relatively to national income".

Lewis's answer to this question is that the share of saving on national income is directly related to a change in the income distribution favourable to the saving class. And in backward economies, the saving class corresponds to the capitalist class since the wages do not differ too much from the subsistence level. As profits are the major source of saving, in a closed economy, the gap between real wages and labour productivity in the modern sector favours long-run economic development if it results in extra-profits retained by the domestic capital and reinvested in the industrialization of the country. As the modern sector grows in consequence of the capital accumulation, the labour surplus of the traditional sector shrinks until it disappears, and from this point forward, real wages start to increase in line with labour productivity growth. In Lewis's view, therefore, classical and neoclassical models correspond to two different phases of the economic development process, the stage of industrial take-off and the stage of the industrial maturity, respectively. According to him, this was the case of Britain and other Western first comers during the Industrial Revolution.

Until now, the analysis has been carried out under the assumption of a closed economy. The removal of this hypothesis with the introduction of foreign trade leads Lewis to formulate very different conclusions about the path of latecomers in the process of industrial modernization. The domestic dualism existing within backward economies is replicated in the world economy. In fact, as opposed to what happens in peripheral countries, the labour market of central countries is nationally integrated and the real wage is set equal to the productivity level. The world labour market too, therefore, is divided in two spatially separate fields, the neoclassical labour market with variable real wages in the Centre, and the classical labour market with fixed real wages in the Periphery. In a situation of free trade and capital mobility, both classical and neoclassical theories share the same conclusions about the equalization of profit rates among all trading countries. The combination of this assumption with Lewis's hypothesis of labour market dualism has profound implications regarding the effects of productivity growth on the terms of trade and the geographical distribution of trade benefits.

In central economies, the growth in labour productivity results in increasing real wages without affecting the prices of produced and exported commodities. Conversely, in a small open peripheral economy, since both wage and profit rates are fixed, at the subsistence level, the former, and at the international level, the latter, the growth in productivity ultimately results in lower prices of the commodities produced and exported by the modern sector. As a consequence, the terms of trade of less developed countries tend to deteriorate in parallel with the expansion of their modern sector, so that in them "(p)ractically all the benefit of increasing efficiency in export industries goes to the foreign consumer" (Lewis, 1954, p. 449). For this reason, Lewis concludes that the Ricardian law of comparative advantages is a valid argument for free trade in advanced industrial economies and, vice versa, for protection in countries with an unlimited supply of labour.

From this framework, it follows that in the world economy the labour market dualism is reflected in a dualistic trade structure characterized by developed countries specialized in high wage sectors on the one hand, and less developed countries specialized in low wage sectors, consisting of primary and tropical goods as well as mature manufacturing productions, on the other hand. Because of this specific geographic localization of industrial branches, in the world economy, the wages earned by comparable workers depend on the sector in which they come to be employed, in analogy with the case of domestic labour markets in backward countries. In neoclassical trade models, the international and intersectoral wage differentials are the effect of industrial specialization in high or low productivity sectors deriving from the given capital, labour, and skill endowments of each country. By contrast, in Lewis's model, the causal link is reversed as it goes from the exogenous determination of wages in the labour markets to the structure of production and trade. Here, the observed intersectoral wage differentials at the international level depend on the dualistic structure of the world economy, and as such, they represent an autonomous source of unequal exchange in international trade.

As we have seen, the constraints imposed by economic dualism give rise to a drain of resources from the Periphery to the Centre in the form of a systematic bias in relative prices of exports and imports as a cause of unequal exchange. In Lewis's model, this term of trade effect relies on purely supply side factors operating through dualistic labour markets. In structuralist development theory, the same adverse terms of trade effect for peripheral economies has also been proposed on the basis of a mixed supply and demand side approach by what is known as the "Prebisch–Singer thesis" to which we now turn our attention.

2.2.2 The "Prebisch–Singer thesis"

In May 1950, two groundbreaking works were published independently of each other, thus starting a long debate in international and development economics. The first was an essay written by the Argentinian economist Raul Prebisch (1950a,b), executive director of the ECLAC, and the second an article of the German-born British economist Hans Singer (1950), who worked at the United Nations Department of Economic Affairs. The thesis advanced by both economists had to do with the existence of a long-run structural trend in the world economy towards the worsening of the net barter terms of trade of primary products relative to manufactured goods, and the consequent impact on the development strategies of the peripheral economies.[26] Both contributions were based on an empirical study, drawn up the previous year by the United Nations (1949) and mostly written by Singer, showing that at the end of 1930s, a given quantity of primary exports only exchanged on average 60 per cent of the quantity of manufactured goods that it could have bought in the 1870s. Given the prevailing international division of labour at that time, the detected path of relative prices in the world economy would force the less developed countries to export a continuously increasing quantity of agricultural commodities and raw materials in return of the same quantity of manufactured goods from industrialized countries. Furthermore, the secular downward trend of the terms of trade of the primary products was aggravated by the extreme short-run volatility of their prices, which prevented the peripheral countries from any reasonable investment planning that necessarily requires more advanced imported foreign technology.

According to Prebisch and Singer, this anomalous pattern was explained by two sets of reasons operating on both the demand and supply side of the world market. The first reason involves the different income elasticities of demand for manufacturing and agricultural commodities resulting from an extrapolation of Engel's law, by which the share of income spent on foods tends to fall as income increases. The operating of this law at the world level would imply a declining relative international demand for primary goods during the process of economic development, and consequently, a similar long-run decline in their prices relative to industrial commodities. The second reason relates to the monopolistic structure of the supply side in the manufacturing sector compared with the competitive structure of primary production, in terms of both labour and goods markets.

Prebisch stressed the role of well-organized trade unions in central countries during the cyclical economic slumps as a source of downward nominal wage rigidity, differentiating the labour markets of the industrialized centre from the perfectly flexible nominal wages prevailing in the agricultural periphery. Alternatively, Singer emphasized the market power of large corporations producing industrial manufactured goods, where prices are fixed according to a cost plus pricing rule by adding a mark-up in order to obtain extra-profit, while the prices of primary goods follow the competitive rule of the unit cost of production plus the normal profit. In both cases, the divergent path of terms of trade between manufacturing and primary commodities depends on the monopolistic structure of the supply side in developed central countries in contrast with the perfectly competitive markets of underdeveloped peripheral economies. Indeed, during the downswing of the cycle, the wage and price stickiness amplifies the negative effects on unemployment and production in the centre, giving rise to a dramatic reduction of demand for primary products of the periphery. Because of the flexible nature of primary markets, this extra pressure exerted by the centre leads to a decrease in income and prices in the periphery even greater than that would be required by the restoration of a competitive equilibrium. At the beginning of the new upward phase of the economic cycle, therefore, the periphery will be in a weakened competitive position vis-à-vis the centre as compared with the previous cycle. In short, the peripheral economies find themselves forced to passively adjust to the constraints imposed by the specific monopolistic structure of the central economies, thereby absorbing the highest costs of the recurrent market crisis. This structural mechanism of subordination of the Periphery to the economic needs of the Centre is at the origin of the notion of dependent economies as a core concept of the related "dependency theory" of underdevelopment.

The Prebisch–Singer thesis was in contrast to a common belief held among economists since the 19th century, according to which the terms of trade of manufacturing goods relative to agricultural and primary products would tend to decline as the economy developed. This conventional wisdom was based on the fact that technological progress was biased in favour of industrial production. Consequently, the growth of productivity would be higher in secondary than in primary activity; the latter was also burdened with the scarcity of natural resources, thus resulting in declining relative prices of manufacturing goods. What the statistical data elaborated by the United Nations showed was, instead, that the gains deriving from the faster technical progress in manufacturing were distributed to the producers in the form of a rise in income, be it wage or profit, whereas the gains deriving from the slower technical progress in agriculture and primary production was distributed to consumers through falling prices. Since the large part of raw materials and agricultural goods produced by peripheral countries was intended for the foreign market, the benefits of the increasing labour productivity in these sectors were passed abroad. In such circumstances, the application of an export-led growth model turned out to be counterproductive.

The conclusion drawn by the two authors was that the gains from international trade were not equally distributed, because all the benefits would have remained in the developed countries leaving the less developed countries with nothing. As Singer pointed out, in a dualistic international economic system

> (t)he industrialized countries have had the best of both worlds, both as consumers of primary commodities and as producers of manufactured articles, whereas the underdeveloped countries had the worst of both worlds, as consumers of manufactures and as producers of raw materials.
>
> (Singer, 1950, p. 479)

Under these circumstances, the inequalities in per capita income between countries increase by the growth of trade, which represents an obstacle to economic development rather than an opportunity for peripheral economies. For the latter, in fact, the adverse international specialization in low-income and low-price exporting sectors would lead to a continuous decline in terms of trade and a growing outward transfer of the gains deriving from their technical progress.

The lesson learnt from this analysis was that underdeveloped agricultural countries should refrain from adopting a free trade policy, and instead impose tariffs on the import of manufacturing goods to protect national industries from foreign competition in a bridging update of the 19th century List's "infant industry argument". In this view, the process of economic development in peripheral countries has to necessarily go through a phase of rapid industrialization because, given the dualistic structure of the world economy, only in this way can the fruit of modern technological progress be put at the service of the well-being of the national collectivity, thus preventing the resulting improvement in productivity enjoyed by other countries. To achieve this goal, therefore, an import substitution strategy aimed at the domestic production of substitutes for manufactured imported goods was recommended to peripheral countries. In the 1950s and 1960s, this recommendation exerted a widespread influence on decision makers, particularly in Latin America, where it became the official approach to development policies advocated by the ECLA under the direction of Raul Prebisch.

To summarize, in the Prebisch–Singer argument the different demand elasticities between primary and manufactured commodities and the non-competitive structures of labour and goods markets of central countries cause the intersectoral differences in wage and profit rates that can be observed in the world economy. Given the existing international division of labour, these differences represent a source of unequal exchange in international trade. With respect to Lewis's version of unequal exchange, on the supply side the dependency approach added the behaviour of monopolistic firms, acting in the world market of manufactured goods, to the main drivers of the draining of resources from peripheral to central countries through international trade. The emphasis on the role of commercial and technological monopolies as a font of exploitation of the Centre on the Periphery, typical of the structuralist unequal exchange theory, is also shared by other approaches in the Marxist tradition, particularly with regard to the power of transnational corporations.

2.3 Marxist unequal exchange

Marx did not leave us a systematic account of the labour theory of value at the international level, although this issue was an integral part of his original writing project on the critique of political economy. The international law of value will be discussed in the following chapters on the basis of his scattered notes and suggestions on the subject. Here, we will briefly discuss some Marxist contributions on the topic of unequal exchange in international trade published after Marx's death. As a general principle, the basic methodological element that distinguishes Marxist from the structuralist approach on unequal exchange is the concept of value as the ultimate determining factor in the price formation mechanism. This carries with it a different conception of the economic surplus that forms the subject of the unequal distribution of the gains deriving from international trade.

In the structuralist approach, the nature of inequality in exchange is defined in terms of the deviation of the actual terms of trade from the ideal relative prices corresponding to a situation of perfect competition in all markets. The two terms of comparison, actual and ideal prices, pertain to two different levels of analysis, the positive defining what is and the normative defining what ought to be. The structuralist critique to mainstream neoclassical economics concerns the adoption of a deductive method that, through an abstract normative analysis, postulates an automatic mechanism of adjustment of economic disequilibria by means of the free play of market forces, leading to an optimal and efficient allocation of resources. By contrast, structuralist economics is based on an inductive method that, using a positive analysis of the existing historical and institutional structures, maintains that market equilibrium can be suboptimal or, put differently, a stable market disequilibrium can occur in the presence of the cumulative and circular processes operating in a dualistic world economy. This latter situation is what happens under free trade, thus resulting in long-run economic stagnation of peripheral economies.

In the structuralist disequilibrium framework, the prices are ultimately determined by the power positions and the strategic and tactic behaviour of the contracting parties.[27] In trade relations between countries, the object of bargaining is the appropriation of the productivity gains or "innovation surplus", representing the fruits of technical progress. This "innovation surplus" is a form of distribution surplus measured in terms of units of general purchasing power and expressed by the net barter terms of trade. When perfectly competitive market equilibrium prevails, as in neoclassical models, there is a balance of power between trading partners and the surplus distribution is neutral or equal. On the contrary, there is unequal exchange in situations of stable market disequilibrium arising out from the breach of competition rules in labour or goods markets. Strictly speaking, in a structuralist approach, the unequal exchange implies neither a drain of material resources nor a transfer of economic surplus, but rather a loss of potential gain from trade for peripheral countries, caused by the dualistic structure of the world economy preventing them from appropriating the fruits of their own technical progress. Similar to neoclassical theory, therefore, in structuralist analysis, there is no room for the concept of an objective value determinable outside of the act of exchange, around which the market price orbits.

Conversely, the concept of value is central in the Marxist approach in which the exchange can be defined as unequal when the value realized in circulation, expressed by the market price of the commodity, differs from the underlying value (or price of production), expressing the labour time socially necessary to its production. Unlike the structuralist approach, the Marxist notion of unequal exchange involves international transfers of economic surplus in the form of a decoupling between value produced and value realized by different countries. Before the publication of Emmanuel's seminal work in the 1960s, on which we will return extensively in the next paragraph, the theme of unequal exchange in trade received little or no attention among Marxist economists, despite the central role gained by the question of imperialism in socialist theoretical and political debate since the turn of the 20th century with the works of Lenin, Luxembourg, and Hilferding, to name only the main authors.[28] Marxist analysis of imperialism was indeed centred more on capital exports from capitalist countries to colonies to find new market opportunities and cheaper raw materials or on the search of new outlets for the realization of excess surplus value, than on trade relations between the Centre and Periphery of the world capitalist system. This lack of engagement may be explained by both political and theoretical considerations.

First, on a political level, the emphasis on the conflictual trade relations between nations could overshadow the centrality of the class conflict between workers and capitalists within each nation, thereby encouraging the nationalistic, conciliatory, and petty-bourgeois tendencies in the labour movement. Furthermore, following some insights contained in early writings of the young Marx about Corn Laws,[29] in the socialist movement, the predominant opinion supported free trade against protectionism, at least up to the beginning of the decolonization process in the mid-20th century. The former, indeed, was considered as an economic policy promoting the rapid development of industrial capitalism, and with it, the intensification of the class conflict between bourgeois and proletariat, thus accelerating the collapse of the system, while the latter favoured the interests of the most reactionary sectors of the ruling class, like landlords and merchant capitalists. The tribute to free trade and capitalist globalization made by some prominent Marxist theorists was equal if not greater than that of liberal neoclassical economists, as evidenced by this passage from the influential book of Hilferding from 1910 (1981, p. 310): "There can be no doubt, therefore, that… free trade, which would amalgamate the whole world market into a single economic territory, would ensure the highest possible labour productivity and the most rational international division of labour". Finally, last but not least, after the Second World War, the question of trade within the Soviet bloc became a burning issue for the communist movement, involving, in particular, the asymmetric bargaining power between the Soviet Union and its satellite countries of Eastern Europe. The general political climate, therefore, did not encourage Marxist scholars to devote a great deal of research to the unequal distribution of trade gains between countries.

Second, and perhaps more importantly, on a theoretical level, an equilibrium approach by nature is not very suitable for investigating the issue of unequal exchange as a structural feature of the world capitalist system deriving from a persistent discrepancy between value created in production and value realized in circulation. At the time of the unequal exchange debate, the prevailing interpretations of Marx's labour theory of value, whether productivist or circulationist[30] as will be discussed in more detail in the next chapters, shared the common trait of an equilibrium analytical framework despite their profound differences. On the one hand, the traditional orthodox theory, associated with the leading figures of Maurice Dobb, Paul Sweezy, and Ronald Meek, considers value as wholly determined within the sphere of production, and ultimately reduced to the quantity of embodied labour time, in a way similar to the labour input coefficients of input-output analysis. In this view, not fundamentally different from Ricardo's theory of value, the sphere of circulation pertains to the surface appearance of the capitalist economy, and, as such, it strictly depends on the technical process of production to which it passively conforms. Consequently, the economic categories of money, price, and exchange play no role in explaining the inner dynamic of capitalism. These categories eventually come into play only at a later, more superficial stage of analysis, that of the individual market prices fluctuating around a long-run average regulated by the value created in production. On the other hand, the rival interpretation, freely inspired by the works of the Soviet economist Isaac Rubin, conceives the substance of value, abstract labour, as the money form of a commodity in exchange, ultimately expressed by the quantity of labour purchasable with a given quantity of money, in a way similar to a dialectical version of Adam Smith's labour commanded. According to this approach, the value created in production and the value realized in circulation are practically identical by assumption, since the former can be quantitatively measured only *ex post* by the latter.

To sum up, in both prevailing interpretations of Marx's theory of value, the exchange is always deemed equal, in the sense that the long-run equilibrium market price reflects the underlying value or price of production of the traded commodity, being production and circulation mirror the other. Hence, the same consideration made by Emmanuel (1972, p. 93) to the neoclassical theory of value shall apply to both prevailing Marxist approaches too: "If equivalence is an *ex post* phenomenon of the market, there is no such thing as equivalence or non-equivalence in themselves", and the issue of international value transfers through unequal exchange in trade is ruled out in advance.

In this theoretical framework, differences between value in production and value in circulation can only be conceived as short-run temporary phenomena devoid of any structural meaning in the theoretical analysis of the capitalist economy. Two exceptions are allowed to this rule: the case of prices of production resulting from the equalization of profit rates among sectors with a different organic composition of capital, and the presence of monopolistic markets dominated by large transnational corporations retaining their power by means of economic and political coercion. These limited exceptions are at the root of the two Marxist approaches to unequal exchange that we are now going to consider.

2.3.1 *Non-equivalent exchange*

According to Marx's labour theory of value, in a capitalist economy, the market price ultimately depends on the price of production rather than the value. Price of production results from the redistribution of surplus value between sectors with different organic compositions of capital, defined as the ratio between constant and variable capital, leading to the equalization of profit rates in the whole economy. This mechanism, described by Marx in the third volume of *Capital*, is triggered by the competition between many individual capitals moving towards the more profitable sectors where the profit per unit of capital invested is higher. Under the assumption that the average rate of surplus value[31] is identical for all sectors as a result of inter-industry workers mobility, if the commodities are sold at their values then the rate of profit will be higher in the industries with a lower organic composition of capital. In such a situation, given the social demand, intersectoral capital mobility would increase (reduce) the supply of commodities using relatively less (more) constant capital, thus determining a market value lower (higher) than labour value, the price of production. The corresponding regulating price, around which short-run market price fluctuates, assures the equalization of profit rates between industries. As a consequence, the value created in the production of a capitalist commodity is normally different from the value realized in circulation. The intersectoral transfers of value from lower to higher capital-intensive industries, resulting from the formation of prices of production, is a structural law of the capitalist economy, in which exchanges are regulated by prices different from the underlying values, except for industries with an organic composition of capital by chance identical to that of the average social capital.

By applying this scheme to regions or countries distinguished by different industrial specializations, the intersectoral value transfers are combined with spatial value transfers by means of trade relations. For this to happen, what is needed is the presence of capital mobility between industries leading to both intersectoral and geographical equalization of profit rates. Since Marx's concept of technical progress is capital-using and labour-saving with constant returns to scale,[32] in this framework, a higher organic composition of capital is associated with higher labour productivity, and consequently, the international division of labour is marked by more developed countries specialized in capital-intensive productions, and less developed countries specialized in labour-intensive ones. Under the hypothesis of a comparable rate of exploitation between countries, the direction of value transfers involved in the formation of international prices of production, therefore, would be from less to more developed countries.

The first to use the price of production argument in a geographical context was one of the outstanding representatives of Austro-Marxism, Otto Bauer, who, during the first third of the past century, occupied important political positions within the Austrian Social Democrat party, covering the role of secretary of the Social Democrat parliamentary group in the Habsburg Empire and later foreign minister of the first Austrian Republic. In his book on *Social Democracy and the Nationalities Question* published in 1907, Bauer (2000) addresses the issue of the national rivalries within the multinational Habsburg monarchy. In fact, at that time, national and ethnic conflicts were a major political problem for the Austrian Social Democrat movement because they undermined the class solidarity between workers, making it difficult to carry out a common labour struggle against capitalists for claiming social and political rights. In the third chapter on the multinational state, Bauer examined the economic aspects of the national question by looking in particular at the situation in Bohemia, where the industrial and more developed regions were predominantly German, while the agrarian and less developed regions were Czech. Given that the industrial production required a higher organic composition of capital than primary production, Bauer argued that the surplus value was asymmetrically distributed through interregional trade because of the domestic integration of the capitalist market, characterized by a common set of prices of production and the equalization of profit rates between different regions of the Austro-Hungarian Empire. Consequently, behind the ethnic and cultural rivalry between the two national groups, there was actually an economic antagonism, deriving from the net value transfers from Czech to German regions. To sum up, in Bauer's analysis, nationalism and revanchism, that infected the working class, were ultimately a consequence of the uneven capitalist development of the different regions of the multinational state.

Bauer has made use of the price of production schema to investigate the historical situation of the Austro-Hungarian multinational state by highlighting the transfers of value hidden behind the interregional trade between "town" and "country" within an integrated domestic market. About two decades later, the Polish Marxist economist Henryk Grossmann returned to the subject in more general and theoretical terms in his work on *The Law of the Accumulation and Breakdown of the Capitalist System* published in 1929, by applying the same argument to the case of international trade. According to Grossmann, since at the stage of modern industrial capitalism the level of price is no longer determined on a national basis but on the world market,

> international trade is not based on an exchange of equivalents because, as on the national market, there is a tendency for rates of profit to be equalised. The commodities of the advanced capitalist country with the higher organic composition will therefore be sold at prices of production higher than value; those of the backward country at prices of production lower than value... In this way circulation on the world market involves transfers of surplus value from the less developed to the more developed capitalist countries
>
> (Grossmann, 1992, p. 105)

In Grossmann's analysis, the enlargement of the world market thorough international trade represented a countervailing tendency to the fall in the rate of profit, thus acting as a slowdown factor in the inevitable breakdown of capitalism.

The transfers of value deriving from the formation of international prices of production occur between industries having different organic compositions of capital by means of inter-industry capital competition. A variant of the same mechanism can be identified in the case of intra-industry capital competition when firms produce the same kind of commodity using different methods of production. Indeed, within a given industry, firms with higher-than-average sectoral productivity have an individual unit labour cost lower than the sectoral average unit labour cost, at which the general profit rate applies to form the price of production. The determination of an identical market price for all the firms of the same branch regulated by the price of production, therefore, will involve different rates of profit between them. The higher profit rate of the more efficient firms comes from their lower unit labour costs compared with the average cost of the industry. As Shaikh (2016, p. 262) points out "competition within an industry tends to disequalize profit margins and profit rates precisely because it tends to equalize selling prices". In other words, the individual profit rate differs between firms producing the same commodity in direct relation with their individual efficiency because of the difference existing between individual and average unit labour costs of production.

Some authors[33] have applied this analytical framework to the formation of international market prices in world competitive markets. They argue that within the same industry, the more efficient national capitals benefit from extra-profits originated by national unit labour costs lower than the international average. In this context, the structure of international trade is determined by the absolute advantages, as in domestic trade, rather than by comparative advantages. Since the production efficiency is higher for more developed countries than less developed countries, in competitive markets the formation of a common international price entails an asymmetrical distribution of trade gains to the benefit of the former. The nature of these intra-industry asymmetries in the distribution of trade gains between countries is similar to that of inter-industry transfers of value because both ultimately depend on the organic composition of national capital. In fact, in a classical political economy framework, the growth in labour productivity is determined by the rate of technical progress, which, in turn, is directly related to the organic composition of capital. Consequently, within a given world industry, more efficient national productions will make use of more capital-intensive techniques than the less efficient, which, on the contrary, use more labour-intensive techniques.

As with inter-industry value transfers, likewise asymmetric intra-industry trade gains result from differences in relative national capital accumulation. The two cases differ between them because international transfers of value in the proper sense happen only in the case of the equalization of the profit rates between different industries. By contrast, within the same industry, the higher profit rates of the more efficient national capitals derive from the higher relative surplus value extracted from national workers, which is subtracted from the international equalization of profit rates because of their technological monopoly. In other words, more developed countries gain more from international trade than less developed countries, without the latter being impoverished. In both cases, however, there is no difference between domestic and international trade, and therefore the law of value that governs both domestic and international markets is the same, as is the unit of measurement of value. The trade advantages, indeed, derive from the normal functioning of the law of value in an integrated world capitalist economy, in which international prices diverge from social and individual values in exactly the same way as happens between sectors and firms within a national economy.

It is the inner structural logic of the capitalist mode of production that commodities exchange at prices different from values, and therefore, the distribution of economic surplus resulting from this discrepancy corresponds perfectly to capitalist social rationality, either at a national or international level. The capitalist exchange of commodities is a non-equivalent exchange of values by its very nature, even in perfectly competitive markets, and there is no peculiarity of foreign trade in this respect. For this reason, in the Marxist debate, the international transfers of value and the asymmetric distribution of gains, involved in trade between countries at different levels of development, have been called non-equivalent exchange or unequal exchange "in the broad sense", rather than unequal exchange "in [the] narrow or strict sense", to indicate that they do not entail a particular form of exploitation of one country by another.[34] In short, non-equivalent exchange does not allow the identification of any essential modification of the law of value at the international level with respect to the national one. It simply reflects the physiology of capitalistic social relations. In the prevailing interpretations of Marx's labour theory of value, based on an equilibrium framework, a situation of unequal exchange in the strict sense can only find a place by resorting to pathologic extra-economic factors breaking the iron rules of perfect competition. This is the case of neo-Marxist theories of monopoly capitalism.

2.3.2 Unequal exchange and monopoly capitalism

The focus on the role of commercial and technological monopolies as a source of exploitation by capitalist developed countries on underdeveloped peripheral economies characterizes a neo-Marxist approach to unequal exchange, known as "monopoly capitalism".[35] This approach combines Marx's analysis of the increasing centralization and concentration of capital with underconsumption theories of economic stagnation. It argues that, in advanced capitalist economies, the market is dominated by a few large oligopolistic firms able to fix prices through a mark-up mechanism aimed at profit maximization. In monopolistic competition, the decline in costs of production, due to technical progress and higher labour productivity, results in increasing extra-profits rather than market prices reduction. The widening of profit margins at firm level translates, at the macroeconomic level, into a growing economic surplus determined by the difference between total output and aggregate necessary costs of production, wages included, both absolutely and as a share of national income. This enlarging gap generates a permanent lack of correspondent effective aggregate demand able to absorb the excess surplus, thus determining a constant tendency towards macroeconomic stagnation.

The productive reinvestment of monopolistic profits does not represent a viable long-term solution to this problem, because it would only widen the structural gap by setting in motion a vicious circle made of further technical progress, reduction of costs of production, and even greater economic surplus. For this reason, monopoly capital requires a constant expansion of unproductive expenditure, made by the government as well as a growing mass of rentiers. This superfluous demand, representing an enormous waste of resources in social terms, is directed towards sectors like advertising, marketing, insurance and finance, luxuries, wholesaling and retailing distribution, passive entertainment, mass media distraction and manipulation, private and public security, and so on. Among these wasteful expenditures, military spending plays a central role in the government absorption of surplus, because of ideological prejudice and opposition to the public supply of socially useful goods and services, such as welfare spending, by competitor private interests. According to the monopoly capital approach, the formation of a military-industrial complex in central capitalist countries reinforces the phenomenon of imperialism that has marked the history of capitalism since its inception in the 16th century.

The relevance of imperialism is crucial in the analysis of the causes of underdevelopment in peripheral countries made by the Russian-American Marxist economist Paul Baran. His book on *The Political Economy of Growth*, published in 1957, has inspired many of the subsequent neo-Marxist and neo-dependency research on the issue of unequal exchange. Baran ascribes the origins of peripheral underdevelopment in past centuries to colonialism, primarily through the direct plunder of colonial resources during the era of merchant capitalism, and later, the industrial policies aiming at destroying the concurrent traditional colonial manufactures, as was the case of Indian textiles after the British Industrial Revolution. After the end of the Second War World, the transformation of the former colonies into new independent national states changed the institutional form of the imperialistic domination, but the substance remained the same.

The constant threat of military intervention, direct or indirect, by the imperialist powers against any attempt of autonomy and national independence of the governments of peripheral countries is the cornerstone of neo-colonialism. As a result, the new post-colonial regimes are in fact politically and militarily subordinate to the Western capitalist powers because of the political hegemony of an indigenous comprador bourgeoisie, totally dependent on the neo-imperialistic model, which draws its earnings from the services rendered to the foreign multinational corporations and the remnants of feudal socio-economic structures. In such situations, the drain of economic surplus from peripheral to central countries takes places through several mechanisms: the pattern of peripheral trade involving the import of manufacturing goods at monopolistic prices and the export of primary products at competitive prices; the super-exploitation of labour and the repatriation of profits on capital invested in former colonial territories by multinational corporations; the foreign control of strategic resources in poor countries; and the burden of foreign debt activated by comprador social groups to finance their unproductive expenditures. In Baran's view, the engine of economic development is the productive use of economic surplus in an accelerating national accumulation of capital to promote industrialization and modernization. The neo-imperialistic siphoning of surplus from peripheral to central economies is, therefore, a relevant factor in explaining the continuous reproduction of the dualistic structure of the capitalist world economy, characterized by an ever-growing inequality in wealth and welfare between advanced and backward regions.

Baran's analysis of the causes of the economic backwardness of peripheral countries exerted a great influence on subsequent development studies. Its relevance lies in the integration of a classical Marxist framework with the new theoretical suggestions stemming from the post-war Keynesian and structuralist economic theories. In this vein, during the 1960s and 1970s, a new radical approach became widespread in universities around the world, under the name of neo-dependency theory in Latin America with the leading figure of Andre Gunder

Frank, and world system analysis in European and North American countries inspired by the works of Immanuel Wallerstein and Giovanni Arrighi, among others.[36] In this approach, the emphasis is more on the political dominance of the Centre over the Periphery, exercised through the crucial mediation of the direct intervention of the State, than the specific market mechanisms at the origin of the draining of the economic surplus within the capitalist world economy. In trade relations between countries, bargaining power is the projection of the relative strength of the State in the international political and military arena, which conditions the distribution of gains and losses deriving from commodity exchange. In this sense, as noted by Wallerstein (1979, p. 18), "once we get a difference in the strength of state machineries, we get the operation of 'unequal exchange'". The relative State power would, in turn, be reflected in the different domestic social structures of national societies, marked by a typical modern capitalist relationship of wage workers and entrepreneurs in central countries, and a pre-modern aggregation of servants and semi-slave workers and masters in peripheral countries, resulting from the corruptive influence of foreign capital by means of multinational corporations. The framework of neo-dependency and world system analysis is therefore interested more on the political and sociological aspects of the interdependent global structure, than the strictly economic laws governing it.

Within this cultural movement, an exception is represented by the Egyptian-French economist and Third World activist Samir Amin, who particularly dealt with the issue of unequal exchange in international trade from an economic perspective.[37] The contribution of this prolific and eclectic author is the idea of a law of globalized value resulting in an imperialist rent in favour of central powers. In addition to exclusive access to the planet's material resources, technological monopolies, and control over the globalized financial system, the imperialistic rent benefiting Northern monopoly capital derives from super-exploitation of Southern workers. According to Amin, indeed, the wage differences between North and South workers is greater than the difference between their respective labour productivity, so that the double factorial terms of trade between countries is systematically distorted from parity.[38] Along these lines, however, another scholar was first and more rigorously and systematically emphasized the crucial role of wage differences as a fundamental cause of unequal exchange in trade between nations, and it to this scholar we now turn our attention.

2.4 Arghiri Emmanuel's theory of unequal exchange

The term "unequal exchange" was first introduced in international trade theory by the Greek economist Arghiri Emmanuel with his book on *L'échange inégal: Essais sur les antagonismes dans les rapports économiques internationaux*, published in French in 1969.[39] Emmanuel defines unequal exchange as:

> the proportion between equilibrium prices that is established through
> the equalization of profits between regions in which the rate of surplus

value is "institutionally' different" – the term "institutionally" meaning that these rates are, for whatever reason, safeguarded from competitive equalization on the factors market and are independent of relative prices.

(Emmanuel, 1972, p. 64)

Let's see what this means.

Emmanuel's starting point is the classical Ricardian trade model with complete specialization of production between countries, to which he changes the basic assumptions concerning the international mobility of factors of production. In Ricardo's original trade theory, both labour and capital are perfectly mobile within national borders but immobile between different countries. Labour immobility, however, does not prevent Ricardo assuming the equalization of wages on a world scale, unlike the equalization of profit rates that would necessarily require the international mobility of capital. In fact, in Ricardo's view, wages are internationally equal even in the absence of worker migration because they are fixed at the subsistence level and are determined by the physiological and biological needs of human beings, which are invariable in space and time. Given the Ricardian conception of wages, the immobility of capital becomes essential to distinguish national from international trade, because "if capital freely flowed towards those countries where it could be most profitably employed, there could be no difference in the rate of profit, and no other difference in the real or labor price of commodities" (Ricardo, 2004, p. 136), and consequently, there could be no comparative advantages between countries. Ricardian trade theory, therefore, is marked by identical wages and different rates of profit between countries in the world economy.

Marx refused the Ricardian conception of the physiological cost of labour power by introducing a moral, historical, and social factor in wage determination, thus allowing for variations of the necessary wage level between nations and between periods. According to Emmanuel, this important difference between Marx's and Ricardo's labour theory of value has not been considered by the few Marxists who have dealt seriously with international trade, as is the case of the Marxist approach to non-equivalent exchange. The latter, indeed, on the one hand, allowed for intersectoral capital mobility leading to the formation of world prices of production, and on the other hand, simply replaced the Ricardian physiological wage with the hypothesis of perfect spatial mobility of labour, thus assuming the equalization of both wages and profit rates between countries. In this case, however, the specificity of international trade vanishes, and there is no difference between national and world economies. In Emmanuel's view, on the contrary, what distinguishes the international from the national law of value is just the different hypothesis made on the mobility of factors of production in the two cases, as it was for Ricardo.

In this respect, the novelty of Emmanuel's analysis was the introduction of a dual hypothesis on international factors mobility, which is perfect mobility of capital combined with null or imperfect mobility of labour, while the other fundamental assumptions of the classical trade theory remain unchanged, notably free trade in a world of perfect competitive goods markets and complete specialization of national productions.[40] According to him, this hypothesis was more appropriate in describing the historical conditions of modern capitalism, characterized by a growing integration of the world financial market and the existence of legal and cultural barriers to free mobility of the workforce. The absence of competition in the labour market on an international scale results in different national wages paid to workers with comparable skills, thus determining a situation of divergent costs of labour power, alongside equal rewards per unit of capital between countries. In this setting, Emmanuel continues, the level of national wages becomes the independent variable of the system that has to be explained outside the model by resorting to extra-economic considerations. His explanation is that the wage level depends on the market bargaining power of the trade unions, which comes to represent the fundamental political and institutional factor in determining international wages differences. And, since trade unions are more powerful in more developed countries than less developed countries due to the historical and political evolution of different societies, the reward for labour directly reflects the uneven development of capitalism on a world scale, with wages higher in richer than in poorer countries. Regarding the low trade unions power in underdeveloped countries, Emmanuel (1975) identified the causes in the repressive policy of colonial and neo-colonial regimes and the narrow margins of surplus redistribution due to the draining of resources by imperialist countries. In this sense, the institutional exogenous variable at the origin of the unequal exchange is a product of the uneven political and economic structure of the capitalist world economy, as a cause becoming the effect of itself in a circular and cumulative process of underdevelopment.

From these premises, Emmanuel infers three relevant conclusions. First, peripheral workers are more exploited by capitalists than central workers because the rate of surplus value is higher in less developed countries. Second, given the international equalization of profit rates and complete trade specialization, an autonomous change in wage level in one country determines changes in the same direction of the price of production of the commodities produced in that country, and in the opposite direction of the general rate of profit. Consequently, the terms of trade are directly related to the level of national wages, thus involving transfers of value from low to high wage countries through the unequal exchange mechanism. Given the hypothesis of complete specialization, in Emmanuel's model, the international value transfers occur between industries and not within industries. Finally, wage growth in more developed countries acts as the ultimate cause of the continuing deterioration of the terms of trade for less developed countries, and consequently, central workers are the primary beneficiaries of the super-exploitation of the peripheral proletariat through the transfers of value deriving from unequal exchange.

The latter point was by far the most provocative, and it triggered the start of a heated discussion among Marxist scholars and political activists of the North and

South. Emmanuel did nothing to mitigate the political and practical implications of his thesis, but rather he stressed them in their whole scope. In fact, he argued that the increases in wages of central workers are paid for the most part by the surplus labour extracted to the peripheral workers, and to a lesser extent by the capitalists of the whole world by a reduction in the international general rate of profit. In this way, Emmanuel resumed and amplified the thesis of the "labour aristocracy" used by Lenin, who explained the opportunism of the British labour movement up to the First World War by the distribution of a small part of the imperialistic super-profits to a privileged upper stratum of the working class for influencing the mass of proletariat towards collaborative positions.[41] Actually, Emmanuel went far beyond Lenin by asserting that the phenomenon of the labour aristocracy cannot be attributed uniquely to a case of "false consciousness" induced by a corrupted fraction of the labour movement, but it is rooted in the material interests of the great majority of the working class of the central capitalist countries. According to Emmanuel, indeed, in capitalist developed countries, the sum of total wages is greater than the total value created by the entire workforce, so that the central workers are net beneficiaries of exploitation because they directly appropriate part of the surplus value extorted to peripheral workers. In other words, the central workers and capitalists of the whole world participate together to the exploitation of the peripheral workers, who then are the sole real producers of the worldwide surplus value.[42] Emmanuel's political conclusion was that the international solidarity of the proletariat is a chimaera, because the central workers are fully aware of their privileges as net receivers of surplus value, and for this reason, they give overall support to the imperialistic policy of the capitalist powers.

Another important implication of Emmanuel's theory concerns the obstacles to the economic development of peripheral countries represented by the transfers of value resulting from the unequal exchange. Since the economic surplus is the fundamental source for productive investment, its draining abroad by means of international trade deprives the backward economies of the opportunity for starting a rapid process of capital accumulation and catching up the economic and technological gap with respect to developed countries. In this sense, Emmanuel maintains that high wages have been a decisive factor in promoting the economic growth of central countries, and this historical example should be followed by peripheral countries too.

Emmanuel's thesis received a very critical reception among Marxist economists, both theoretically and politically. Among several authors participating in the debate following the publication of Emmanuel's book,[43] we shall briefly examine the contributions of two economists who assumed a major role, Charles Bettelheim and Samir Amin. On the theoretical level, the main objections were expressed in the preface to Emmanuel's book written by his academic tutor, Professor Charles Bettelheim, who contested the argument of the institutionally exogenous wage by claiming that it is not a logical and inevitable consequence of the hypothesis of international labour immobility, but rather it represents a crucial, and unjustified, postulate at the base of Emmanuel's entire reasoning. In fact, Bettheleim (1972), while recognizing the historical character of the value of labour power, argues that the wage level is determined in the sphere of production, because it is related to the "objective" structure of production relations and productive forces and, therefore, to the stage of economic development reached by each country, and not to the "subjective" political circumstances of wage settlements. By contrast for Emmanuel, the wages along with other primary incomes like profits and rents are "claims" to a share in the social product, directly connected to the market exchange ratio between commodities that are determined in the sphere of circulation and distribution. Here, the different conception of the theory of value between the two authors is explicitly manifested. Bettelheim adheres to a traditional Marxist interpretation in considering the exchange value as a mere superficial form of the "absolute value" created in the sphere of production, in which the phenomenon of exploitation materializes. Emmanuel, for his part, objects that the exchange is an essential moment, inextricably linked to capitalist production, that necessarily results in value in the form of the price of production, rather than vice versa. In his opinion, whereas values are in the abstract measurable in terms of quantity of labour, actual capitalist prices of production are necessarily expressed in monetary terms as the sum of factor remunerations. Hence, the astonishing conclusion for a professed Marxist: "Exploitation is not a fact of production but of appropriation" (Emmanuel, 1972, p. 329).

During the dispute, however, Emmanuel soon realized that his thesis was difficult to reconcile with Marx's labour theory of value because it implies a mere technical concept of the economic surplus arising from the material organization of labour existing in every possible form of society, with or without classes. In his view, the relations of production assume a particular historical social configuration in the process of distribution, characterized by the struggle between established "claims" for the appropriation of the net product, which in capitalist economies occurs in the sphere of circulation through the exchange of commodities once the technical process of production is accomplished. For this reason, in the later versions of the model Emmanuel preferred to use a Sraffian framework of analysis.[44] In doing so, however, the radical charge of his original message faded because the unequal exchange ceases to be a mechanism of exploitation of the peripheral workers inscribed in the inner economic structure of the capitalist world system, which only a revolution can eliminate. It became, instead, a political and ethical question concerning a more or less fair distribution of the surplus of an otherwise rational and efficient technical process of production and international division of labour. In coherence with this vision, the solution proposed by Emmanuel is framed along reformist lines in envisaging international mechanisms of income redistribution at world level, similar to that operating within Western developed countries by means of welfare state policies and progressive fiscal systems, in a sort of worldwide Keynesianism.

The second strand of objections to Emmanuel's theory was based on the practical validity of his thesis. Provided that the theoretical assumptions of his model are regarded as correct, the exploitation of peripheral workers by their colleagues of the central countries is an empirical question because we need to see if there is a positive difference between the wages perceived and the surplus produced by the workers of more developed countries. Or, put in Marxist terms, it is not sufficient to observe a difference between central and peripheral rates of exploitation of comparable workers, but it must be demonstrated that central workers are not exploited at all by their capitalists and their reward incorporates an imperialistic rent, additional to the value created by their living labour expended in production. If this is not the case, the higher wages would represent a partial refund of the surplus value extorted by capitalists, without direct consequence on peripheral workers conditions. Emmanuel (1975) thought to give empirical proof by contradiction by multiplying the average US nominal wage in dollars for the total number of workers worldwide for the year 1969, arguing that American workers were a net receiver of surplus value since the result was greater than the total world income at factor prices.

However, Emmanuel's calculation was not entirely convincing. As Amin pointed out, the wage comparison should take account of the levels of productivity, because unequal exchange can arise only when unequal wages correspond to equal productivity; otherwise, the higher wages may simply be the result of the greater value produced by more productive workers for an identical rate of exploitation. In more technical terms, Amin (1976) argued that unequal exchange is properly defined by double factorial terms of trade different from unity, indicating a situation in which wage differentials are greater than productivity differentials. A similar argument was used by Bettelheim in reproaching Emmanuel for considering only the extraction of absolute and not relative surplus labour, which would have implied a higher rate of exploitation of central workers than peripheral ones, despite the higher wages of the former. Considering the productivity levels, however, is not an easy task to perform. In fact, what should be compared is the physical or real productivity and not the nominal productivity, because the latter is calculated by means of observable market prices formed on the basis of already distorted factor remunerations. But, real productivity, measured in terms of physical quantities, can be compared only within a given industry producing goods of the same kind, while it cannot be compared between different industries because there would be no common unit of measurement.[45] Consequently, since Emmanuel's model necessarily includes the hypothesis of complete specialization in production and trade in specific commodities for each partner, the double factorial terms of trade cannot be applied and, therefore, it is impossible to empirically verify its validity. The failure in the empirical validation of the model predictions was then a decisive factor in bringing into question the scientific status of the whole theory.

2.5 A taxonomy of the forms of unequal exchange

The selected review of the literature showed that the unequal exchange in international trade has been justified in a variety of ways, often heterogeneous between

Table 2.1 Forms of unequal exchange in the literature

Cause	Differences	Main authors
Structure of production and industrial specialization	Intersectoral wages Intersectoral profit rates Organic composition of capital	Lewis Prebisch and Singer Classic Marxist theory (Bauer, Grossmann)
International distribution of income	International wages International profit rates	Emmanuel Monopoly capitalism theory (Baran, Sweezy, Amin)

them. In an attempt to give a logical order, we can classify the different typologies shown in Table 2.1, where they are divided according to the nature of the independent and exogenous factor at the origin of the unequal exchange, and the form by which it affects the terms of trade between countries.

Foremost, we found a fundamental divide between theories based on differences in the structure of production and industrial specialization between countries, and theories based on the process of international distribution of income, as the ultimate cause of unequal exchange. In the former, there are the structuralist approaches that attribute the divergent terms of trade to differences in factor remunerations between sectors in which countries specialize, along with Marxist non-equivalent exchange due to different national organic compositions of capital. In the latter, there are the monopoly capitalism and neo-dependency approaches along with Emmanuel's thesis, which derive the unequal exchange from the institutional market power of transnational corporations and Western trade unions, respectively, over the international distribution of income.

The different sources and forms of unequal exchange highlighted in the literature lack a unified theoretical framework that is able to incorporate all of them. This fact surely represents one major weakness of the unequal exchange thesis, because the international transfers of value appear more as exceptions and special cases of a normally balanced trade, rather than the rule of a globalized capitalist world economy. However, it is my opinion that a general model of unequal exchange can be derived on the basis of Marx's international law of value, as will be shown in the following chapters.

Notes

1 A thorough examination of mercantilist thought is beyond the present scope, and here the analysis will be strictly limited to some points bearing on the modern unequal exchange debate. For an up-to-date critical review of the historiographic and economic debate on mercantilist political economy, see Magnusson (2015).
2 In the course of this book, unless otherwise indicated, we will use the concept of net terms of trade, indicating the relative price of exported goods in terms of imported goods, that is, the number of units of imported goods of equal value obtainable for each unit of exported good. On the different concepts of terms of trade, see Findlay (2018).

3 See Perrotta (2004), pp. 210–220.
4 "The Design or End of Commerce, is the drawing to one's self Gold and Silver; which I call the grand real Measure or Denominator of the real Value of all things". So Isaac Gervaise, a prominent merchant and mercantilist writer, wrote in his influential *The System or Theory of the Trade of the World* published in 1720 (in Magnusson, 1995, p. 2).
5 See Perrotta (1991).
6 On Marx's interpretation of the "monetary and mercantile system", see Wiltgen (1989). In chapter 23 of *The General Theory of Employment, Interest, and Money*, Keynes explicitly regards mercantilists as his predecessors, see Keynes (2018).
7 On the accumulation by dispossession practices in capitalism, see Harvey (2003) and Glassmann (2006).
8 From a Marxist perspective, the role played by mercantilism in the birth of capitalism is particularly stressed by Dobb (1946) and, more recently, Perelman (2000) and Heller (2011).
9 See Hattori (2012).
10 See Magnusson (2015), pp. 37–41.
11 See Thirlwall (1998).
12 What authors should be included in the definition of classical political economy is a controversial issue, see Milonakis and Fine (2009, pp. 13–16). Marx's definition included economists from Petty and Boisguillebert to Ricardo and Sismondi, in Britain and France, respectively, with Adam Smith as a central figure (Marx, *MECW*, vol. 29, p. 292).
13 On the notion of "ideological unconscious" in Marx, see Read (2017).
14 For a critical analysis of Ricardo's theory of comparative advantages and free trade principle, see Baiman (2017).
15 See Semmel (1970).
16 This difference is expressed in International Political Economy by the distinction between "malevolent" and "benign" mercantilism, see Gilpin (1987).
17 On the List's attitude about free trade and protectionism, see Shafaeddin (2005), Selwyn (2009), and Pradella (2014).
18 On Keynes's views about trade protection, see Eichengreen (1984).
19 For an extensive and detailed review of the unequal exchange debate from mercantilism to ecological approach, see Brolin (2007). A more selective survey can be found in Raffer (1987) and Brolin (2016).
20 On the evolution of thinking at the ECLAC during its first 60 years of existence, see Bielschowsky (2009).
21 See Arndt (1985).
22 See Chenery (1975).
23 On the ontological opposition between structuralism and individualism, see Karsten (1983), Jackson (2003), and Charusheela (2013).
24 See Myrdal (1957). For an extensive discussion on the use of the principle of circular and cumulative causation in heterodox political economy, see the book edited by Berger (2009).
25 Lewis presented the model first in his famous article in *The Manchester Journal*, see Lewis (1954). Later, he returned to the topic with particular attention to the foreign trade aspects in Lewis (1969), (1978), and (1979). A comprehensive survey of the developments of Lewis's model is in Kirkpatrick and Barrientos (2004). On unequal exchange in a Lewis-type dual economy, see Evans (1989).
26 On the "Prebisch–Singer thesis", see Toye and Toye (2003).
27 On the structuralist conception of value, prices, and surplus, see Di Filippo (1980) and (2009).

28 For a critical survey of Marxist theories of imperialism, see Brewer (2002).

29 In 1888, Engels published some of Marx's speeches and writing of the 1840s in a pamphlet titled "On the question of free trade". In the preface, he wrote: "forty years ago, Marx pronounced, in principle, in favor of Free Trade as the more progressive plan, and, therefore, the plan which would soonest bring capitalist society to that deadlock" (Engels, *MECW*, vol. 26, p. 535). On the position of the young Marx on free trade and protectionism, see Ghorashi (1995).

30 For a critical review of these interpretations, see Fine and Harris (1976) and Saad-Filho (2019, chap. 2).

31 The rate of surplus value, or rate of exploitation, is given by the ratio between surplus labour, or unpaid labour, and necessary labour, or total wages.

32 See Kurz (2010).

33 See Shaikh (1980), Carchedi (1988) and (1989), and Seretis and Tsaliki (2012) and (2015).

34 On this point, see, in particular, the debate between Emmanuel (1972) and Bettelheim (1972) on the distinction between unequal exchange in "the broad sense" and in "the narrow sense".

35 The classical text of the theory of monopoly capital is Baran and Sweezy (1966). For a representative collection of the main authors adhering to this approach, see the volume edited by Bellamy Foster and Szlajfer (1984). For a review of the Marxist theory of monopoly capitalism, see Bellamy Foster (1986) and Sawyer (1988). The relation between monopoly capitalism and unequal exchange theories is discussed by Dunn (2017).

36 Gunder Frank (1967) and (1969) are the most influential works of this author. A collection of his selected writings is in Chew and Lauderdale (2010). For an introduction in world system analysis made by one of its architects, see Wallerstein (2004). On the issue of unequal exchange in world system analysis, see also Boles (2002).

37 Amin was a very prolific author. For an overview of the evolution of his thought on the issue of unequal exchange, see Amin (1974) and (2018). On the cultural and political legacy of Samir Amin, who died in 2018, see Kvangraven (2020).

38 "Precise analysis of the significance of the worsening of the terms of trade for the underdeveloped countries requires that systematic studies be undertaken in order to compare the evolution of relative prices (net barter terms of trade) with that of productivities. The concept of double factorial terms of trade answers to this need, as it is the quotient of the net barter terms of trade by the index of progress in comparative productivities" (Amin 1976, p. 168).

39 For recent critical reviews of Emmanuel's theory, see Sheppard (2012), Edwards (2015) and Lichtenstein (2016).

40 This is how Emmanuel (1972, p. xxxiv) summarizes the basic condition of his thesis: "Mobility of the capital factor-immobility of the labor factor, with rejection of Ricardo's assumption about the physiological cost of labor power. Sufficient mobility of capital to ensure that in essentials international equalization of profits takes place, so the proposition regarding prices of production remains valid; sufficient immobility of labor to ensure that local differences in wages, due to the socio-historical element, cannot be eliminated".

41 See Lenin (2010). On the concept of labour aristocracy in British political debate, see Pelling (1979). Hobsbawn (2012) discusses Lenin's position on the subject. A critique of the concept of labour aristocracy is in Post (2010). For a review of Marxist debate on labour aristocracy, see Kerswell (2019). Recently, the debate on labour aristocracy has been revived by Cope (2012).

42 See Emmanuel (1975, p. 63): "Today, the vast majority of American workers, and even those in other large OECD countries, are no longer donors but receivers of surplus

value; and naturally this surplus can only come from the labour of workers of other nations, even though it is not directly extorted by those at the end of the line... This is enough to make these sections, who know very well what they are doing, turn their faces resolutely against any kind of fraternal socialistic world".

43 In the controversy following the publication of Emmanuel's works, different strands of criticism emerged, among them the lack of consideration of the transformation problem from values to prices of production (Palloix, 1970; Somaini, 1973); the restriction of the analysis to complete specialization and unable to treat non-specific, intra-industry trade (De Janvry and Kramer, 1979); the assumption of an identical technological level between countries (Houston and Paus, 1987); and the extreme assumption of worldwide identical rates of profit, not substantiated by empirical evidence (Bernal, 1980).

44 For a discussion of Sraffian versions of Emmanuel's unequal exchange, see Bacha (1978), Evans (1984), and Barnes (1985).

45 As argued by Howard and King (1992, p. 194), the problem faced by Emmanuel's theory is analogous to that of the reduction of heterogeneous into homogeneous labour in Marx's labour theory of value. As we will see later, the purchasing power parity can be used to determine the real productivity of different economies. At the time of Emmanuel's debate, however, reliable data on PPP was not yet available.

Bibliography

Amin, S. (1974). *Accumulation on a world scale: A critique of the theory of underdevelopment*. New York: Monthly Review Press.

Amin, S. (1976). *Unequal development: An essay on the social formations of peripheral capitalism*. New York: Monthly Review Press.

Amin, S. (2018). *Modern imperialism, monopoly finance capital, and Marx's law of value*. New York: Monthly Review Press.

Arndt, H. W. (1985). The origins of structuralism. *World Development, 13*(2), 151–159.

Bacha, E. L. (1978). An interpretation of unequal exchange from Prebisch-Singer to Emmanuel. *Journal of Development Economics, 5*(4), 319–330.

Baiman, R. (2017). *The global free trade error: The infeasibility of Ricardo's comparative advantage theory*. London: Routledge.

Baran, P. (1957). *The political economy of growth*. New York: Monthly Review Press.

Baran, P., and Sweezy, P. M. (1966). *Monopoly capital: An essay on the American economic and social order*. New York: New York University Press.

Barnes, T. J. (1985). Theories of interregional trade and theories of value. *Environment and Planning A, 17*(6), 729–746.

Bauer, O. (2000). *The question of nationalities and social democracy*. Minneapolis: University of Minnesota Press.

Bellamy Foster, J. (1986). *The theory of monopoly capitalism*. New York: New York University Press.

Bellamy Foster, J., and Szlajfer, H. (1984). *Faltering economy. The problem of accumulation under monopoly capitalism*. New York: New York University Press.

Berger, S. (Ed.). (2009). *The foundations of non-equilibrium economics: The principle of circular and cumulative causation*. London: Routledge.

Bernal, R. L. (1980). Emmanuel's unequal exchange as a theory of underdevelopment. *Social and Economic Studies, 29*(4), 152–174.

Bettelheim, C. (1972). Theoretical comments. In *Unequal exchange: A study of the imperialism of trade*. Auth.: A. Emmanuel. New York: Monthly Review Press, 271–322.

Bielschowsky, R. (2009). Sixty years of ECLAC: Structuralism and neo-structuralism. *Cepal Review*, *97*, 171–192.

Boles, E. E. (2002). Critiques of world-systems analysis and alternatives: Unequal exchange and three forms of class and struggle in the Japan US silk network, 1880–1890. *Journal of World-Systems Research*, *8*(2), 150–212.

Brewer, T. (2002). *Marxist theories of imperialism: A critical survey*. London: Routledge.

Brolin, J. (2007). *The bias of the world: Theories of unequal exchange in history*. Lund: Lund University.

Brolin, J. (2016). Unequal exchange. In *The Palgrave encyclopaedia of imperialism and anti-imperialism*. Eds: I. Ness, Z. Cope. London: Palgrave Macmillan, 1160–1177.

Carchedi, G. (1988). Marxian price theory and modern capitalism. *International Journal of Political Economy*, *18*(3), 1–112.

Carchedi, G. (1989). Comparative advantage, unequal exchange and socialism: A reply to Tsang and Woo. *Economy and Society*, *18*(3), 360–364.

Charusheela, S. (2013). *Structuralism and individualism in economic analysis: The "contractionary devaluation debate" in development economics*. London: Routledge.

Chenery, H. B. (1975). The structuralist approach to development policy. *The American Economic Review*, *65*(2), 310–316.

Chew, S., and Lauderdale, P. (Eds.). (2010). *Theory and methodology of world development: The writings of Andre Gunder Frank*. Berlin: Springer.

Cope, Z. (2012), *Divided world, divided class: Global political economy and the stratification of labour under capitalism*. Montreal: Kersplebedeb.

De Janvry, A., and Kramer, F. (1979). The limits of unequal exchange. *Review of Radical Political Economics*, *11*(4), 3–15.

Di Filippo, A. (1980). Economic development and theories of value. *Cepal Review*, *11*, 77–114.

Di Filippo, A. (2009). Latin American structuralism and economic theory. *Cepal Review*, *98*, 175–196.

Dobb, M. (1946), *Studies in the development of capitalism*. London: Routledge and Sons.

Dunn, B. (2017). Class, capital and the global unfree market: Resituating theories of monopoly capitalism and unequal exchange. *Science and Society*, *81*(3), 348–374.

Edwards, C. (2015). *The fragmented world: Competing perspectives on trade, money and crisis*. London: Routledge.

Eichengreen, B. (1984). Keynes and protection. *Journal of Economic History*, *44*(2), 363–373.

Emmanuel, A. (1972). *Unequal exchange: A study of the imperialism of trade*. New York: Monthly Review Press.

Emmanuel, A. (1975). *Unequal exchange revisited*. IDS Discussion Paper No. 77. Brighton: University of Sussex.

Evans, D. (1984). A critical assessment of some neo-Marxian trade theories. *The Journal of Development Studies*, *20*(2), 202–226.

Evans, D. (1989). Alternative perspectives on trade and development. In *Handbook of development economics*, Vol. 2. Eds. H. Chenery, and T. N. Srinivasan. Amsterdam: Elsevier, 1241–1304.

Findlay, R. (2018), Terms of trade. In *The New Palgrave dictionary of economics*, Third edition. Eds: M. Vernengo, E. Perez Caldentey, B.J. Rosser Jr. London: Palgrave Macmillan, 13557–13562.

Fine, B., and Harris, L. (1976). Controversial issues in Marxist economic theory. *Socialist Register*, *13*, 141–178.

Ghorashi, R. (1995). Marx on free trade. *Science and Society*, *59*(1), 38–51.

Gilpin, R. (1987). *The political economy of international relations*. Princeton: Princeton University Press.

Glassman, J. (2006). Primitive accumulation, accumulation by dispossession, accumulation by 'extra-economic' means. *Progress in Human Geography*, *30*(5), 608–625.

Grossmann, H. (1992). *The law of accumulation and breakdown of the capitalist system*. London: Pluto Press.

Gunder Frank, A. (1967). *Capitalism and underdevelopment in Latin America*. New York: New York University Press.

Gunder Frank, A. (1969). *Latin America: Underdevelopment or revolution*. New York: Monthly Review Press.

Harvey, D. (2003). *The new imperialism*. Oxford: Oxford University Press.

Hattori, M. (2012). Noboru Kobayashi and his study on the history of economic thought. *The History of Economic Thought*, *54*(1), 1–21.

Heckscher, E. F. (2013). *Mercantilism*. London: Routledge.

Heller, H. (2011). *The birth of capitalism: A 21st century perspective*. London: Pluto Press.

Hilferding, R. (1981). *Finance capital: A study of the latest phase of capitalist development*. London: Routledge and Kegan Paul.

Hobsbawm, E. (2012). Lenin and the "Aristocracy of Labor". *Monthly Review*, *64*(7), 26-34.

Houston, D., and Paus, E. (1987). The theory of unequal exchange: An indictment. *Review of Radical Political Economics*, *19*(1), 90–97.

Howard, M. C., and King, J. E. (1992). *A history of Marxian economics: Volume II: 1929–1990*. London: Macmillan International Higher Education.

Jackson, W. A. (2003). Social structure in economic theory. *Journal of Economic Issues*, *37*(3), 727–746.

Karsten, S. G. (1983). Dialectics, functionalism, and structuralism in economic thought. *American Journal of Economics and Sociology*, *42*(2), 179–192.

Kerswell, T. (2019). A conceptual history of the labour aristocracy: A critical review. *Socialism and Democracy*, *33*(1), 70–87.

Keynes, J. M. (1933). National self-sufficiency. *The Yale Review*, *22*(4), 755-769.

Keynes, J. M. (2018). *The general theory of employment, interest, and money*. Berlin: Springer.

Kirkpatrick, C., and Barrientos, A. (2004). The Lewis model after 50 years. *The Manchester School*, *72*(6), 679–690.

Kurz, H. D. (2010). Technical progress, capital accumulation and income distribution in Classical economics: Adam Smith, David Ricardo and Karl Marx. *The European Journal of the History of Economic Thought*, *17*(5), 1183–1222.

Kvangraven, I. H. (2020). Samir Amin: A pioneering Marxist and third world activist. *Development and Change*, *51*(2), 631–649.

Lenin, V. I. (2010). *Imperialism: The highest stage of capitalism*. London: Penguin Books.

Lewis, W. A. (1954). Economic development with unlimited supplies of labour. *The Manchester School*, *22*(2), 139–191.

Lewis, W. A. (1969). *Aspects of tropical trade 1583–1965.* Stockholm: Almqvist & Wiksell.

Lewis, W. A. (1978). *The evolution of the international economic order.* Princeton: Princeton University Press.

Lewis, W. A. (1979). The dual economy revisited. *The Manchester School, 47*(3), 211–229.

Lichtenstein, P. M. (2016). *Theories of international economics.* London: Routledge.

List, F. (2016). *The natural system of political economy.* London: Routledge.

Magnusson, L. (Ed.). (1995), *Mercantilism vol. 4.* London: Routledge.

Magnusson, L. (2015). *The political economy of mercantilism.* London: Routledge.

Milonakis, D., and Fine, B. (2009). *From political economy to economics: Method, the social and the historical in the evolution of economic theory.* London: Routledge.

Myrdal, G. (1957). *Economic theory and under-developed regions.* London: Gerald Duckworth.

Palloix, C. (1970). La question de l'échange inégal: Une critique de l'économie politique. *L'Homme et la Société, 18,* 5–33.

Pelling, H. (1979). *Popular politics and society in late Victorian Britain.* London: Macmillan Press.

Perelman, M. (2000). *The invention of capitalism: Classical political economy and the secret history of primitive accumulation.* Durham: Duke University Press.

Perrotta, C. (1991). Is the Mercantilist theory of the favorable balance of trade really erroneous?. *History of Political Economy, 23*(2), 301–336.

Perrotta, C. (2004). *Consumption as an investment.* London: Routledge.

Post, C. (2010). Exploring working-class consciousness: A critique of the theory of the 'Labour-Aristocracy'. *Historical Materialism, 18*(4), 3–38.

Pradella, L. (2014). New developmentalism and the origins of methodological nationalism. *Competition and Change, 18*(2), 180–193.

Prebisch, R. (1950a). Crecimiento, desequilibrio y disparidades: Interpretación del proceso de desarrollo económico. In *Estudio económico de América Latina,* 1949-E/CN. 12/164/Rev. 1-1950-p. 3–89.

Prebisch, R. (1950b). *The economic development of Latin America and its principal problems.* New York: United Nations.

Raffer, K. (1987). *Unequal exchange and the evolution of the world system: Reconsidering the impact of trade on north-south relations.* London: Macmillan.

Read, M. K. (2017). Towards a notion of the ideological unconscious: Marx, Althusser, Juan Carlos Rodríguez. *Historical Materialism, 25*(4), 139–165.

Ricardo, D. (2004). *The works and correspondence of David Ricardo. Vol. 1: On the principles of political economy and taxation.* Ed. Piero Sraffa. Indianapolis: Liberty Fund.

Saad Filho, A. (2019). *Value and crisis: Essays on labour, money and contemporary capitalism.* Leiden: Brill.

Sawyer, M. C. (1988). Theories of monopoly capitalism. *Journal of Economic Surveys, 2*(1), 47–76.

Selwyn, B. (2009). An historical materialist appraisal of Friedrich List and his modern-day followers. *New Political Economy, 14*(2), 157–180.

Semmel, B. (1970). *The rise of free trade imperialism: Classical political economy the empire of free trade and imperialism 1750–1850.* Cambridge: Cambridge University Press.

Seretis, S. A., and Tsaliki, P. V. (2012). Value transfers in trade: An explanation of the observed differences in development. *International Journal of Social Economics, 39*(12), 965–982.

Seretis, S. A., and Tsaliki, P. V. (2015). Absolute advantage and international trade. *Review of Radical Political Economics*, *48*(3), 438–451.

Shafaeddin, M. (2005). Friederich List and the infant industry argument. In *The pioneers of development economics: Great economists on development*. Ed. K.S. Jomo. London: Zed Books, 42–61.

Shaikh, A. (1980). On the laws of international exchange. In *Growth, profits, and property: Essays in the revival of political economy*. Ed. E. J. Nell. Cambridge: Cambridge University Press, 204–235.

Shaikh, A. (2016). *Capitalism: Competition, conflict, crises*. Oxford: Oxford University Press.

Sheppard, E. (2012). Trade, globalization and uneven development: Entanglements of geographical political economy. *Progress in Human Geography*, *36*(1), 44–71.

Singer, H. W. (1950). The distribution of gains between investing and borrowing countries. *The American Economic Review*, 40(2), 473–485.

Smith, A. (2010). *The Wealth of Nations: An inquiry into the nature and causes of the Wealth of Nations*. Petersfield: Harriman House.

Somaini, E. (1973). Sulle differenze tra i livelli salariali in diversi paesi: Critica delle tesi di Arghiri Emmanuel. In *Salari, sottosviluppo e imperialismo: Un dibattito sullo scambio ineguale*. Eds: E. Somaini et al. Torino: Einaudi, 3–50.

Thirlwall, A. P. (1998). The balance of payments and growth: From mercantilism to Keynes to Harrod and beyond. In *Economic dynamics, trade and growth*. Ed: A. P. Thirlwall. London: Palgrave Macmillan, 179–211.

Toye, J. F. J., and Toye, R. (2003). The origins and interpretation of the Prebisch-Singer thesis. *History of Political Economy, 35*(3), 437–467.

United Nations. (1949). *Relative prices of exports and imports of under-developed countries: A study of post-war terms of trade between under-developed and industrialized countries*. New York: Dept. of Economic Affairs, United Nations.

Wallerstein, I. (1979). *The capitalist world-economy*. Vol. 2. Cambridge: Cambridge University Press.

Wallerstein, I. (2004). *World-systems analysis*. Durham: Duke University Press.

Wiltgen, R. (1989). The evolution of Marx's perspective of Mercantilism. *International Journal of Social Economics, 16*(7), 48–56.

3

THE SOCIAL ALGORITHM OF VALUE

Andrea Ricci

3.1 The Marxist debate on abstract labour

As we have seen in Chapter 2, in all the different theoretical approaches, the phenomenon of unequal exchange refers to a persistent discrepancy of a country's export and import prices from an ideal long-run equilibrium condition. In the Marxist approach, it concerns the essential dimension of value rather than the phenomenal dimension of market price fluctuations. Unequal exchange can be defined as systematic divergence between the value created in the sphere of commodity production and the value realized in the sphere of commodity circulation. For an individual country, unequal exchange involves both export and import sides. On the export side, it results from a quantitative discrepancy between the international value created by domestic labour in the production of exported commodities, and the international value realized in money from their sale on the world market. On the import side, vice versa, it results from a quantitative discrepancy between the international value created by foreign labour in the production of the imported commodities, and the sum of international money given in payment for them by domestic purchasers. Therefore, transfers of value in international trade derive from the geographical and spatial mismatch between value created in production and value realized in circulation.

In Marx's theory of value, the possibility of the divergence between value created in production and value realized in circulation does not represent a peculiarity of international trade, but it is a general feature of the capitalist exchange. The same applies to more efficient firms with higher than industry average labour productivity, which benefit from a quasi-rent in the form of extra profit deriving from an individual unit value temporarily lower than social unit value, at the expense of firms with lower labour productivity having a lower-than-average profit rate. A difference between value in production and value in circulation also occurs in the case of intersectoral equalization of profit rates, where the price of production of the industries with an organic composition of capital higher than the social average is greater than the value produced by them, and vice versa for the industries with a lower organic composition of capital.

In this chapter, we will show how the potential for decoupling value in production and value in circulation arises from the twofold character of the socially necessary labour, or abstract labour, constituting the substance of value. In the capitalist mode of production, not only does the commodity as a product of labour have a dual existence, resulting in the distinction between concrete labour producing use value and abstract labour producing exchange value, but abstract labour is itself dual. The duality originates from the private character of the process of production and reproduction of capitalist society, which distinguishes it from all other previous forms of social organization. To fully understand what this duality consists of, it is first necessary to clarify what abstract labour and value are.

Without going into the details of a debate lasting over a century, it is possible to note the existence of two opposing lines of interpretation of abstract labour in Marx's value theory.[1] The first interpretation, which goes back to the traditional orthodox and productivist approach to Marx's value theory outlined by Sweezy (1942), considers abstract labour as a transhistorical and asocial category derived from human labour in general.[2] In this context, abstract labour is reduced to its purely physiological aspect of expenditure of human physical and mental energy in production, regardless of the concrete and particular way in which this expenditure takes place. Abstract labour, therefore, would merely be the conceptual generalization of what Marx calls simple labour, which every average worker can do, and to which complex labour that requires special skills can always be quantitatively reduced as its multiple. It would be determined entirely within the labour process, considered in a mere technical sense, irrespective of the specific social form taken by the product of labour, without any relation to money and commodity circulation or to other specific historical features of capitalism. Such an undifferentiated notion of labour can therefore be applied to any form of human society, historically antecedent or subsequent to capitalism. This physiological and naturalistic concept of abstract labour as the substance of value leads the orthodox Marxist approach to the immediate identification of value with the labour time embodied in the production of the commodity. It recalls a Ricardian interpretation of value theory substantially different from that of Marx, who criticized Ricardo precisely for having ignored the specific historical social form assumed by the product of the value-creating labour in capitalism, which is the money form.[3]

This traditional Marxist conception of abstract labour as physiological labour was later embraced by neo-Ricardians, who, however, drew opposite conclusions about the theory of value in an apparently paradoxical way. Sharing the purely naturalistic notion of labour as the real social cost of production, applicable to every historical form of society, neo-Ricardians consider as abstract labour the natural labour the products of which circulate as commodities.[4] On the immutable substratum of natural labour is added the mercantile exchange that gives the specific form of exchange value to the real social cost of production now consisting of wage goods. In capitalism, the value is thus determined only in the sphere of circulation of commodities because it is just the market exchange making capitalism different from all other modes of production. Therefore, what distinguishes capitalism is the form of price, as the only visible expression of exchange value, and not the form of value, which thus becomes a useless metaphysical ornament devoid of any cognitive significance.[5] Consequently, for neo-Ricardian scholars, the economic analysis of capitalism begins and ends within the sphere of commodity circulation with the determination of relative prices, since the social distribution of the net product between social classes would be determined by extra-economic factors of a political nature.[6] In this way, neo-Ricardian theory, although originating from classical roots, aims to replace neoclassical theory as the theory of general economic equilibrium, thus losing the connotations of the critique of political economy essential in Marx's discourse.

Curiously, the second prevailing interpretation of Marx's value theory arrives at the same circulationist view in considering value and abstract labour as exclusively originating from the commodity exchange, rather than from the labour effectively performed in production, on the basis, however, of a completely different theoretical framework than the neo-Ricardian one. The modern interpreters of this approach are the authors belonging to the Value Form school[7] who have reassessed the circulationist argument according to a social and historical, rather than natural, concept of abstract labour. This modern approach is characterized by two main theoretical roots. The first root is the rediscovery in the 1970s of the work on value by Isaac Rubin, who in the 1920s had earlier emphasized abstract labour as a social phenomenon in opposition to labour as a physiological human activity.[8] The second root lies in the revaluation of Hegelian dialectics as an indispensable tool for a correct interpretation of Marx's value theory, in reaction to the naturalistic and positivistic character of orthodox Marxism.[9] Unlike Hegelian idealism, however, the Value Form school considers the forms of expression of abstract categories as social and historical, rather than general and immutable. Despite the variety of individual contributions, it shares a common premise in considering the mercantile form as the specific social form of economic categories in capitalism. The formal analysis of the market exchange would therefore be the only valid method to grasp the historical specificity of labour in capitalism compared with other social economic formations, where the social forms of the products of labour are different. In this way, the circulation of commodities becomes the privileged moment over that of production, which instead complies with universally valid technical rather than social constraints. In this approach, production, when regarded as separated from circulation, looks as a purely instrumental procedure, an ideal conceptual representation of the human metabolism with nature, detached from the process of social constitution that would be determined only in the sphere of distribution, and in capitalism exclusively through the exchange of commodities. Everything upstream or downstream of the moment of exchange, be it the production or consumption of goods, is thus seen as belonging to a private sphere, and as such is not involved in defining the historical form of capitalist society. Even if through other ways and drawing opposite conclusions, then the Value Form school comes to consider production in the same naturalistic, asocial, and technical way as the traditional Marxist and neo-Ricardian approaches to which it is confronted. Following these theoretical premises, abstract labour would be constituted as the social form of value-creating labour in commodity circulation, since labour in production would be heterogeneous and incommensurable, as a private labour devoid of social quality. Therefore, labour becomes abstract only when it takes the form of money in the expression of price, which would be the only measure of value without any reference to labour time. In this way, however, abstract labour loses all connection with living labour,[10] which, to use Marx's expressions, objectifies, crystallizes in the value of commodities, and the very notion of exploitation of labour by capital disappears into the formal equality of the seller and the buyer, both subject to the common alienation of social commodification.

In the controversy between circulationist and productivist notions of value and abstract labour, Marxist economics seems to revive in itself the old opposition between Smith's labour-commanded and Ricardo's labour-embodied concept of value in classical political economy,[11] even though Marx deemed to have definitely overcome it. In Marxist literature, however, there are some exceptions from authors mostly sympathetic to the Value Form school, such as Murray (2016) and Bellofiore (2009), who have proposed alternative readings of Marxian texts on abstract labour, aware of the inner limits of the two main opposite interpretations. These authors, in criticizing both the "production-only" and the "exchange-only" views of Marx's theory, claim that value arises from the totality of the monetary circuit of capitalist production and circulation and there is no possibility to determine an ontological priority of one of the two moments. Value, as an intrinsic social property of the commodity, remains "latent", "potential", and "ideal" as abstract labour in production, becoming "actual" and "practical" as money in circulation by means of the social validation of the exchange.

Murray's contribution considers purely physiological labour as a general analytical category of thought, "abstract labour in general", which in capitalism finds its real specific social and historical form in value-producing labour expressed by money in circulation, the "practically abstract labour". Between the two notions of "abstract labour in general" and "practically abstract labour", there is no direct connection because they stand on different conceptual levels. "Abstract labour in general" is a pure concept devoid of any materiality, obtained by removing from the concept of labour in general the purpose, the form, and the natural matter. What remains is the empty idea of pure human energy expenditure, which Murray (2016, p. 240) defines as the "pure labour (labour 'in itself')". Bellofiore has a slightly different view in considering abstract labour not merely as a mental generalization, but as a real abstraction that imposes its dominion on the concrete living labour of workers through the action of capital inside the material production process. Abstract labour acting in production as a real abstraction is latent and ideal money, in which capital wants to transform the product of living labour through the sale of commodities on the market. Abstract labour, as the substance of value, has the form of ideal money even within production since "the content, in a sense, is already always form-determined" (Bellofiore, 2009, p. 191). In both views, there is an inescapable incommensurability between the invisible dimension of abstract labour in production and its social form of expression as the price in commodity circulation, without any possibility of determining whatsoever the quantitative relationship between money and labour time in production, being the latter always a concrete and heterogeneous labour time in Murray or a pure potentiality waiting to be actualized as money in Bellofiore. In this collapse of content and form in the black hole of money, this approach is unable to truly incorporate the moment of production into the determination of value, which remains anchored in a "practical sense" only to the one-sided monetary dimension. Value as distinct from price is thus reduced to a purely abstract notion, a "ghost", devoid of the operational character that it instead has in Marx. In that manner, value theory becomes a noteworthy philosophical and political critique of capitalist modernity, without however providing practical analytical tools for the concrete investigation of the ordinary phenomena of actual capitalist economy.

Another interesting attempt to overcome the dilemma between productivist and circulationist concept of abstract labour is the one pursued on an original theoretical basis by Kicilsof and Starosta (2007a, b, 2011). While rejecting the naturalistic notion of embodied labour, these authors differ from the Value Form school in considering abstract labour as a general category of human activity in its individual and material corporeality, rather than a pure category of thought. They define abstract labour as "the universal or general aspect of the materiality of the labour of the individual (i.e. the expenditure of brains, nerves, muscles, etc., regardless of its particular form)"[12], which exists in every historical form of human society as physical and mental effort and fatigue, in the meaning that Genesis (3:19) tells us "By the sweat of your brow you will eat your food". What is distinctive of capitalism is the separate and independent social form of value in which the materiality of abstract labour objectifies because of the private character of production. As long as production was immediately social and the division of social labour occurred according to the criteria of collective cooperation or personal dominance, as in patriarchal, ancient, and feudal societies, abstract labour remained a private dimension of the individual experience of each worker. The autonomous and independent social form of value, as the objectified abstract labour in capitalism, provides a criterion for the division of social labour realized through private production and the exchange of commodities. The purely physiological aspect of labour, previously merged with the concrete individual labour activity, becomes in capitalism the vector of social commensurability of the different privately produced use values, transforming them into exchange values. The visible social equivalence established by money in commodity exchange would be based on the commensurability of abstract labour in its material aspect of individual expenditure of human energy. In this sense, value-producing labour is "privately performed (socially necessary) abstract labour".[13]

The problem that arises with this interpretation of abstract labour is how a purely individual and subjective dimension of working human activity can become a social category and provide the objective basis for the division of social labour in capitalism. The answer cannot be that it is the levelling action of the exchange between commodity and money that determines the social equivalence of individual material working experiences since this would lead to a vicious logical circle, given that it is abstract labour objectified in an autonomous social form that should represent the foundation of the exchange value as a vector of the division of social labour and not vice versa. An answer of this kind would make this interpretation of abstract labour similar to that of the circulationist approach, albeit in a substantialist and physicalist version. The effort and fatigue of concrete labour, which according to Kicillof and Starosta (2011, p. 298) define "the abstract or general materiality of individual labour (i.e. of abstract labour)", are subjective aspects of the work experience that vary from individual to individual depending on strictly personal biological and psychological factors.[14] Time is not the unit of measurement of the physiological expenditure of human energy, since the individual effort and fatigue of a given concrete work are irreducible to the length of time measured by the clock. The same identical labour activity, performed over the same period of time with the same intensity, does not require the same effort and fatigue in two different individuals. From a purely biological point of view, the unit of measurement could rather be the calories needed by each individual to perform a specific action, but this would fail to account for the psychic component. The material abstraction of individual labour as effort and fatigue has a purely qualitative character. It belongs to the general definition of concrete labour, which by its nature is socially incommensurable, and from which in no way can it detach itself and give rise to the autonomous social form of the exchange value. As with the formalist notion, then, the substantialist and physicalist notion of abstract labour does not seem able to solve the dilemma of what is to be understood by the concept of abstract labour in Marx.

3.2 Social labour in general

To understand the notion of abstract labour in Marx, it is first necessary to start with a proper definition of labour. According to Marx, "Labour is, in the first place, a process in which both man and Nature participate, and in which man of his own accord starts, regulates, and controls the material reactions between himself and Nature" (*MK1*, p. 127) in order to satisfy his needs. However, the labour process does not indicate an abstract ontological metabolism of Man with Nature, because in Marx the real ontological foundation of the human being always has a specific social character. Consequently, labour in every historical epoch, since primordial times, is always a social activity, and what really exists is the metabolism of human society with nature. Marx's starting point, therefore, is not pure and simple human labour in general, but a human activity socially performed, that is, social labour in general.[15] Along these lines, I will define abstract labour as the specific historical social form taken in capitalism by social labour in general,[16] to which corresponds the institution of wage labour as the dominant form of labour relationship in capitalism.

Let us now examine in more detail the concept of social labour in general. Its two constituent elements are labour and sociality that represent in their historically inseparable unity a universal characteristic of human life resulting from the mediated character of human experience in the world. Animality becomes humankind when it begins to manufacture the instruments of labour, the production tools, to obtain means of subsistence, not simply use them as they are found in nature.[17] The formal transformation of natural objects to instruments of labour gives rise to a new type of force that acts on animate and inanimate matter alongside and together with natural forces. This new force is labour as a human intentional activity aimed at the transformation of external objects by means of tools in accordance with the specific goal of procuring the livelihoods and satisfying human needs. Labour as an intentional activity mediated by manufactured tools implies a detachment from the immediacy of a purely perceptive experience. To see in a natural object a possible production tool, obtained through the transformation of its immediate form into an artefact necessary to produce other artefacts, it is necessary to imagine oneself in the future, being aware of one's body and mind detached from the immediate natural context in which one finds oneself at that moment. This reflexive consciousness can only be achieved through the language that transforms the animal's cry, the lip-smacks of the ape, in words organized in speech and thought. Through language, the immediate interiority of perception is projected outside the self and is objectified, allowing to imagine oneself beyond the immediate self of the instant. As the transformation of the external nature is mediated by manufactured tools, so too the inner transformation of the animal becoming man is mediated by words. Language and labour, word and tool, together mark the advent of a new animal species named humankind.[18] Both of these two constituent categories of humanity have from the beginning, by their very essence, a social character. Nor can they be thought and defined outside of a social link between different individuals living together. What applies to language, as the structure of individual thought and simultaneous social communication, applies in the same way to production and labour, as the structure of the reproduction of individual and simultaneous social life. In his criticism of the individualistic solipsism of bourgeois political economy, Marx is ironic on this point when in the *Grundrisse* he says:

Production by an isolated individual outside society – a rare exception which may well occur when a civilized person in whom the social forces are already dynamically present is cast by accident into the wilderness – is as much of an absurdity as is the development of language without individuals living together and talking to each other.

(Marx, *MG*, p. 18)

Just as language is by its very nature a social phenomenon, so labour is always by its very nature social labour even when it is conducted by a single individual isolated from the rest of the human community.

Social labour is a general concept, applicable to every historical form of human society. It consists of the coordinated working activities of the individuals belonging to a given community, aimed at satisfying the social needs through the production of the goods necessary for the reproduction of the collective and individual life of all its members. Social labour is structured in two general moments, that of production and reproduction through the consumption of the produced goods. The general moment of reproduction, in turn, incorporates both particular types of productive consumption, in the form of intermediate goods and means of production, and unproductive consumption, in the form of final consumer goods. It is in social labour that the two moments of social production and social reproduction join together to establish a given human society, which lasts from generation to generation. To achieve this function of social constitution, the concept of social labour implies a proper distribution of individual activities in accordance with the social needs of the community. Ultimately, Marx notes in the *Grundrisse*,[19] the economic organization of all forms of society concerns the distribution of available individual and collective time between the activities of material and intellectual production and consumption of resources necessary for the reproduction of the physical and moral life of human beings. What differentiates the modes of production that have followed one another throughout human history, from prehistoric communist communities to today's globalized capitalism, is the specific form in which the division of social labour is realized. It is, therefore, the specific form, through which the division of social labour among the members of the society occurs, that defines the specific historical character of the social modes of production in the course of successive ages, as Marx points out very clearly to Kugelmann in his letter of July 11, 1868:

> Every child knows a nation which ceased to work, I will not say for a year, but even for a few weeks, would perish. Every child knows, too, that the masses of products corresponding to the different needs required different and quantitatively determined masses of the total labor of society. That this *necessity* of the *distribution* of social labor in definite proportions cannot possibly be done away with by a *particular form* of social production but can only change the *mode* of its *appearance*, is self-evident. No natural laws can be done away with. What can change in historically different circumstances is only the *form* in which these laws assert themselves.
>
> (Marx, *MEC*, July 11, 1868)

The notion of division of social labour does not coincide with that of social division of labour. The latter refers exclusively to the moment of production, indicating the division of working tasks among the members of a productive unit or branch of production. This type of division of labour becomes particularly important within capitalist manufacture, while in the previous modes of production it was poorly developed due to the polyvalent character of traditional agricultural and craft work. The former, instead, defined by Marx (*MECW*, vol. 30, p. 199) as the division of "the labour of society as a whole", has a broader and universal meaning because it refers to the social distribution of the labour of the whole society among all the different branches producing all kinds of goods, in accordance with the social needs to be satisfied. This division of social labour has existed in every historical form of society, even in the simplest form of division of productive and reproductive tasks between generations and between genders. Marx reproaches Smith for not distinguishing between the two forms of division of labour, thus giving a universal meaning to the social division of labour which, unlike the division of social labour, is instead a prominent feature of the capitalist mode of production alone.[20]

The division of social labour is simultaneously the division between members of society of the labour activities, on the one hand, and of goods and services produced for their productive and unproductive consumption, on the other hand. Due to the inherent nature of social labour, a necessary coherence has to exist between the two aspects of its division, so that a given form of social production is necessarily associated with a corresponding form of social distribution of the goods produced. In pre-capitalist societies, the division of social labour took place on the basis of personal relationships that bound the individual members of the community, each with its own social role defined by traditions and customs, in compliance with criteria of a political, religious, or cultural nature. The specific form taken by these personal ties in the process of division of social labour defines the different modes of production that succeeded prior to the advent of capitalism. We can thus distinguish modes of production of an egalitarian type, such as primitive communistic communities, and modes of production based on hierarchical relations of class domination, such as those of the patriarchal, ancient slavery, Asian and feudal type. In all these historically different forms of society, the division of social labour took place according to a direct and unitary planned process, in which the two distinct moments of production and consumption coincided immediately at the time of the definition of the social role assumed or inherited by each member. In these societies, therefore, individual labour was directly and consciously aimed at satisfying social needs that were concretely and personally established in advance of production. "The labour of the individual is posited from the outset as social labour" (Marx, *MG*, p. 102). Under these historical conditions, the labour of individuals was always and exclusively concrete labour, the producer of specific use values corresponding to the socially assigned task to each individual worker and intended for socially pre-determined specific consumers. The division of social labour coincided with the pre-determined distribution of concrete working activities and use values between individuals.

In these historical circumstances, social labour in general did not take an independent and autonomous form with respect to the rest of the process of social reproduction but remained perfectly integrated within the unitary structure of the direct personal relationships of cooperation and mutual dependence between the members of the community. For this reason, the economic sphere had not yet separated itself, becoming autonomous and independent from the political and religious spheres, as will happen with capitalism. In pre-capitalist societies, social labour is lacking an autonomous specific form of expression, and it remains concealed within the totality of social relations. What assumes a specific character is the modality of division of social labour, which, however, takes place on the basis of criteria and mechanisms of a political, religious, and cultural nature, rather than strictly economic considerations, thus defining the specific historical form of each traditional mode of production. Primitive domestic labour, slavery and serfdom are general institutions that govern every aspect of the social and cultural life of individuals, unlike what will happen in capitalism with wage labour. It is only with the system of wage labour that social labour takes on a specific mode of expression as abstract labour, becoming autonomous from the rest of the social relations that constitute an organized community of individuals.

The planned distribution of social labour among the members of traditional societies does not imply, however, a rational and consciously self-directed process of social production and reproduction. The rules, criteria, and aims underlying the plan for the division of social labour are in fact subtracted from the free choice of the community and rigidly determined according to customs and traditions handed down from generation to generation. Ultimately, they are dictated by magical and religious beliefs in supernatural entities of various kinds, from totems to monotheistic gods, which require the continuous repetition of the same social practices. These magical entities, taking the form of fetishes, represent the imaginary mental transposition of the dominant social structure and the alienated power of social cooperation of individuals belonging to the same community. While this spirit of preservation ensures the reproduction of social life in ordinary circumstances, it is a heavy obstacle to change and innovation in the face of unexpected and extraordinary events. It blocks the development of social productive forces and compels traditional societies to a permanent stagnation, characterized by the continuous recurrence of the same cycles in individual and collective life. The historical evolution of traditional societies is thus typically characterized by long phases of stability followed by sudden moments of crisis and rapid dissolution. With the advent of capitalism, the regulating principle of the social order determining the division of social labour, previously projected in an imaginary form outside of society, moves inside society, becoming the spontaneous product of the myriad of independent individual practices that find their only connection point in the market and in commodity exchange. The old magical and religious idols of transcendent nature are thus replaced in their practical economic functions by a new idol, immanent but always subtracted from the conscious human will, which reigns supreme over capitalist society, the value.

3.3 The social algorithm of value

The real historical evolution of pre-capitalist societies is, of course, more articulated than the picture described in the previous paragraph, especially during the phases of transition from one mode of production to another, mainly due to the effect of trade, which is playing an increasingly important role as we approach the bourgeois era by eroding ancient social foundations. What remains unquestionable, however, is that before the advent of capitalism as the dominant mode of production, the division of social labour did not require the involvement of value and abstract labour as an autonomous and independent form of social labour in general. The things are different in a capitalist society, where instead the division of social labour occurs indirectly and unconsciously through the market mechanism, as Marx states in the remainder of his letter to Kugelmann reported previously:

> And the form in which this proportional distribution of labor asserts itself, in the state of society where the interconnection of social labor is manifested in the private exchange of the individual products of labor, is precisely the exchange value of these products.
>
> (Marx, *MEC*, July 11, 1868)

To show the logical origin of the concepts of value and abstract labour as vectors of the division of social labour in capitalism, we will follow the same path as Marx in the first book of *Capital*, starting with a hypothetical society of independent private producers who exchange their products on the market in order to obtain the necessary means of subsistence. As we will discuss in more detail later, this starting point does not concern historical time but logical time, since it does not refer to a past period of human social evolution but rather to the investigation of the capitalist mode of production from its simplest and most abstract categories. As Tombazos (2014, p. 10) points out with an incisive expression: "The object of the first part of *Capital* is not a pre-capitalist commercial order, but instead a capitalism without capital, which is obviously contradictory". But this is a necessary contradiction. In fact, it is precisely from the development of this contradiction, between the formal equality of exchange and the emergence of the capitalist surplus in the form of profit, that Marx's analysis moves in search of the dialectical element capable of overcoming, and at the same time preserving, the initial antinomy. Marx's decisive discovery was to identify this element in the concept of labour power, distinct from that of labour, as the special commodity whose use value consists in increasing, and valorizing, the exchange value represented by it in the form of wages. However, the presentation of this discovery necessarily requires the equivalence of the exchange to pose as a starting premise, from which the contradiction and finally the dialectic solution spontaneously arise. Capital and profit logically originate from the law of value in its simplest and purest form of exact equivalence of exchange in the first book of *Capital,* and only after their emergence do they modify the law of value in the final form of prices of production in the third book. In the same way, the further modification of the law of value at the international level, which is the object of my research, requires to start from the equivalence of the simple market exchange in which the law of value acts in its simplest and purest form.

In a society of private producers, the division of social labour is no longer determined *ex ante*, before production, according to the political, religious, and cultural order of past traditional societies, but is the *ex post* result of the commodity circulation and market exchange.[21] In this case, the two moments of social production and consumption are incarnated by two independent social figures, the producer-seller and the consumer-purchaser, linked together only by the market exchange of the commodity. The roles played by real individuals in this relationship are not fixed and immutable, but variable and interchangeable both in a diachronic sense, over time, and in a synchronic sense, within the single act of exchange. The vendor sells its privately produced good to obtain in exchange the good privately produced by the buyer, and vice versa, since it is only through the reciprocal alienation that everyone can acquire their own means of subsistence. The dual social role that each individual simultaneously assumes in market exchange gives each of the two exchanged goods the simultaneous dual character of use value, indicating their qualitative property to satisfy a particular human need, and exchange value, indicating the determined quantitative ratio at which the goods are exchanged. This twofold character imparts the social form of commodity to the exchanged objects. In this way, the commodities become the objectification of a social relation between individuals, and their social form of exchange value becomes the impersonal and unconscious vector of the division of social labour. Thus, the foundational social link of the capitalist society, the one ensuring its continuous reproduction as an organized community of independent private producers, appears as the objective property of the material objects bearing the form of commodity and acquires the character of a fetish.[22]

Let us now return to the moment of exchange and consider the case of a reproducible commodity that is exchanged with a multitude of other commodities according to a consistent market exchange ratio that is without any possibility of arbitrage. As we will discuss later, we are therefore examining the exchange of a capitalist commodity. By abstracting from the material qualities that make the commodity an object of use, within the act of market exchange, "something" operates that allows the mutual formal transformation of two intrinsically different entities one into the other according to a given market exchange ratio. This "something" is what Marx calls value.

Some authors argue that this "something" is a "third thing" that exists in each of the two commodities regardless of their mutual exchange, on the grounds of which the market exchange ratio is determined, and they identify this "third thing" with a common social property, or substance, shared by all commodities as products of labour.[23] This "third thing" is what would define the concept of value as "intrinsic value", defined as "a quantum of abstract labour congealed in commodities" (Kliman, 2000, p. 92), distinct from the formal expression of exchange value that constitutes the "extrinsic value". In this way, however, a misunderstanding specularly opposed to that typical of the Value Form school is made. If the latter leads to the collapse of abstract labour as the substance of value in the formal relation of exchange, in this case, the opposite happens with the complete detachment of abstract labour, unilaterally identified with social labour in production,[24] from the social form of value. In this way, the dialectical tension, the conceptual dualism, is no longer inside each of the two determinations of substance (abstract labour) and form (exchange value) of value, as in Marx, but is projected outside as external opposition between them. The two moments of substance, defined as the "intrinsic value", and form, defined as the "extrinsic value", lose conceptual autonomy and reduce to rigidly opposed unilateral determinations.

Both productivist and circulationist approaches to Marx's theory of value interpret the dualistic character of value as a dialectical opposition between substance and form, "intrinsic value" and "extrinsic value", abstract labour and exchange value, and socially necessary labour time and money, except that each of them privileges only one of the two moments of the alleged dialectical opposition. Value and substance of value are identified in social labour objectified in production, to the point that it becomes impossible to distinguish the concept of value from that of abstract labour. The exchange value as the form of value is in turn confined to the partial determination of the market exchange ratio. In this way, different levels of abstraction are placed on the same conceptual level by merging value and substance of value[25] and contrasting value and value-form. Substance and form, abstract labour and exchange value, placed in mutual opposition must, however, find a synthesis, otherwise, the dialectical movement of the commodity remains frozen in a fruitless logical antagonism. The way out is recourse to the concept of interdependence between value and form of value, between value as abstract labour time and exchange value as price.[26] It is this, however, a purely formal solution that reveals the loss of conceptual autonomy suffered by the one-sided definitions of substance and form of value. Interdependence implies indeed that neither of the two determinations can be defined independently one from the other, and this leads to a logical vicious circle in which value refers to price and price to value.

In Marx, the "third thing" acting as a vector of commensurability in exchange is abstract labour, which, however, as the substance of value should be logically distinct from value itself. In fact, value and abstract labour are not synonyms that define the same conceptual entity, but separate concepts each having its own specific and autonomous meaning within their mutual interconnection. Value is indeed unity of substance and form; it is what gives form to substance and substance to form. The dualism of value does not derive from the opposition between substance and form, because in a materialistic conception of dialectics they are complementary and necessarily corresponding to each other. This kind of dualism is typical of idealism, which opposes a universal transcendent substance, existing in itself, to a particular material form without substance of its own. The dualism of value, on the other hand, derives from the fact that substance and form are both dual inside themselves, and the two moments of their internal dualism correspond with each other. Thus, we have abstract labour as the substance of value that is composed of the two moments of social labour necessary for production and reproduction/consumption, to which corresponds the dual form of exchange value in production and circulation, in turn, expressed by the dual measure of abstract labour time and money.

Up to this point, the substance of value, abstract labour, has been defined as the specific form of social labour in capitalism, manifesting itself in the social form of exchange value, but it still remains to consider the nature of value as an indissoluble link between form and content. So, what is value? The answer is not a simple and immediate one since "(t)urn and examine a single commodity, by itself... yet in so far as it remains an object of value, it seems impossible to grasp it" (Marx, *MK1*, chap. 1, p. 33). In fact, even when it takes its own specific social form in the act of exchange, value remains invisible to the eyes and mind of the buyer and seller, because what is observable is only the determined quantitative relation of equivalence between two commodities. The "something" called value we can neither see nor touch, but it exists, it is operating in the act of exchange, because without it no consistent equivalence relation could be determined between two heterogeneous entities, and therefore, their market exchange could not even be conceived. In criticizing the "vulgar economist" Bailey, the answer of Marx is that:

> As values, commodities are social magnitudes, that is to say, something absolutely different from their "properties" as "things". As values, they constitute only relations of men in their productive activity... In actual fact, the concept "value" presupposes "exchanges" of the products. Where labour is communal, the relations of men in their social production do not manifest themselves as "values" of "things". Exchange of products as commodities is a method of exchanging labour, [it demonstrates] the dependence of the labour of each upon the labour of the others [and corresponds to] a certain mode of social labour or social production. In the first part of my book, I mentioned that it is characteristic of labour based on private exchange that the social character of labour "manifests" itself in a perverted form – as the "property" of things; that a social relation appears as a relation between things... Thus he, the wiseacre, transforms value into something absolute, "a property of things", instead of seeing in it only something relative, the relation of things to social labour, social labour based on private exchange, in which things are defined not as independent entities, but as mere expressions of social production.
>
> (Marx, *MTSV*, chap. XX, 817)

Value is neither the common property of commodities as objects of exchange as in the circulationist approach, nor the common property of commodities as products of labour as in the productivist approach, but it is a relation between individuals as members of a society, which is expressed by a relation between things in the form of exchange value.[27] Exchange value represents the link between a given commodity and social labour, as defining the part of social labour that is dedicated to satisfying the social needs to which the commodity is devoted in a society of private producers[28]. As social relation, value is therefore always relative, yet not in a passive sense as a mere reflection of the market ratio of equivalence between two commodities, but in an active sense as a means of connection of individuals between them. Value in capitalism is an abstract real procedure of building the social link between persons through the establishment of a link between things expressed in the form of exchange value. It generates the ratio of equivalence between the parts of total social labour represented by the commodities in exchange, which is expressed by a market exchange ratio between them. In this sense, value can be reduced neither to mere social form as exchange value, nor to mere intrinsic content as abstract labour, but it is the social relation that gives both social form and content to the commodities. "Value is their [*of the commodities, ndr*] social relation, their economic quality" (Marx, *MG*, p. 71).

Therefore, it is not correct to speak of extrinsic and intrinsic value because value is a primal and as such unitary concept, which manifests its dualistic substance of abstract labour in the dualistic social form of exchange value having a dual extrinsic and intrinsic measure. The concept of value contains in itself the specific dualistic determinations of substance, form, and measure, but it is not dual itself. Value, in fact, is the unilateral transposition into the social dimension of the pure objectivity of commodity, that is, of the commodity as a mere thing, which is coupled with the other unilateral transposition of use value into the individual private dimension. Value and use value express, one in social form and the other in private form, the relationship existing in capitalism between the human subjectivity and the bare objectivity of the commodity as a "thing". Through value, the "thing" commodity becomes a vehicle of the capitalist social relationship of individuals among themselves, while through use value it becomes a vehicle of the relationship between the interiority of individual needs and the external world. Both value and use value are therefore a one-sided, and as such internally unitary, expression of the original dualism of the commodity as Marx notes in a fundamental yet often misunderstood passage from *Notes on Adolph Wagner*:

> I do not divide value into use-value and exchange-value as opposites into which the abstraction "value" splits up, but the concrete social form of the product of labour, the "commodity", is on the one hand, use-value and on the other, "value", not exchange-value, since the mere form of expression is not its own content.
>
> (Marx, *MNW*)

The dualism of the determinations of substance and form of value does not come from an alleged dualism of value, which instead is a unitary concept, but from the original dualism of the commodity, of which value represents the unilateral social expression. The unitary character of value derives from representing the commodity, as the material product of the concrete labour, in the social world of the market, in the same way that use value represents the same material object in the private world of individual human needs. Value and use value join together in the bare objectuality of the commodity as a "thing" considered outside any social or private interrelation with human subjectivity. The commodity as a mere thing, a bare object, is the material bearer of value and use value, the former as a social form of relationship between individuals expressed through a relationship between things, and the latter as a private form of relationship between individuals and things. The commodity, stripped of its private relation of an object useful to the buyer, as a purely social expression, remains with only one, single unilateral dimension, that of value. Value is the social objectuality of the commodity, to which the private objectuality of use value is opposed. It is the material commodity considered from the one-sided perspective of sociality. In capitalism, a material product of concrete human labour acquires social character through value. Therefore, value indicates the objective social process that gives the material product of concrete labour the dimension of sociality, transforming it into a commodity.

The establishment of the social relationship institutive of capitalist society, that is, the division of social labour through private exchange, is not posed as in traditional societies through a conscious and recognized decision, but through an impersonal and unconscious mechanism determining individual and collective behaviour. As such, value is a real abstraction. Formally, it is a pure abstract operator or, to use a term that has become of current use in our time, an algorithm of social equivalence between commodities, or more precisely, between individual labours satisfying different social needs. In simple terms, an algorithm is an abstract logical procedure consisting of an ordinate and finite sequence of successive steps needed to solve a problem. Algorithms are, for example, the sets of rules that allow the four elementary arithmetic operations to be performed. What we observe in these operations is the external form of the relationship between two numbers, that is, the arithmetic sign of the operation (plus, minus, per, and divided) and its final result (sum, subtraction, multiplication, and division). However, we are not able to observe the logical procedure that leads to the correct result, which remains hidden and invisible, abstract inside our mind. Unless we are logicians or mathematicians, we are normally not even fully aware of the ordered set of logical steps that led us to solve the operation. Yet, the sequence of logical steps really exists and produces factual results. It constitutes the algorithm of the arithmetic operation.

Similarly, inside the market exchange, there is an algorithm that determines an equivalence relation between commodities. Only that, unlike the elementary arithmetic operations, this algorithm exists outside our minds, outside the minds of the seller and the buyer, it is not a pure act of human thought, but a generative social structure existing independently of our will. It is an objective social procedure, a *social* algorithm, a real abstraction. The algorithm operating within the social relation of the market exchange, which allows us to determine the equivalence relation transforming qualitatively different commodities in quantitatively identical exchange values, is what Marx defines value:

the transformation of the commodity into exchange value does not equate it to any other particular commodity, but expresses it as equivalent, expresses its exchangeability relation, vis-à-vis all other commodities. This comparison, which the head accomplishes in one stroke, can be achieved in reality only in a delimited sphere determined by needs, and only in successive steps.

(Marx, *MG*, p. 74)

Value is this set of successive steps leading to the determination of the exchange value as a formal expression of objectified abstract labour constituting the social substance of a commodity. Value is therefore the *social algorithm* of market equivalence between commodities and between the individual concrete labours that produced them. The social process of value determines simultaneously at the same time the equivalence between two commodities as a market exchange ratio and as an objectified quantity of abstract labour. A given market exchange ratio and a given quantity of objectified abstract labour are the mutually equivalent results of the social algorithm of value expressed in the form of a given exchange value. The social algorithm of value adds to the material and merely bodily form of object of use, the social form of exchange value as the equivalence between market exchange ratio with other commodities and quantity of objectified abstract labour.

In formal terms, an equivalence relation is characterized by the properties of reflexivity, symmetry, and transitivity. Let us now show how the commodities are placed in an equivalence relation within the act of market exchange. Given a set of commodities, C, composed of three commodities, x, y, and z, there is an equivalence relation (denoted by the symbol $\sim$) between them if the following three formal properties apply:

a) reflexivity $(x \sim x)$;
b) symmetry: (if $x \sim y$ then also $y \sim x$);
c) transitivity (if $x \sim y$ and $y \sim z$ then also $x \sim z$, and therefore $x \sim y \sim z$).

It is immediate to note that the act of exchange of commodities respects all three properties that define an equivalence relation. These three properties correspond to the initial steps from which all the more complex forms of value are developed by Marx in the first chapter of the first book of *Capital*. Reflexivity in the exchange is an obvious property since two absolutely identical commodities exchange each other as equals. Regarding the other two properties, the symmetry indicates the relative form of value and the transitivity indicates the equivalent form of value. The social algorithm of value is the set of real steps operating within the act of market exchange that puts the commodities in an equivalence relation, where these three formal properties are verified.

Looking more closely at the form of capitalist commodity, we find that the dualism consists of its twofold existence as use value and value, the latter expressed in

69

the form of a determined exchange value. It is important at this point to stress the logical difference between value and exchange value. Between the two concepts, there is a relation similar to that existing between the sum as a logical operation of calculation and the sum as a result of this operation. The sum we observe is the solution of a calculation procedure, an arithmetic algorithm, we call sum or addition. Similarly, the exchange value is the visible result, the form of expression of value as a social procedure, as the social algorithm that operates in the market exchange. When we refer to an already determined magnitude of value, such as that of a given commodity, we are referring to the social form of expression of value, that is exchange value. Vice versa, when we intend to consider the origin of the determined exchange value, from where it comes out, we refer to value as a social algorithm.

The definition of value as a social algorithm provided here contrasts with the idea of value commonly present in Marxist debate. Generally, value is conceived as a "substantial concept", in the sense of an objective qualitative property of a commodity deriving from a social substance objectified in it, termed abstract labour, quantitatively expressed in the social form of exchange value. This property, conferred to all commodities by the social substance of abstract labour, is alternatively understood as being the commodity of the product of human labour in the productivist approach or being it endowed with general market exchange-ability in the circulationist approach. Usually, the discussion is about what the substance of value consists of and how it is measured, be it labour time embodied in production or money realized in circulation.

In such a view, value would be nothing other than a plain linguistic expression denoting the union of social content with its form, and as such a derived, static definition of the relation between them. On a logical level, it is the determinations of substance and form of value that give meaning to the concept of value, rather than the opposite. The derived character of the concept of value contains in a nut-shell the opposition between substance and form of value that characterizes the debate between productivists and circulationalists. In fact, depending on which moment is considered as primary, the purely formal link of the derived concept of value implies that the social form would express what the social substance already logically is, or the social substance would consist in what is already logically expressed by the social form. In the productivist approach, the form is nothing but the superficial and visible expression of an already existing social substance, while in the circulationist approach, the substance is only the abstract generaliza-tion of the specific social form of commodity.

In both cases, the misunderstanding arises from not distinguishing the sub-stance of value, abstract labour, from the objectified labour that is past, already performed, "dead" labour. The value-creating labour is instead labour in motion, work in progress, living labour considered just at the moment in which it is pro-ducing commodities, that is, labour as a pure creating activity. And this value-creating labour is not the concrete labour of the individual worker, but the labour of the whole society, social and as such abstract labour, an abstraction really existing in capitalism. Abstract labour as the substance of value has the character of potentiality, it expresses what it can be but is not yet, the becoming, rather than the actuality, what is already present, the being. Abstract labour passes from the state of potentiality to that of actuality only when it is finished, objectifying itself in the external form of exchanged commodity and thus assuming the social form of exchange value. The exchange value represents the objectification, the actualization of the abstract labour, as the use value represents the objectification, the actualization of the concrete labour. Objectified abstract labour is therefore a characteristic of the social form of value not of its substance. The substance of value, abstract labour, is pure subjectivity that objectifies itself in the form of exchange value by means of the social algorithm of value. Value is precisely what gives a specific, actual social form to the potentiality of social living labour in motion, what transforms concrete social labour producing objects of use in the abstract labour producing commodities, fixing itself in the social form of exchange value. Value is the process that transforms the living social subjectivity of abstract labour into the dead social objectivity of exchange value. Both moments of social subjectivity as creating activity, potentiality, and social objectivity as form, actuality already achieved, are present as moments, partial determinations, of value, which thus acquire the nature of real abstraction, objective subjectivity, and subjective objectivity at the same time.

In this sense, value should be conceived as a "processual concept", a social algorithm, a generative relational structure, representing an abstract procedure deriving from a real social process, which continuously transforms abstract labour from potentiality into actuality, giving it an objective, a specific and quantitatively determined social form as exchange value. Since in capitalism the social substance of value, abstract labour, is dual, simultaneously reflecting the social labour necessary in production and the social labour necessary to satisfy social needs, the social form of value, exchange value, is dual too as it simultaneously represents a given market exchange ratio and a given quantity of objectified abstract labour. The dualism of value is not between substance and form, therefore, but inside each one of them. Value is that social process that momentarily resolves the dualisms inherent in substance and form, which continuously reappear in the commodities produced and exchanged on the market, placing them in a relation of equivalence. As a transformative process, value is neither object nor subject, but both things together in a social algorithm, because it is what transforms the subjectivity of its substance as abstract labour into the objectivity of its form as exchange value. In this sense, Marx's concept of value is different from the Hegelian concept of Absolute Spirit, since it is not a transcendent subject from which social reality derives and to which it continuously returns, but on the contrary, value is an immanent structure that itself is a product of the immediate capitalist social reality. As real abstraction, the algorithm of value is the unconscious and spontaneous result of the concrete and material social practices of a multitude of individuals, the fruit of the myriad of exchange activities that take place at every moment on the market.

71

This idea is clearly expressed in the following passage of Marx, where the analogy between the code of language and the code of value as social products returns again:

> whenever, by an exchange, we equate as values our different products, by that very act, we also equate, as human labour, the different kinds of labour expended upon them. We are not aware of this, nevertheless we do it. Value, therefore, does not stalk about with a label describing what it is. It is value, rather, that converts every product into a social hieroglyphic. Later on, we try to decipher the hieroglyphic, to get behind the secret of our own social products; for to stamp an object of utility as a value, is just as much a social product as language.
>
> (Marx, *MK1*, chap. 1, p. 49)

Value is the procedure, the algorithm that converts the concrete, immediate, actual product of human labour into a commodity. Just as language is the code that transforms the sounds of the individual into socially communicable concepts, so value is the code that transforms individual labour into social labour. The discovery of this algorithm allows Marx to find the key to decipher the social hieroglyphic of the commodity.

The relational, processual, and dynamic nature of value gives it a constant expansionary character, "endowed with a motion of its own" (Marx, *MK1*, 107-8). When the social algorithm of value comes to apply to its own subjective substance, establishing the capitalist social relation of wage labour with the purchase and sale of labour power, it becomes capital, self-valorizing value. "Value therefore now becomes value in process, money in process, and, as such, capital" (Marx, *MK1*, 108). And the only way in which value really exists in the history of human societies is as capital. As capital, the social algorithm of value goes beyond the Pillars of Hercules of social production and reproduction within which it logically originates, to also invade with its abstract code human and non-human nature. In this incessant expansion, value turned into capital finds its limits, and the inner dualism of its determinations become ever more arduous to restore to a coherent unity. This continuous expanding movement of value as capital does not have a teleological character but remains a spontaneous, socially objective process without a planning subject, similar in this respect to the processes of self-organization of complex natural systems.[29] The search for profit is the conscious aim of capitalists, that is to say of individual capitals in constant struggle with each other, in the same way that individual living organisms instinctively pursue the goal of survival. But just as natural reality as a whole is devoid of purpose, so capital, in general, does not represent a unitary teleological entity, but an impersonal, decentralized, and objective processual social structure, acting as a (pseudo)subject without Subject. Just as the biological code does not require the help of a conscious creator act, equally, the social algorithm of value operates without the presence of a conscious director.

In the first German edition of the first book of *Capital*, published in 1867, there is a passage in which Marx clearly expresses the processual nature of value. As is well known, in subsequent editions Marx revised the first chapter in depth to make it more comprehensible to readers unaccustomed to dialectical language, and this passage disappeared. However, it is worth mentioning it for its importance and clarity:

> As values the commodities are expressions of the same unity, of abstract human labour. In the form of exchange value they appear to one another as values and relate themselves to one another as values. They thereby relate themselves at the same time to abstract human labour as their common social substance. Their social relationship consists exclusively in counting with respect to one another as expressions of this social substance of theirs which differs only quantitatively, but which is qualitatively equal and hence replaceable and interchangeable with one another. As a useful thing, a commodity possesses social determinacy insofar as it is use-value for people other than its possessor, and hence satisfies social needs. But it is indifferent just whose needs the commodity's useful properties relate it to. The commodity nevertheless can only become through these properties in all cases only an object related to human needs, but not a commodity for other commodities. Only what *transforms* mere objects of use into commodities can relate each other as commodities and hence set them into social relation.[30] *But this is just what value is.*
>
> (Marx, *MKFGE*, emphasis added)

According to Marx, therefore, value is what *transforms* "mere objects of use", simple things having a bodily form suitable for human use, into commodities in social relation between them, and, as such, it is not a static property, rather a process, a social algorithm. To someone the analogy between the concept of value in Marx's theory and the notion of an algorithm may seem risky and forced, especially since the logical and mathematical definition of an algorithm was rigorously elaborated only in the 20th century. As a matter of fact, Marx, who, among his many scientific interests, also cultivated an interest in mathematics, has somehow foreshadowed the notion of algorithms in the interpretation of differential calculus in Marx's Mathematical Manuscripts (MMMs) written in the last years of his life. It is therefore worth dedicating some attention to this work, often ignored or neglected by Marx's interpreters.

3.3.1 *The notion of algorithm in Marx's Mathematical Manuscripts*[31]

"But in every single field which Marx investigated – and he investigated very many fields, none of them superficially – in every field, even in that of mathematics, he made independent discoveries". These words of Friedrich Engels, in the funeral speech for Karl Marx on 17 March 1883,[32] remained for a long time incomprehensible. No one suspected that Marx had a serious interest in mathematics, beyond the knowledge necessary for his economic studies. A few years later, Engels returned to the matter by announcing the publication of MMMs, but he failed to keep his promise.[33] After the posthumous publication of the second and third volumes of *Capital*, in which there were some errors of calculation, the belief in Marx's poor mathematical attitude was widespread. The interest in MMMs resumed only after the October revolution when, in the 1920s, the director of the Marx-Engels Institute of Moscow, David Rjazanov, commissioned a German mathematician, Emil Gumbel, to order, classify, and publish Marx's mathematical writings. In 1931, however, the arrest of Rjazanov, a victim of the Stalinist purges, blocked the project. During the Stalinist era, the interest in MMMs completely disappeared, and it was not until 1968 that a large portion of the manuscripts was published by Sofya Yanovskaya of the Moscow University. Since then, many translations have appeared in the main Western and Oriental languages, but nevertheless, the circulation and study of these notes are still very limited.[34]

Marx received his first mathematical education at the Lyceum Gymnasium in Trier where, at the time of graduation, in 1835, his knowledge of mathematics was judged to be good. In the next two decades, however, there are no indications revealing Marx's interest in mathematics. Only after he undertook the systematic study of political economy, in London, during the 1850s, Marx felt the need to rediscover mathematics in conjunction with the revival of Hegel's Logic, in which the notion of infinitesimal is strongly criticized. Some of his letters to Engels show that the only intellectual activity that he could carry out, in the most difficult moments of his life, was just mathematical studies.[35] In the last years of Marx's life, mathematics assumed an increasing role in his theoretical work, and the vast majority of mathematical manuscripts were written in this period.[36] Seeing this constant interest, it can be safely said that, at the end of his life, Marx considered his mathematical works as an integral part of his scientific legacy.

The MMMs consist of notes on arithmetic, algebra, geometry, and analysis, as well as a series of mathematical applications to problems of political economy concerning the differential rent, the process of circulation of capital, the rates of surplus value and profit, and the analysis of economic crises, for a total of over a thousand handwritten pages. The degree of elaboration ranges from simple notes and reading extracts to essays ready for publication. The greater part of them is devoted to the logical and conceptual foundations of differential calculus and the history of its development. Over the course of the previous two centuries, the discovery of differential calculus had transformed mathematics from the science of constant quantities to the science of variable quantities. The practical application of this new method to non-uniform motion had contributed decisively to the construction of the first industrial machines, acting as an important productive force in the development of industrial capitalism.

Marx taught himself advanced mathematics. The only one, apart from Engels, to whom Marx showed some of his mathematical manuscripts was Samuel Moore, a lawyer and a member of the First International, who, however, did not manage to fully grasp their meaning. The textbooks used by Marx to study differential calculus were those used at the time at the University of Cambridge, strongly influenced by the great mathematicians of Newtonian tradition of the 17th and 18th centuries. In the period when Marx wrote his manuscripts, modern classical analysis was beginning to be built in continental Europe by mathematicians such as Weierstrass, Dedekind, and Cantor on the basis of the notion of limit in the sense of Cauchy. However, in English universities, these new research directions remained practically unknown for a long time and began to penetrate only a few decades later, at the beginning of the 20th century. This is probably the reason Marx, limited by the concrete availability of study material, was never aware of the new developments in the field of differential calculus.

Despite this cultural isolation, the problem faced by Marx was the same as that of modern analysis, namely the dissatisfaction with how differential calculus had been up to then logically and conceptually founded. The problem arose from the fact that the passage from the algebra of ordinary numbers, the expression of actual processes, to differential calculus, the expression of potential properties concealed within real processes, occurred through an unjustified logical jump, devoid of coherent conceptual foundations. And yet, despite its theoretical inconsistency, differential calculus had contributed to a significant increase in the understanding of physical phenomena of the real world, somewhat like classical political economy with respect to economic phenomena.

Marx's method is historical-genetic, identical to that used in his critique of political economy. It starts from the critical analysis of the theoretical development of differential calculus in order to set out the internal logical contradictions and the attempts to resolve them. Marx identifies three different methods in the history of differential calculus. The first is the "mystic" method of Newton and Leibniz, whose mathematical procedure used infinitely small quantities, defined as differentials. Differentials were sometimes considered as positive numbers, and sometimes suppressed and treated as numerical zero, thus contravening the most elementary algebraic rules. Because of this strange behaviour, differentials appeared to orthodox mathematicians of the time as mysterious metaphysical entities, almost as the concept of value appeared to post-Ricardian "vulgar economists" criticized by Marx, and later to neoclassical economics. The amazing thing was that, through what Marx calls "jugglery", correct results were obtained "by a positively incorrect mathematical procedure" (Marx, *MMMs*, p. 78), in which the solution intuitively known from the beginning was the hidden assumption of the whole argument.

The second method is the "rational" one formulated by D'Alembert and Euler, who replaced the infinitely small quantities with finite increments to which the ordinary algebraic rules are applied since they are ordinary numbers. The differentials are introduced only in the final equation, where in the right part they disappear as numerical zero, while in the left part their ratio remains, replacing the expression 0 over 0. The final result is identical to that of Newton and Leibniz but obtained without "jugglery". However, although free from formal errors, this method lacks logical consistency because the ratio $0/0$ is an indeterminate expression that can assume any value and its equivalence to the value of the derivative represents an arbitrary imposition, justified only by the need to obtain the correct result already known at the outset. While representing undeniable progress, the rational method did not solve the contradictions of the differential calculus, whose conceptual foundations remained shrouded in mystery, susceptible of being understood only intuitively.

The third method is the "purely algebraic" method of Lagrange, who defines the derivative as the first coefficient of Taylor's series of a function, without addressing the question of the logical contradictions of differential calculus. Moreover, Lagrange never succeeded in demonstrating the general and universally applicable character of his solution. But this way, according to Marx, Lagrange provides at most a practical calculation technique, without modifying the precarious logical foundation of differential calculus established by his predecessors.

As can be seen, the similarity between the historical analysis of differential calculus and the political economy conducted by Marx is not only limited to the methodological aspect. Comparing the historical reconstruction of differential calculus in the MMMs with that of political economy in the *Theories on Surplus Value*, parallelism can be found in the phases of theoretical development of the two disciplines identified by Marx, from the intuitive discovery of labour as the source of value in the physiocracy and in some English economists, such as Petty and Torrens, to the rational systematization of Smith and the formal rigour of Ricardo. It is difficult to escape the idea that Marx believed that his contribution to the two disciplines should be placed at the same point of their development, that of the scientific and rational foundation of their theoretical bases.

Despite its limitations, the purely algebraic method of Lagrange remains the most advanced point of the classical theory of differential calculus from which Marx moved in his research. He wanted to find a method to obtain the derivative of a function in such a manner that its algebraic and real origin is met. To do this, he changed the starting point. Previous methods started from a sum, where the increment is added as a separate quantity which exists independently of the process of variation and has the nature of a constant. Marx starts from a difference, where the increment is the result of the variation of the variable itself and, as such, it cannot be defined independently of the change, thus representing an effectively variable quantity. At the end of Marx's differentiation procedure, the increments appear only on the left side of the equivalence, as a ratio, while the right-hand side only contains the ordinary algebraic variables.

This fact, Marx argues, is not accidental but expresses a qualitative difference between the two sides of the equation: the left-hand side has a symbolic nature, while the right-hand side has an algebraic real nature. The first one represents the purely symbolic expression of the actual process of variation that takes place entirely in the right-hand algebraic side of the equation. The zeroing of the increments has effect only on the left side, which is reduced to the 0 over 0 ratio, leaving the right member unchanged. This time, however, the 0 over 0 ratio does not denote an arithmetic operation but is a purely logical operator, which can be replaced by the differential ratio without any contradiction given its symbolic nature. Unlike the previous methods in which the differentials appeared as distinct entities having substantial content, they are now inseparably connected in the differential ratio symbolically representing the process of differentiation. This ratio now represents only the symbolic form of an abstract procedure through which the qualitative leap takes place from the algebra of the constant quantities to the differential calculus of the variable quantities. In other words, for Marx, the differential ratio is a mere symbolic operator devoid of any content of its own, an algorithm, which denotes an ordered sequence of logical and algebraic operations necessary to compute the derivative of a function. In the end, therefore, the final result of the derivative, a purely algebraic expression of a concrete and factual nature, proves to be the product of an algorithm, a purely abstract expression of an ordered and finite set of successive logical steps.

The interest that today the MMMs can still arouse does not concern the technical and formal aspects since, even while Marx was writing, the differential calculus was finding a solid logic foundation in the precise definition of the concepts of limit and continuity. The interest is rather historical and methodological because the definition of the differential as a symbolic operator prefigures the modern concept of algorithm and this makes Marx a precursor of modern computational mathematics.

Moreover, there is also an important theoretical aspect that goes beyond mathematics and involves, albeit indirectly, the central core of Marx's thought, the theory of value. In fact, the mathematical procedure developed by Marx shows how it is possible to obtain from a purely abstract and symbolic process, such as the algorithm of derivation, a real and factual result, such as the function derivative, which is actually operating in nature and whose discovery has allowed important practical applications in a wide range of techniques. As we have previously shown, the concept of value, elaborated by Marx in the economic works of his maturity, presents strong logical analogies with the symbolic operator of derivation in their common structure of algorithm – a purely abstract procedure that produces factual results. The study of MMMs is therefore useful to better understand the meaning of the concept of value in Marx's work.

3.4 The dual nature of substance and form of value

In the previous paragraph, we defined value as a social algorithm operating in market exchange, acting as a symbolic operator of social equivalence between commodities. Let us now analyse this definition in more detail by examining the various elements. As *operator*, value consists of a procedure, an ordered and finite set of steps necessary to achieve a given result. As *symbolic* operator, value is an abstract procedure that applies in commodity market exchange to content or substance logically distinct from itself. As operator of *equivalence*, value determines a quantitative relation, requiring that the substance to which it applies is commensurable and qualitatively identical between commodities, differing among them only quantitatively. As *social* operator, value has a purely social substance, in the sense that it is independent of any physical, natural, and material features of the commodities. As Marx points out, the only possible common feature that meets the criteria of quantitative social equivalence is that the commodities are all the product of human labour. Labour is therefore the substance to which the social algorithm of value applies.

But what kind of labour is it? It cannot be the concrete labour spent in the production of the specific and individual commodities since these concrete working activities are qualitatively different and as such quantitatively incomparable. Concrete labour always refers to an individual dimension of labour, the practical working activity carried out by a given worker to perform a given task. It regards the technical working process considered outside the social dimension in which this process is carried out and realized. In pre-capitalist societies, when the products of human labour had not taken the social form of commodity, concrete labour did not practically exist as a specific individual form of human labour as opposed to the social form, since individual labour was immediately social labour, and vice versa, social labour was also immediately concrete labour of a multitude of individuals belonging to the community, aimed at satisfying pre-determined social needs. In these types of societies, therefore, no conceptual distinction can be made between concrete and abstract labour. When in capitalism both the produced goods and labour power acquire the social form of commodity, individual labour also separates itself from social labour, the former assuming the specific form of concrete labour producing use value, and the latter the specific form of abstract labour producing exchange value. Just as in capitalism any given commodity assumes a dual form, use value and value, so the commodity-producing labour has a dual form, that of concrete labour producing a qualitatively given use value and abstract labour producing a quantitatively given exchange value, this latter representing the specific social form of expression of value. The social algorithm of value applies to abstract labour as its substance to determine a specific exchange value as its final expression. Therefore, it is abstract labour that constitutes the basis of equivalence, the substance of the social algorithm of value that is expressed in the social form of exchange value.

3.4.1 The dual nature of abstract labour

What has been provided so far is a functional definition of abstract labour as labour producing exchange value in opposition to concrete labour producing use value. We will now proceed to define abstract labour in a substantive sense as the specific form taken in capitalism by social labour in general. We have previously defined social labour in general as the coordinated set of working activities performed by individuals belonging to a given society in order to meet social needs. Social labour is an essential constitutive element of any human society that makes the two fundamental moments of social production and social consumption mutually consistent, thus ensuring the continuous reproduction of individual and collective life. In pre-capitalist societies, social labour does not acquire an autonomous and specific form separate from the overall social activity and therefore remains embedded within the general political, religious, and cultural order of the community. The division of social labour among members of traditional social communities derives from direct personal relationships determined by the social roles assumed by each individual, which are established by tradition and transmitted by inheritance, co-optation, or conquered by force. In such circumstances, the moments of social production and social consumption are immediately linked, so that the individual working activities are directly aimed at satisfying specific and identifiable social needs. The division of social labour, in both of its constituent moments, is therefore established and known from the beginning of each cycle of social reproduction. Their possible divergence can only arise later as a result of exceptional and unforeseen events deriving from external causes of natural origin, such as drought and environmental disasters, or historical, such as raids and looting by other peoples.

By contrast, in capitalist societies, the individual and social reproduction are the final results of a mediated and indirect process realized through market exchange between private producers, which gives rise to the possibility of an inconsistency between the two moments of social production and social consumption. In capitalism, individual working activities are no longer immediately directed to the satisfaction of previously established and known social needs, but they have to prove their effective social utility through the market exchange of privately produced goods. If the privately produced good does not find a corresponding purchaser on the market, the individual labour used in its production is of no social utility and does not become part of the total social labour of the community. At the level of society as a whole, when the total supply of a given commodity exceeds the total quantity demanded in the market, the labour spent in its production is "squandered" and does not count as social labour.[37] While in pre-capitalist societies, the social labour available to the community was known before production took place and allocated according to traditional criteria, in capitalism, social labour is determined only after production when the goods are exchanged on the market. In this way, the two elements that compose social labour, namely working activity and social needs, once indissolubly linked in an entanglement of personal relations, now become actually divided into two separate moments. These two moments are personified by the two distinct and interchangeable social figures of seller and buyer, supply and demand, which have to be reunified in the impersonal mediation of the market through the social algorithm of value. What was previously the general presupposition of the social constitution, social labour, now becomes the spontaneous result of a myriad of individual actions that find their coordination, necessary to ensure the continuous reproduction of society, in the unconscious social structure of the market.

To produce social order, however, the blind functioning of the market must be governed by criteria that restore to general coherence uncoordinated individual practices, namely by an equally unconscious and objective law acting within the mercantile institutional structure. This law is the law of value conceived as a social algorithm, an abstract and objective procedure operating through the actors of the market, producers and consumers, sellers and buyers, regardless of their conscience and will. The law of value asserts itself through the mechanism of capitalist competition, which entails an incessant conflict among individual capitals to survive and prosper. The law of value is full of individual successes and failures, victories and defeats, births of new enterprises and deaths of old ones. By the operation of this law, the social labour effectively required for the reproduction of society is determined, and it thus comes to take a specific and autonomous social form separated from the other social practices with which it was once merged – the value form of the commodity. In this way, the social relation of the division of social labour among the members of the society manifests itself as a property of things in the value of commodities. In capitalist society, the social algorithm of value, operating in market exchange, is the generative structure of social reproduction.

The specific social form assumed by social labour in capitalism is abstract labour, which is the substance to which the social algorithm of value applies to produce social order. Both value and its substance share the same abstract, impersonal, and social character. The two social moments of production and consumption, which in traditional societies were merged together, now form the two components of the specific dual form assumed by social labour in capitalism as abstract labour. The elements of this dual form are socially necessary labour in production and socially necessary labour in circulation, which both in their unity constitute abstract labour.

As with the dualistic nature of the commodity, the dualistic nature of abstract labour likewise derives from the private and mediated character of the capitalist social reproduction. The total abstract labour of a capitalist society is the general social labour necessary on the one hand to produce any kind of commodity, given the normal level reached by productive forces at any particular time, and, on the other hand, to satisfy any kind of solvable social need, given the tastes and preferences prevailing at a given historical period. It is important to underline that in capitalism the needs recognized as social are only those that are solvable, meaning that they provide a market counterpart to that required to satisfy them. The solvable social needs are only those of the buyer on the market, that is, those that manifest themselves within the sphere of commodity circulation. Abstract labour in capitalism has, therefore, the dual character of socially necessary labour in production and socially necessary labour in circulation, which are continuously led to coherence by the spontaneous and blind functioning of the social algorithm of value. It is precisely in the intimate connection between these two moments of the general process of reproduction of the capitalist society, the production and circulation of commodities, that abstract labour is determined as the substance of value.

Since what is immediately visible in capitalist society is the phantasmagorical pinwheel of buying and selling all kinds of goods and services, abstract labour materializes and appears on the surface of the capitalist economy as an "immense accumulation of commodities" stored on real or virtual sales counters, that is, in its attribute of objectified socially necessary labour in circulation. The complementary attribute of socially necessary labour in production remains instead invisible and hidden within the walls of the warehouses and offices of firms, where it materializes as command of capital over living labour, as the capitalist organization of the labour process and as exploitation of the labour power. However, both these two dimensions, the apparent and visible one of circulation and the hidden and secret one of the production of commodities, together constitute in their unity the social form of abstract labour as the fundamental engine of the process of reproduction of capitalist society. In this generating process, abstract labour is composed of two attributes, which are different but not opposed, and only in their unity is it constituted as the substance of value. In the dual nature of abstract labour, in which there is a difference in identity rather than a contradiction of opposites, Marx's dialectical method seems closer to Spinoza's legacy than to that of Hegel.[38]

3.4.2 The dual nature of exchange value

The social form of value, corresponding to abstract labour as its substance, is the exchange value of the commodities. Abstract labour as substance of value and exchange value as form of value are both the result of the operation of the social algorithm of value in the market exchange of privately produced commodities. The social algorithm of value establishes a quantitative relation of equivalence between the two attributes of abstract labour, as social labour objectified in production and social labour objectified in circulation, thus determining a given magnitude of value that appears in the form of exchange value, visible in the market exchange ratio agreed between seller and buyer at the conclusion of their transaction. The dual nature of abstract labour is reflected in the dual nature of the exchange value, as exchange value created in production and exchange value realized in circulation, which manifests itself in the real confrontation occurring in the process of market exchange between seller and buyer concerning supply price and demand price, the real cost of production,[39] and the final price of the commodity. As Marx wrote in the *Grundrisse*, exchange value

> is at the same time the exponent of the relation in which the commodity is exchanged with other commodities, as well as the exponent of the relation in which it has already been exchanged with other commodities

(materialized labour time) in production; it is their quantitatively determined exchangeability.

(Marx, MG, p. 71)

We will see later that the dual character of exchange value implies the possibility of a contradiction, of a lack of equivalence, between the two moments of which it is composed.

The dual nature of exchange value, resulting from the dual character of abstract labour, determines a correspondingly dual measure of its magnitude since each of the two moments of the exchange value has its own specific measure, one intrinsic or immanent and the other extrinsic or phenomenal.[40] Both measures indicate in a different form the magnitude of the exchange value of the commodity, the intrinsic measure as social labour objectified in production and the extrinsic measure as a given market exchange ratio with other commodities. The former is hidden and invisible inside the production process, while the latter appears in the form of the market price of commodities. In their equivalence, the socially necessary labour in production and the socially necessary labour in circulation are reunited, defining the magnitude of value of the commodity as a given quantity of objectified abstract labour. Let us now see what these two measures of exchange value consist of and how they are expressed.

We have seen that abstract labour is the specific capitalist form of social labour in general, defined as the amount of labour available to produce the goods necessary to meet the needs of society as a whole over a given period of time. Social labour in production is thus given by the total amount of individual working time that society uses to produce all the commodities sold on the market, and it can be calculated by multiplying the working time performed by each worker by the number of people at work. Since the natural measure of labour is time, labour time represents the intrinsic measure of abstract labour as substance of value of the commodities, but in the actual market exchange, this common measure never appears. In fact, commodities are exchanged on the market because of their qualitative difference rather than their common quantitative identity. The exchange of commodities is motivated by the exchange of two qualitatively different use values, and never by the exchange of two quantitatively identical exchange values. For this reason, the dual nature of the commodities implies that the quantitative basis of their equivalence, the abstract labour time as a common measure of their value, is necessarily expressed in a form different from itself, otherwise, the exchange would lose all meaning.

The market exchange is not only a formal and abstract process of quantitative exchange of equivalents but first of all a material and concrete process of qualitative exchange of differences. The purpose of the market exchange is the reciprocal transformation of material objects, which may be tangible or intangible, possessed by the contracting parties. The seller wants to replace his commodity with that of the buyer through the market exchange, and vice versa. Both are interested in acquiring the use value of the commodity in the hands of the other

82

trader, even if the use value is represented by its ability to appropriate or generate more exchange value in the future, as in the case of financial transactions or capitalist purchase of labour power, respectively. If the objects exchanged were not qualitatively different from each other, the exchange would not make sense, because there is no point in exchanging, for example, glasses for identical glasses, or dollars for dollars. What we observe in the market exchange is precisely the mutual passage of different material objects, different use values, between the two parties, while their common objectified value substance, as materialized abstract labour time, remains hidden and invisible behind the surface of the exchange.

Therefore, the ratio of equivalence, which appears externally in the exchange, is that between two quantities of heterogeneous material objects, and this market exchange ratio constitutes the extrinsic, visible measure of the equivalence of the exchange, so that we notice, for example, that glasses are exchanged for dollars and vice versa. This extrinsic measure is always by its nature a relative measure, which finds its justification precisely in the differences that distinguish the exchanged commodities. But this market exchange ratio between different objects must necessarily be founded on common ground shared by both of them, which makes it possible to set the basis of the quantitative equivalence expressed by it. The commensurability of the exchanged commodities can only result from an underlying identity, hidden behind their qualitative differences and derived from their common substance, as objectified abstract labour time. The measure of this common substance constitutes the intrinsic measure of the exchange value of each commodity, the basis of all the various extrinsic measures of the exchange value that a commodity can assume relative to all the other commodities. And since the natural unit of measurement of labour in general is time, the intrinsic measure of the exchange value of a commodity is the abstract labour time objectified in it.

Consequently, behind every extrinsic measure of the exchange value of a capitalist commodity, consisting of the visible market exchange ratio it has with another commodity, there is always a corresponding intrinsic measure consisting of the abstract labour time objectified in them. This intrinsic measure, however, is not visible and is expressed externally in the form of extrinsic measure. The existence of two measures of the exchange value, one extrinsic and visible, the other intrinsic and invisible, makes possible the discordance between them. The quantitative correspondence between intrinsic and extrinsic measures of the exchange value defines an equivalent exchange. When, on the other hand, the two measures diverge, there is non-equivalent exchange. In the equivalent exchange, the market exchange ratio between the commodities is defined by the respective abstract labour time objectified in each of them in production. By contrast, in non-equivalent exchange, a given amount of objectified abstract labour time is exchanged with a different amount of abstract labour time objectified in the production of the other commodity. In the latter case, we have value transfer in trade, since market exchange ratio and relative objectified abstract labour time differ from each other.

Unequal exchange, therefore, derives from the discrepancy between the two measures of the exchange value. These two measures, in turn, originate from the dual nature of exchange value as a reflection of the dual nature of abstract labour as the substance of value. It is important to underline how this definition of unequal exchange differs from the existing approaches in the literature examined in Chapter 2. In the structuralist approach, the unequal exchange derives from the difference between the market price and an ideal, or natural, competitive equilibrium price, both expressed in monetary form. In traditional Marxist approaches, it derives instead from the difference between market price and value, or price of production, both expressed in the form of labour time embodied in commodities. In both cases, unequal exchange arises from the gap between an intimate ideal dimension of the natural price or value, and an apparent phenomenal dimension of the market price. In the definition given here, the unequal exchange concerns the difference between two measures of the same magnitude of value, represented by the given exchange value of the commodities, once expressed in terms of market exchange ratio and once in terms of labour time. As will be clear later on, unequal exchange is the result of the non-equivalent conversion of the two units of measurement used to determine the same magnitude of a given exchange value.

Notes

1 On the Marxist debate on abstract labour, see Roberts (2017).
2 Other prominent authors supporting such an interpretation of abstract labour are Dobb (1955) and Meek (1956).
3 "This circumstance – the necessity of presenting labour contained in commodities as uniform social labour, i.e. as money – is overlooked by Ricardo" (Marx, *MTSV*, chap. XX, 817).
4 Lippi (1979) expresses the most systematic and coherent exposition of the neo-Ricardian concept of labour: "Labor as a measure of the difficulties that must be overcome, as real social cost, is the immanent measure of the product, whatever the historical mode of production...Value is merely the form assumed by real cost when the objects in question are commodities, products to be exchanged" (p. xv–xvi). For a criticism of Lippi's positions, see Bellofiore (1998).
5 All neo-Ricardian economists share these views on value formulated by Joan Robinson: "The awkwardness of reckoning in terms of value... accounts for much of the obscurity of Marx's exposition, and none of the important ideas which he expresses in terms of the concept of value cannot be better expressed without it" (Robinson, 1966, p. 20). And: "One of the great metaphysical ideas in economics is expressed by the word 'value'... What is it? Where shall we find it? Like all metaphysical concepts, when you try to pin it down it turns out to be just a word" (Robinson, 1962, p. 26). On Robinson's view on labour theory of value, see Hunt (1983).
6 In the debate of the last century on Marx's theory of value, the circulationist approach was supported by Neo-Ricardian authors such as Steedman (1977) and Hodgson (1982).
7 For more than 20 years, the main forum of debate for Value Form interpretation has been the International Symposium on Marxian Theory (ISMT). The long-standing members of this research group are Chris Arthur, Tony Smith, Geert Reuten, Riccardo Bellofiore, Martha Campbell, Roberto Fineschi, Fred Moseley, and Patrick Murray.

Eleven books have been published resulting from the ISMT conferences, see: https://ch risarthur.net/international-symposium-on-marxian-theory-ismt/. Other relevant contributions are, among others, Backhaus (1980), Eldred and Hanlon (1981), Arthur (1986, 2004), Murray (1988), Reuten and Williams (1989), Tony Smith (1990), Heinrich (2012), and, specifically on abstract labour, Bonefeld (2010).

8   "One of two things is possible: if abstract labor is an expenditure of human energy in physiological form, then value also has a reified-material character. Or value is a social phenomenon, and then abstract labor must also be understood as a social phenomenon connected with a determined social form of production. It is not possible to reconcile a physiological concept of abstract labor with the historical character of the value which it creates" (Rubin, 1972, p. 135).

9   On the influence of positivism on the traditional and orthodox interpretation of Marx's theory of value see Taylor (1988). In this respect, the Value Form school is closely linked to the Frankfurt critical theory, see Reichelt (1982) and O'Kane (2020).

10 This point is critically underlined by Bellofiore (2016). For a more general criticism of the Value Form school, particularly in the version of Arthur's so-called "systematic dialectics", see Likitkijsomboon (1995), Bidet (2005), Carchedi (2009), and Lange (2016).

11 In Ahumada (2012), this opposition takes the form of the distinction between mercantile value and value of the commodity.

12 Kicillof and Starosta (2011), p. 298.

13 Ibid., p. 299.

14 For a critique of this substantive-physicalist conception of abstract labour, see Screpanti (2019, chap. 1).

15 There are many passages of Marx expressing this thesis. From the *Grundrisse*: "Individuals producing in society – hence socially determined individual production – is, of course, the point of departure" (Marx, *MG*, p. 17). "All production is appropriation of nature on the part of an individual within and through a specific form of society" (Marx, *MG*, p. 21). From *Capital I*: "from the moment that men in any way work for one another, their labour assumes a social form" (Marx, *MK1*, chap. 1, p. 47).

16 See what Marx writes in the *Economic Manuscript of 1861–63* (*MECW*, vol. 30, emphasis added): "Spinning adds value to cotton in so far as it is reduced to equal *social labour in general*, reduced to this abstract form of labour" (p. 77). "The fact that value is added to them derives merely from spinning labour's being labour in general, *abstract social labour in general*" (p. 126).

17 In *Capital I*, Marx (35, p. 188–9) describes the work process in this way: "The elementary factors of the labour-process are 1, the personal activity of man, i.e., work itself, 2, the subject of that work, and 3, its instruments... An instrument of labour is a thing, or a complex of things, which the labourer interposes between himself and the subject of his labour, and which serves as the conductor of his activity... (T)he first thing of which the labourer possesses himself is not the subject of labour (natural raw materials, *ndr*) but its instrument... The use and fabrication of instruments of labour, although existing in the germ among certain species of animals, is specifically characteristic of the human labour process, and Franklin therefore defines man as a tool-making animal" (Marx, *MK1*, chap.7, p. 127–8).

18 In this sense, Marx states: "By thus acting on the external world and changing it, he (man, *ndr*) at the same time changes his own nature" (Marx, *MK1*, chap. 7, p. 127). On the homology between language and labour in Marx, see Rossi-Landi (1977).

19 "Economy of time, to this all economy ultimately reduces itself. Society likewise has to distribute its time in a purposeful way, in order to achieve a production adequate to its overall needs; just as the individual has to distribute his time correctly in order to satisfy the various demands on his activity" (Marx, *MG*, p. 103).

20 See Marx, *MECW*, vol. 30, p. 266–8.
21 I use the term "market exchange" and not simply 'exchange' because, as anthropological research has highlighted, objects that are not commodities can be exchanged outside of any market relationship even in traditional societies, as entangled objects, sacred things, gifts, and even parenthood, by means of alternative institutional patterns based on the principles of reciprocity and redistribution. As Polanyi (1957) pointed out, only in an idealistic and Western-centred view, these acts of exchange can be thought as exchanges of value.
22 "(T)he fetishistic notion, peculiar to the capitalist mode of production and arising from its essence, (is) that the formal economic determinations, such as that of being a commodity, or being productive labour, etc., are qualities belonging to the material repositories of these formal determinations or categories in and for themselves" (Marx, *MECW*, vol. 34, p. 450). On the fetishistic character of capitalist economic categories in Marx's thought, see Rovatti (1972).
23 See Kliman (2000, p. 94) : "since two commodities that exchange are qualitatively equal, they share a common property, and that what is meant by value is precisely this common property, substance, or 'third thing' that they both contain, not the one commodity or the other". On the same line is Brown (2008, p. 132) talking of "the 'third thing' termed 'value'".
24 "(N)o reference to exchange of the products is needed in order to determine either the abstract labour extracted from workers or the products' values" (McGlone and Kliman, 2004).
25 See, for example, Foley (1986, p. 13): "Marx views value as a substance contained in definite quantities in every commodity"
26 See Wolff, Callari, and Roberts (1984), which derive the interdependence of value and value-form from the Althusserian concept of over-determination. This interpretation is the basis of the post-structuralist approach to Marx's value theory.
27 "Value is a relation between persons expressed as a relation between things" (Marx, MK1, chap. 1, p. 56).
28 "(A)ll commodities, in so far as they are exchange-values, are only *relative* expressions of social labour-time and their relativity consists by no means solely of the ratio in which they exchange for one another, but of the ratio of all of them to this social labour which is their substance" (Marx, *MTSV*, 527).
29 The teleological character of Capital as a subject endowed with its own "will" is supported by Tombazos (2020) in a polemic with Callinicos (2014) who instead defines Capital as a pseudo-subjectivity.
30 In the German-English translation, Albert Dragstedt uses here the expression "the kind of thing" to translate the German words "was" used by Marx (*MK1FGE*, p. 28). In the text I use instead a more literal translation ("what") of this sentence, in accordance with the Italian translation (*MEOC*, p. 1063), to avoid interpretative misunderstandings.
31 This paragraph is a revised version of a previous article, published in *Lettera Matematica International Edition* to which I refer for further details, see Ricci (2018).
32 See Frederick Engels' Speech at the Grave of Karl Marx available at: www.marxists.org/archive/marx/works/1883/death/burial.htm.
33 So Engels (*MECW*, vol. 25, p. 13) wrote in the Preface to the second edition of 1885 Anti-Dühring: "For the present I... must wait to find some later opportunity to put together and publish the results which I have arrived at, perhaps in conjunction with the extremely important mathematical manuscripts left by Marx"
34 On the *MMMs*, see Struik (1948), Smolinski (1973), Alcouffe (1985), Gerdes (1985), Baksi (1994), Kennedy (2006), Carchedi (2008), and Ricci (2018).
35 On November 23, 1860, while he was taking care of his wife suffering from smallpox, Marx wrote to Engels that "the only occupation that helps me maintain the necessary

quietness of mind is Mathematics" (*MECW*, vol. 41, p. 216). A few years later, during a period of intense work of drafting *Das Kapital*, on July 6, 1863, Marx revealed to his friend that "My spare time is now devoted to differential and integral calculus" (*MECW*, vol. 41, p. 483), and again in a May 20, 1865, letter: "I am working like a horse... In between times, since one cannot always be writing, I am doing some differential calculus dx/dy. I have no patience to read anything else at all" (*MECW*, vol. 42, p. 159).

36 On August 18, 1881, Engels expressed to his friend his entirely positive impressions of two manuscripts about the notions of function and differential, given to him by Marx some time before. And again, on November 22, 1882, in one of his last letters, Marx, whose health conditions were rapidly deteriorating, returned to differential calculus, in response to a request from his friend.

37 "(I)f this commodity has been produced in excess of the existing social needs, then so much of the social labour-time is squandered and the mass of the commodity comes to represent a much smaller quantity of social labour in the market than is actually incorporated in it" (Marx, *MK3*, chap. 10, p. 134).

38 Also with regard to the dual expression of the commodity as use value and exchange value, Marx (*MK1*, chap. 3, p. 72) uses the Spinozian term of "unity of differences". On the difference between Spinoza's materialistic dialectic and Hegel's idealistic dialectics, see Macherey (2011).

39 The real cost of production differs from the capitalist cost of production because the former includes normal and average profit. "He (*the capitalist, ndr*) sells not only what has cost him an equivalent, but he sells also what has cost him nothing, although it has cost his workman labour. The cost of the commodity to the capitalist and its real cost are different things" (Marx, *MVPP*, chap. 10).

40 Marx uses the term "immanent or intrinsic measure of value" to indicate the labour time spent in commodity production in several passages of the *Theories of Surplus Value*, particularly in the critique to Ricardo and Bailey. "The connection between value, its immanent measure – i.e., labour time – and the necessity for an external measure of the values of commodities is not understood or even raised as a problem [by Ricardo, *ndr*]" (Marx, *MTSV*, 542). "[Smith] confuses – as Ricardo also often does – labour, the intrinsic measure of value, with money, the external measure, which presupposes that value is already determined" (Marx, *MTSV*, 654). Also in Book I of *Capital*, Marx clearly defines this expression as follows: "Labour is the substance, and the immanent measure of value" (Marx, *MK1*, chap. 19, p. 379). As an alternative to intrinsic and extrinsic measure of value, Marx sometimes uses the terms of absolute and relative expression of value, respectively: "Its [of the value, *ndr*] absolute expression would be its expression in terms of labour-time and this absolute expression would express it as something relative, but in the absolute relation, by which it is value" (Marx, *MTSV*, 819).

Bibliography

Ahumada, P. (2012). The mercantile form of value and its place in Marx's theory of the commodity. *Cambridge Journal of Economics*, 36(4), 843–867.

Alcouffe, A. (1985). Marx, Hegel et le "Calcul". In *Les Manuscrits Mathematiques*. Marx, K. (Ed.). Paris: Economica, 9–109.

Arthur, C. J. (1986). *Dialectics of Labour; Marx and His Relation to Hegel*. Oxford: Blackwell.

Arthur, C. J. (2004). *The New Dialectic and Marx's 'Capital'*. Leiden: Brill.

Backhaus, H. G. (1980). On the dialectics of the value-form. *Thesis Eleven*, 1(1), 99–120.

Baksi, P. (1994). Special supplement. In *Mathematical Manuscripts*. Marx, K. (Ed.). Calcutta: Viswakos Parisad, 386–408.

Bellofiore, R. (1998). The concept of labor in Marx. *International Journal of Political Economy*, *28*(3), 4–34.

Bellofiore, R. (2009). A ghost turning into a vampire: The concept of capital and living labour. In *Re-Reading Marx: New Perspectives after the Critical Edition*. Bellofiore, R., and Fineschi, R. (Eds.). London: Palgrave Macmillan, 178–194.

Bellofiore, R. (2016). Marx after Hegel: Capital as Totality and the Centrality of Production. *Crisis and Critique*, *3*(3), 31–64.

Bidet, J. (2005). The dialectician's interpretation of Capital. *Historical Materialism*, *13*(2), 121–146.

Bonefeld, W. (2010). Abstract labour: Against its nature and on its time. *Capital and Class*, *34*(2), 257–276.

Brown, A. (2008). A materialist development of some recent contributions to the labour theory of value. *Cambridge Journal of Economics*, *32*(1), 125–146.

Callinicos, A. (2014). *Deciphering Capital: Marx's Capital and Its Destiny*. London: Bookmarks Publications.

Carchedi, G. (2008). Dialectics and temporality in Marx's Mathematical Manuscripts. *Science and Society*, *72*(4), 415–426.

Carchedi, G. (2009). The fallacies of 'new dialectics' and value-form theory. *Historical Materialism*, *17*(1), 145–169.

Dobb, M. (1955). *On Economic Theory and Socialism: Collected Papers*. London: Routledge and Kegan Paul.

Eldred, M., and Hanlon, M. (1981). Reconstructing value-form analysis. *Capital and Class*, *5*(1), 24–60.

Gerdes, P. (1985). *Marx Demystifies Calculus*. Minneapolis: MEP Publications.

Foley, D. K. (1986). *Understanding 'Capital': Marx's Economic Theory*. Cambridge, MA: Harvard University Press.

Heinrich, M. (2012). *An Introduction to the Three Volumes of Karl Marx's Capital*. New York: New York University Press.

Hodgson, G. (1982). Marx without the labor theory of value. *Review of Radical Political Economics*, *14*(2), 59–65.

Hunt, E. K. (1983). Joan Robinson and the labour theory of value. *Cambridge Journal of Economics*, *7*(3/4), 331–342.

Kennedy, H. (2006). *Negation of the Negation: Karl Marx and Differential Calculus*. Concord, CA: Peremptory Publications.

Kicillof, A., and Starosta, G. (2007a). Value form and class struggle: A critique of the autonomist theory of value. *Capital and Class*, *31*(2), 13–40.

Kicillof, A., and Starosta, G. (2007b). On materiality and social form: A political critique of Rubin's value-form theory. *Historical Materialism*, *15*(3), 9–43.

Kicillof, A., and Starosta, G. (2011). On value and abstract labour: A reply to Werner Bonefeld. *Capital and Class*, *35*(2), 295–305.

Kliman, A. J. (2000). Marx's concept of intrinsic value. *Historical Materialism*, *6*(1), 89–114.

Kliman, A. J., and McGlone, T. (1999). A temporal single-system interpretation of Marx's value theory. *Review of Political Economy*, *11*(1), 33–59.

Lange, E. L. (2016). The critique of political economy and the new dialectic. Hegel, Marx, and Christopher J. Arthur's' Homology Thesis'. *Crisis and Critique*, *3*(3), 235–272.

Likitkijsomboon, P. (1995). Marxian theories of value-form. *Review of Radical Political Economics, 27*(2), 73–105.

Lippi, M. (1979). *Value and Naturalism in Marx*. London: New Left Books.

Macherey, P. (2011). *Hegel or Spinoza*. Minneapolis: University of Minnesota Press.

McGlone, T., and Kliman A. (2004). The duality of labour. In *The New Value Controversy and the Foundations of Economics*. Freeman, A., Kliman, A., and Wells, J. (Eds.). Cheltenham UK: Edward Elgar Publishing, 135–150.

Meek, R. L. (1956). *Studies in the Labor Theory of Value*. New York: New York University Press.

Murray, P. (1988). *Marx's Theory of Scientific Knowledge*. Atlantic Highlands, NJ: Humanities.

Murray, P. (2016). *The Mismeasure of Wealth: Essays on Marx and Social Form*. Leiden: Brill.

O'Kane, C. (2020). The critique of real abstraction: From the critical theory of society to the critique of political economy and back again. In *Marx and Contemporary Critical Theory*. Oliva et al. (Eds.). London: Palgrave Macmillan, 265–287.

Polanyi, K. (1957). *Trade and Market in the Early Empires*. Glencoe: Free Press.

Reichelt, H. (1982). From the Frankfurt School to value-form analysis. *Thesis Eleven, 4*(1), 166–169.

Reuten, G., and Williams, M. (1989). *Value-Form and the State*. London: Routledge.

Ricci, A. (2018). The mathematics of Marx. *Lettera Matematica, 6*(4), 221–225.

Roberts, B. (2017). Abstract labor. In *Routledge Handbook of Marxian Economics*. Brennan et al. (Eds.). London: Routledge, 59–68.

Robinson, J. (1962). *Economic Philosophy*. New York: Anchor Books.

Robinson, J. (1966). *An Essay on Marxian Economics*, Second Edition. New York: St Martin's Press.

Rossi-Landi, F. (1977). *Linguistics and Economics*. Berlin: De Gruyter Mouton.

Rovatti, P. A. (1972). Fetishism and economic categories. *Telos, 1972*(14), 87–105.

Rubin, I. I. (1972): *Essays on Marx's Theory of Value*. Detroit: Black and Red.

Screpanti, E. (2019). *Labour and Value. Rethinking Marx's Theory of Exploitation*. Cambridge: Open Book Publishers.

Smith, T. (1990). *The Logic of Marx's Capital: Replies to Hegelian Criticisms*. New York: State University of New York Press.

Smolinski, L. (1973). Karl Marx and Mathematical Economics. *Journal of Political Economy, 81*, 1189–1204.

Steedman, I. (1977). *Marx after Sraffa*. London: New Left Books.

Struik, D. (1948). Marx and Mathematics. *Science and Society, 12*(1), 181–196.

Sweezy, P. M. (1942). *Theory of Capital Development*. Oxford: Oxford University Press.

Taylor, C. (1988). The Contradictions of Positivist Marxism. In *Value, Social Form and the State* (pp. 62-79). Ed: M. Williams. Palgrave Macmillan, London, 62–79.

Tombazos, S. (2014). *Time in Marx: The Categories of Time in Marx's Capital*. Leiden: Brill.

Tombazos, S. (2020). Capital as 'abstraction in action' and economic rhythms in Marx. *Cambridge Journal of Economics, 44*(5), 1055–1068.

Wolff, R. D., Callari, A., and Roberts, B. (1984). A Marxian alternative to the traditional "transformation problem". *Review of Radical Political Economics, 16*(2–3), 115–135.

4

THE DUAL MEASURE OF VALUE

Money and labour time

Andrea Ricci

4.1 "Money as general commodity"[1]

As we have seen in Chapter 3, the extrinsic measure of the exchange value not only expresses itself directly as the relative market exchange ratio of the commodity, but at the same time, it also indirectly expresses the underlying intrinsic measure as objectified abstract labour time. In a barter, the extrinsic measure of the exchange value of a given commodity is represented by the physical quantity of the other commodity with which it exchanges. In the case of bartering, therefore, we have as many extrinsic measures of the exchange value as there are possible relative market exchange ratios of a commodity with all other commodities. In the absence of arbitrage opportunities, all these measures are mutually equivalent, in the sense that the three formal properties of reflexivity, symmetry, and transitivity are verified. The case is different for a monetary exchange in which the extrinsic measure of the exchange value of a commodity is expressed by a single general market exchange ratio with a given amount of money, which acts as the general equivalent in market exchange. In fact, when market exchange is the dominant form of social reproduction, money logically and necessarily emerges as the universal intermediary of exchange. This is what happens in a capitalist economy that is by its very nature a monetary economy of production. For this reason, from this moment on, we will consider money as the extrinsic measure of the exchange value of the commodity, to which corresponds the objectified abstract labour time as its intrinsic measure. In a capitalist economy, therefore, money simultaneously represents the visible mode of appearance of both measures of the exchange value of a commodity, directly as extrinsic measure and indirectly as intrinsic measure. In other words, both the market exchange ratio of one commodity with other commodities, and the abstract labour time objectified in them, appear in the exchange in the form of a given amount of money. The analysis of the possible divergence between the two measures of exchange value, which defines a situation of unequal exchange, demands an in-depth investigation of the role and nature of money in capitalism as a simultaneous expression of the two measures of the exchange value.

The nature of money is often the subject of lively discussions about whether, in Marx's theory of value, money must necessarily be a commodity or may not be a commodity, or whether money is a commodity only in certain tangible forms, such as gold, and not in other intangible forms, such as inconvertible fiat money or credit money.[2] However, disputes around money often arise from a misunderstanding because, in reality, they concern, sometimes unconsciously, not the general commodity form of money, but rather the specific form of the particular commodity that historically represents money. The first problem relates to the general feature of the commodity form, namely the dual nature of object of use and object of market exchange, whatever the material nature of the "object money" is, be it tangible or intangible. The second problem, on the other hand, relates to the relationship between the extrinsic measure of money as a commodity, that is, the market exchange ratio with other commodities, and the intrinsic measure as a given quantity of objectified abstract labour time. In other words, the issue of money as a commodity in general, that is, the commodity form of money, is often confused with the issue of money as a particular commodity, that is, the physical nature of money, the material support of the social form of money in capitalism.[3] The argument I intend to present can be summarized in the following three points: 1) money is always and necessarily a commodity in general; 2) in capitalism, money can historically take different specific commodity forms, namely both that of a capitalist commodity as specie money and a non-capitalist commodity as fiat money; and 3) whatever specific form of commodity it takes, in capitalism, money always expresses both extrinsic and intrinsic measures of the exchange value of the commodities exchanged with it.[4] To clarify these aspects, after discussing Marx's initial hypothesis about gold as money, we will examine the two essential properties of money according to Marx, namely, money as a medium of circulation and money as a measure of values, respectively.[5]

4.1.1 *The simplifying assumption of gold money in Marx's* **Capital**

The processual concept of value as a social algorithm, resulting in the dual nature of both the substance and form of value, allows for a better understanding of money because the enigma of money is the same of the value form of commodity although in a "fully developed shape".[6] Marx derives money from the development of the simplest and most abstract form of exchange, considered in its logical purity as a mathematical equation ("x commodity A = y commodity B"), outside of any material, historical, or social reference. In this simple exchange, each commodity takes the form of money for the other commodity, because it expresses the exchange value, deriving from the objectified abstract labour, in terms of a given exchange ratio between them. This is how Marx (*MK1*, chap. 3, p. 72) describes this mutual relationship:

> Commodities, first of all, enter into the process of exchange just as they are. The process then differentiates them into commodities and money, and thus produces an external opposition corresponding to the internal opposition inherent in them, as being at once use-values and values. Commodities as use-values now stand opposed to money as

exchange-value. On the other hand, both opposing sides are commodities, unities of use-value and value.

Therefore, in its pure conceptual form, money presupposes the category of commodity in general, in which it occupies a special position as universal equivalent.[7] Given its purely logical and conceptual genesis, the notion of money as a special commodity does not depend on the specific commodity social forms that money has historically assumed in capitalism. The analysis of money carried out by Marx should be basically still valid today after the complete abandonment of the monetary functions of gold, as it was when the monetary circulation had bullion as its base. Should this not be the case, it would imply, willingly or not, the rejection of one of the fundamental characters of the whole of Marx's theoretical construct, because the concept of money is an essential pillar of his value theory. Certainly, Marx's account of money still remains valid in its essential theoretical meaning since some ambiguities of expression are present in the original formulation. These are mainly related to Marx's desire to simplify the argument for the reader of his time, when the total demonetization of gold, which occurred more than a century later with the end of the Bretton Woods system, was not even conceivable yet. For this reason, what follows is not intended to be a philological presentation of Marx's analysis of money, but rather an assessment of his theory of money consistent with the interpretation of the value theory proposed in Chapter 3.

First of all, it is necessary to look at the first sentence with which the third chapter of *Capital I* begins, which is devoted to the analysis of money, after those on commodity and exchange: "Throughout this work, I assume, for the sake of simplicity, gold as the money-commodity" (Marx, *MK1*, chap. 3, p. 67). The meaning of this premise, from which the whole discourse develops, is not further clarified later by Marx and remains implicit in all the subsequent analysis of money. Marx's extreme conciseness has probably contributed to some of the misunderstandings that have arisen around his conception of money and therefore deserves an accurate analysis. There are three things to note in it.

Firstly, it is an assumption, a presupposition of reasoning ("I assume"), which is postulated after the money form has already been introduced by Marx in the two previous chapters, where he showed how money logically comes from the equivalent form in the process of barter commodity exchange. Previously, in introducing the form of money, Marx had explicitly stated that whatever commodity can assume this role the only condition required is that, when used as money, the commodity is separated from all others because it holds the social monopoly of universal equivalent.[8] It is only from the third chapter onwards that money is represented by gold and so a specific commodity is chosen from among all the possible ones.

Secondly, this assumption is not an essential, fundamental, and necessary presupposition, but it is a simplification ("for the sake of simplicity") to make the exposition more comprehensible to the readers of the time. This assumption, therefore, does not derive from the peculiar dialectical method typical of Marx, that of the cycle of the "presupposition-posit",[9] through which the initial postulate becomes at the end of the dialectical procedure the final result, this time, however, in the form of a logically founded concept. In the case of gold as money, it is instead, as Marx wants to emphasize, a mere simplifying hypothesis, without any theoretical necessity, so much so that this initial assumption will never come to be the logical and inevitable result of the dialectical analysis of the money form. Nor is it to be thought that Marx meant to use gold instead of silver or copper, i.e. other precious metals used as currency at that time, because in this respect, there is no advantage in terms of simplicity in using one or the other. Besides, it is certain that such a trivial detail would not have been used by Marx, so careful about the meaning of words and the logical order of speech, to open one of the most important chapters of his work, but at most, it would have been relegated in a note to the text. All the more so because Marx will in fact very often use silver together with gold to indicate the bodily form of money during the following chapters. This premise should, therefore, be regarded as having a wider theoretical meaning in referring to the formal attributes of gold as a representative of a specific social form of commodity.

Thirdly, Marx does not say that for simplicity he takes gold commodity as money, but on the contrary, "gold as money-commodity". The appellation of commodity refers to the concept of money, not to the specific material, gold, which represents it. So, money must be considered a commodity by its very nature, and Marx for simplicity opts for gold, a particular commodity, to give a specific form to the money commodity. My suggestion is that, by assuming gold as money, Marx wants to indicate that he is assuming the specific social form of commodity represented by gold, rather than a *commodity in general* that may have any specific form, merely because this assumption simplifies the presentation of the argument and not because it is logically necessary. As will be shown later, the specific social commodity form of gold is that of a *capitalist commodity*, and more specifically, within the context of the general presuppositions of the first book of *Capital*, it is a capitalist simple commodity.

The simplicity of exposition invoked by Marx, as justification for the assumption of gold as money, derives from two reasons. One is obvious and consists in the fact that at that time gold had historically assumed the social monopoly as universal equivalent in all capitalist societies. As shown by a passage from the second book of *Capital*,[10] Marx was fully aware that metallic money represented only a first stage of the historical development of money in capitalism, followed by symbolic money and credit money, which at the time he wrote, however, were not yet universally adopted. The second reason, less obvious, is instead of a theoretical order and concerns the specificity of the capitalist form of commodity to which gold corresponds. Since the assumption underlying the first book of *Capital*, which deals with total social capital, is that of an equivalent exchange between all the commodities, Marx consistently assumes that money shares this feature too as a capitalistic commodity. This form, indeed, makes it more straightforward to express the measure of the exchange value of other commodities, because both extrinsic and intrinsic measures could be directly and immediately expressed by the single form of price, on the sole condition of knowing the socially necessary labour time required for producing gold. In fact, the general assumption of the first book of *Capital* can also be seen as that of the existence of a single average composite commodity, produced by total social capital, which is exchanged for money at a market exchange ratio corresponding to the abstract labour time objectified in them. It is, therefore, appropriate to examine what are the peculiar characteristics of the capitalist commodity with respect to the general form of commodity.

4.1.2 Commodity in general and specific social forms of commodity

A given good acquires the general form of commodity when it is a traded useful object. The commodity in general is defined by the dual nature of object of use and object of market exchange, that is, by being a use value exchanged on the market, regardless of how the market exchange ratio with other commodities is determined with or without a correspondence between extrinsic and intrinsic measure of the exchange value. The mere existence of the dual nature of object of use and object of market exchange defines a good as a commodity. An object is a commodity in general because of its general market exchangeability, independent of the specific, quantitatively determined, exchange ratio with other commodities. The concept of commodity in general belongs to the category of the general determinations that identifies the common elements of a multitude of really existing entities. The general form of a commodity is an abstract and universal category of market exchange, which manifests its concrete historical existence in a plurality of the specific social form of particular commodities. It is precisely the particular mode of determination of the market exchange ratio that defines the specific social form actually assumed by a given commodity. All the historical social forms of commodity belong to the category of commodity in general, and are distinguished from each other by the different, particular mode of determination of their market exchange ratio. All commodities can be considered as commodities in general that become particular commodities, assuming their concrete and individual existence, when they enter into a given market exchange ratio with other commodities and thus their specific social form is determined.

A particular commodity assumes the specific social form of a capitalist commodity when it is exchanged as a product of capital and acquires real existence only when capitalism becomes the historically dominant mode of production. Commodities, in fact, as well as market trading activities, historically and logically precede capitalism, since they were already present in traditional societies,[11] albeit with a marginal social role, and can also be conceived in the bartering process, regardless of the specific capitalist monetary form of exchange. What distinguishes the capitalist commodity is that it is the result of a capitalistic process of production and circulation. Firstly, the capitalist commodity is a reproducible good,[12] in the sense that it is not characterized by uniqueness, and it can be newly produced and therefore consumed more than once. This, however, is a necessary but not sufficient condition to define the specific capitalist character of a commodity, because it has to be assessed within the whole mode of production and reproduction of the society in which it is exchanged. In traditional societies, for example, the trade of reproducible commodities exists as an interstitial economic activity, mostly related to the exchange of surpluses and luxury goods, often conducted with foreign communities and exercised by marginal social groups. In these situations, the exchange ratio of the commodities is normally determined by fortuitous and accidental circumstances. Besides being reproducible, the capitalist commodity also requires to be freely produced and traded under competitive conditions, and subjected to the operation of the law of value that establishes the correspondence between extrinsic and intrinsic measure of the exchange value in a pure or modified form. In addition to capitalist commodities, the general form of commodity also includes pre-capitalist commodities and other forms of non-capitalist commodities existing in capitalism, which are scarce, non-reproducible, and subjected to natural or artificial monopoly conditions.

Under the general presupposition of the first book of *Capital*, capitalist commodities are simple commodities. Simple commodities are defined by the exact correspondence between the intrinsic and extrinsic measures of the exchange value, meaning that the market exchange ratio is exactly proportional to the objectified abstract labour time of the exchanged commodities. When, in the third book of *Capital*, Marx moves from analysis of the total social capital to the more concrete analysis of many particular capitals in competition with each other, the capitalist commodity is no longer a simple commodity since it is exchanged based on price of production, according to the rule of equalization of the profit rates between all the particular industries into a general rate of profit. Although it is no longer a simple commodity, it remains, however, a capitalist commodity because it is subject to the law of value modified by the existence of industries with different organic compositions of capital. For non-capitalist commodities, instead, extrinsic and intrinsic measures may be completely disconnected since they may be only partially proportional, or even the intrinsic measure may not exist at all when the commodity is not the product of labour, like objects that "have a price without having value".[13] The commodity in general, including both capitalist and non-capitalist forms of commodities, therefore, is defined only by having the extrinsic measure as the relative market exchange ratio, regardless of the intrinsic measure that determines the specific social forms it takes. Consequently, a capitalist commodity is always a commodity in general, while a commodity in general may not be a capitalist commodity.

Some authors have rightly argued, in contrast to Engels' interpretation shared by orthodox traditional Marxism,[14] that since the beginning of *Capital*, Marx presupposes the capitalist mode of production, and therefore the commodity with which the work opens, is already a capitalist commodity rather than a supposed pre-capitalist simple commodity. However, the error of the traditional orthodox interpretation does not lie in considering the form of commodity with which Marx begins *Capital* as a simple commodity, but in considering the simple commodity as a pre-capitalist commodity, that is, in giving a historical meaning, anyway unfounded, to a logical presupposition. In fact, contrary to the traditional approach, the simple commodity is a particular case of capitalist commodity. In the first two books of *Capital*, Marx always assumes that the commodity is a simple capitalist commodity, not a generic simple commodity. The simple capitalist commodity denotes the particular character taken by the specific social form of capitalist commodity when the intrinsic measure of the exchange value, as the objectification of abstract labour time, corresponds to the extrinsic measure, as market exchange ratio. The simple commodity is therefore the appellation given to the capitalist commodity when it is exchanged on the market exactly in proportion to the abstract labour time objectified in it. This situation, however, is an exception in capitalism, since as shown by Marx in the third book of *Capital*, capitalist commodities are normally exchanged on the basis of prices of production different from values. The simple commodity is therefore the particular case of the commodity with an average organic composition of capital, where the sectoral profit rate coincides with the general rate of profit. The simple commodity form of the first book of *Capital* performs the same function as corn in Ricardo's basic model as an invariable measure of value, later developed by Sraffa (1960) in more rigorous terms with the notion of standard commodity.

Exactly the opposite, therefore, of what is stated by the traditional orthodox approach, the simple commodity cannot be a pre-capitalist commodity, because in the modes of production prior to capitalism the commodity did not have an exchange value, but only an exchange ratio with the other commodities, which was determined according to rules different from those of the law of value. Nor did abstract labour, which is the specific form taken by social labour in general only in capitalist societies and does not exist at all in traditional pre-capitalist societies. Marx starts with the simple commodity as a special case of capitalist commodity because in this way it places itself at the highest possible degree of abstraction to derive the concept of value in its purest form, avoiding all the complications arising from the technical differences in the material process of production of the individual commodities. In this way, he can analyse capital in a unitary form as total social capital in order to isolate its nature as general social relation with social labour power from the particular relationships existing among the multitude of individual capitals in competition. On the other hand, it would have been impossible and extremely confusing to derive the concept of value, as the social algorithm of equivalence in commodities exchange, from a commodity in which the dualism of the form of value is expressed in a divergent rather than equivalent way.

This does not mean, however, that the commodities to which Marx refers in the course of his work have always the specific capitalist form, because in capitalism alongside them there are also non-capitalist commodities that Marx deals with several times, for example, in the analysis of ground rent.[15] The non-capitalist commodities existing in capitalism are those commodities that do not comply with the law of value in its simple or modified form for the determination of their market exchange ratio. Consequently, both capitalist and non-capitalist commodities can be encompassed within a more general form, that of the commodity in general, of which each of the two constitutes a specific social form. This general form necessarily brings together all specific forms of commodity existing in capitalism, regardless of how they are produced and traded, as the result of industrial or artistic labour, as privately appropriate gifts of nature or as social goods under state or private monopoly. The thesis argued here is that in capitalism money can historically assume both specific forms of commodity, capitalist and non-capitalist, and therefore, in order to be investigated at the higher level of abstraction, it has to be considered as a commodity in general, without presupposing a specific social form.[16]

At the beginning of the third chapter of *Capital I*, the assumption of gold as money is of the same nature as the one adopted by Marx at the beginning of the first chapter, both regarding the assumption of the simple capitalist commodity as the specific social form taken by the commodity in general.[17] Both assumptions were logically forced at the beginning because otherwise, the presentation of the argument would have been incomprehensible. In fact, as Marx points out in his letter to Kugelmann: "Science consists precisely in demonstrating *how* the law of value asserts itself. So that if one wanted at the very beginning to 'explain' all the phenomenon which seemingly contradict that law, one would have to present science *before* science" (*MEC*, July 11, 1868). Later on, with the development of the discourse in the third book of *Capital*, Marx removes the hypothesis of the simple capitalist commodity in the analysis of value by formulating the concept of the price of production as the specific form assumed by the law of value in capitalism. The same Marx did not have the time to do, in an organic and systematic manner, the hypothesis of gold as a money commodity, and we cannot know if in the unwritten but planned books he would have made this passage. In any case, it is now time to continue the research in order to progress in the knowledge of contemporary social reality, supported by the reading key given to us by Marx and the concrete experience of the historical transformations of capitalism. We must now see, therefore, whether the essential functions of medium of circulation and measure of values can be equally performed by abandoning the simplifying hypothesis of gold money and considering money as a commodity in general rather than a simple capitalist commodity. In such a case, as a commodity in general, money can take any specific form, that of specie money as a capitalist commodity or that of fiat money as a non-capitalist commodity.

4.2 The functions of money

4.2.1 *Money as the medium of circulation*

As the medium of circulation, money has the property to act as a general intermediary of exchanges, replacing the myriad of bilateral barters with a single general form of bilateral exchange between each particular commodity and money. In this way, money replaces the multitude of relative barter exchange ratios with a general exchange ratio between every particular commodity and money and performs the function of universal equivalent. In capitalist societies, where the market exchange of commodities represents the general form of social reproduction, a particular commodity separates itself from all other commodities to perform the function of general intermediary of exchanges, thus becoming as universal equivalent the visible expression of the exchange value of all the commodities in the form of price. The price, or money form of commodity, is precisely the relative exchange ratio of a commodity with all other commodities expressed in the form of a general exchange ratio with money as the universal equivalent, and in capitalism, it directly represents the extrinsic measure of the exchange value, which in particular circumstances exactly corresponds to the intrinsic measure.

The particular commodity turned into money acquires a new use value as a visible form of expression of the exchange value of all other commodities.[18] The use value of money is "represented by the series of expressions of relative value in which it stands face to face with all other commodities" (Marx, *MK1*, chap. 3, p. 72). The specificity of money as commodity in capitalism lies precisely in the fact that its use value consists in being the immediate and general representative of the exchange value of all commodities, made autonomous and independent from the body of any particular commodity other than the money commodity. In this way, money also becomes at the same time the general representative of every use value since it can buy any particular commodity. This new general use value supersedes the particular one the "object" money had previously. In the case that the money commodity also continues to be a particular object of use in production or consumption, as with metals or salt in primitive communities, a curious thing happens. The same single physical commodity acquires a shifting existence as a concrete object depending on the particular circumstances in which it is used. It is a particular use value when destined for specific purposes, and a general use value as money when used as the intermediary of exchanges. One function excludes the other since the commodity performing the function of money can never be particular use value and general use value at the same time, confirming the pure social character of money regardless of the specific material object bearing the monetary function.

The general distinctive property of money as the medium of circulation in capitalism is to be both the bearer of general exchange value for the seller and general use value for the buyer. Only one of all existing commodities can possess this general property, and from the moment this property is universally recognized by society this is sufficient for it to become the medium of circulation. We can draw two conclusions from this. Firstly, the commodity dualism of use value and exchange value is intrinsic in the concept of money as the medium of circulation, independently of the specific social form that it historically takes, and therefore in this function, money is always a commodity in general. Secondly, the commodity dualism of money, as the expression of general use value and general exchange value, is a necessary and sufficient condition to perform the function of the medium of circulation, regardless of the specific commodity form that money assumes in its concrete existence. Money as the medium of circulation, therefore, merely requires the feature of commodity in general, no matter whether it is a capitalist commodity or not. The mere possession of a relative exchange ratio with all other commodities, which qualifies it as an object of market exchange, makes it possible for money to serve as the extrinsic measure of the exchange value of all other commodities, thus providing it with a new use value as general equivalent. For this reason, Marx states that as a medium of circulation money can even just be a symbolic commodity, devoid of any intrinsic value, representing a given amount of value by social recognition.[19] By contrast, the intrinsic measure of money as quantity of objectified abstract labour time does not play any role in defining it as the medium of circulation. In summary, the only quality required of money as the medium of circulation is to be a commodity in general, and consequently, it is not necessary that it should be a capitalist commodity too.

The exchange realized through the intermediation of money does not present any essential difference with the barter exchange. On a purely logical view, it is possible to think of the monetary exchange as a succession of barter exchanges between the commodity money and every other commodity, which replaces the direct barter of all the other commodities among them. This accounts for Marx's claim that any commodity can act as the medium of circulation.[20] Modern anthropological research has shown that the medium of circulation in primitive societies was represented by precious objects of various kinds, having the character of rare and non-reproducible goods, such as pearls, fish teeth, salt, or shells. In this case, the exchange ratio of this "primitive" money, acting as an intermediary in trade with other social groups, resulted from its scarcity rather than from the costs of production in terms of human labour.[21] In the history of humankind, the function of the medium of circulation has been played by the most varied commodities selected on the basis of their material qualities (durability, divisibility, homogeneity) or even their symbolic, social, and sometimes magical properties. In capitalist societies, in which a disenchanted and utilitarian vision of the world prevailed, the purely material and physical properties of the object predominated, and therefore, the function of medium of circulation was historically assumed by precious metals. Gold became the universal intermediary of exchanges in the early stages of capitalism on the basis of a process of natural selection, replacing all other commodities competing for this function because of its peculiar physical characteristics.

Precious metals, such as gold, silver, and copper, possess the features of capitalist commodities, since they are capitalistically produced by a particular branch of production subject to competition like all other industries in the economic system. It is not, however, for being a product of labour nor even less a product of capital that gold has historically emerged as medium of circulation, but it was for its particular material qualities. When this happened, the prevailing use of gold served as the general equivalent of exchanges rather than as a luxury good. The simple social act of placing a commodity as the medium of circulation, universally accepted on the market, determines at the same time its use value. Consequently, even an object lacking any use value of its own acquires the use value of general equivalent when it is socially accepted as money. Moreover, when an object with a use value is not freely and gratuitously available, it also becomes an object of market exchange. For these reasons, it was possible to replace gold as the medium of circulation with a legal tender currency, fiat money, whose forced circulation is socially imposed by the state by virtue of a law obligation. Fiat money is a commodity that appears *ex novo* on the basis of a state decision and replaces gold in the social monopoly of money. Its use value and exchange value are created in the very act of its institution as money, and outside of this function, it is devoid of any use value and exchange value. When this happens, the function of money as medium of circulation, previously performed by a capitalist commodity such as gold, is now performed by a non-capitalist commodity such as fiduciary money devoid of intrinsic value issued by the State in a monopoly regime.

In summary, money as the medium of circulation has to be always, whatever specific form it possesses, whether of tangible or intangible nature, a commodity in general because it always is an object of use and an object of market exchange. In capitalism, therefore, money as the medium of circulation always represents both use value and exchange value, even if it has a special character distinguishing it from all other commodities as the general representative of every use value and every exchange value. By contrast, money assumes the character of a capitalist commodity only in particular circumstances, when as specie money, for example, gold, it is the private product of an ordinary branch of production, that of mining, subject to the same competitive constraints as all other capitalist industries. Throughout the history of capitalism, gold, initially adopted in social use as medium of circulation due to its physical properties, gradually loses its monetary functions to be completely replaced by a form of money, such as fiat money, which is a state monopoly commodity without intrinsic value. We have thus established that logically and historically money as the medium of circulation requires to be a commodity in general, without necessarily taking one or the other of the specific forms of capitalist or non-capitalist commodity, being able to fulfil its proper function as general intermediary of exchanges in both cases.

4.2.2 Money as the measure of values

As the measure of values, money has the property to express in a phenomenal, bodily form the exchange value of all other commodities. In this function, Marx distinguishes two distinct but closely related aspects, that of expression of the measure of values in the proper sense and that of standard of prices. By the former, he means the property of money to represent the intrinsic measure of the exchange value of a commodity as an expression of the abstract labour time objectified in it.[22] By the latter, he means the property of money to represent the extrinsic measure of the exchange value of a commodity as an expression of the general market exchange ratio of a given currency unit. According to Marx, therefore, money is the universal form of expression of the dual measure of exchange value of the commodities in capitalism. Let us now examine what features are required of money to perform the function of measure of values, starting with the simpler aspect of standard of prices.

When a given form of money is socially affirmed as the general intermediary of exchanges, it also takes on the role of the extrinsic measure, as an expression of the general market exchange ratio of commodities, thus becoming the standard of prices. The definition of the standard of price is prerogative of each national state that establishes, by coinage, the currency unit in force for domestic trade by dividing the money according to a specific scale of measurements. The elements of this monetary scale express different quantities of value according to a progressive order, such as pence, shillings, and pounds. When the monetary base was gold or silver, each unit of the scale was the expression of a given weight of gold or silver, and therefore they were the name of the general market exchange ratio of a given amount of gold or silver, that is, of the extrinsic measure of money indirectly expressed. With the advent of the fiduciary state money, the link with gold or silver ceases to exist, and the currency units directly express the extrinsic measure of money. As Marx incidentally notes, the formal distinction between intrinsic and extrinsic measures implies, already at this stage of the analysis, the possibility of their divergence. This divergence in the case of money takes the form of state seigniorage at the time the money is coined or issued, and this is the main reason why gold money was not expressed directly according to the weight of the metal but according to a currency unit established by the state. As far as the aspect of standard of prices is concerned, the only characteristic that money must have is that it is a commodity in general, meaning that it is object of use and object of market exchange as universal equivalent and general intermediary of trade by virtue of a state obligation. In this respect, there is no difference between the various forms of expression of money, be it gold or fiduciary state money. More challenging is the examination of money as an expression of the intrinsic measure of exchange values.

As an expression of the intrinsic measure of the exchange value, money provides the external and visible manifestation of the commensurability between commodities as products of human labour. The exchange values of the commodities are expressed as crystals of objectified abstract labour time through the common money representation. Marx points out that money can serve as a material expression of the objectified abstract labour time only because the commodities are crystals of abstract labour logically before their conversion into money. It is not money that makes the commodities crystals of abstract labour but the opposite, the commodities as crystals of abstract labour give money the faculty to express the intrinsic measure of exchange value. The same applies to the expression of abstract labour in money as it does to the expression of an object's weight in kilos. It is only by weighing a kilo of iron that we can know how much a kilo of iron weighs, but it is not the act of weighing, nor its expression in kilos rather than in pounds that provides the definite given weight to iron. Rather the opposite is true, that is, kilos and pounds express a definite given weight because the objects weighed already have a weight of kilos and pounds on their own.

Another point deserves to be observed. Marx notes that the commodities enter the exchange process with an intrinsic measure expressed in money in "a purely ideal or mental form", that is, in "imaginary or ideal money", which waits to be transformed into real money, into hard cash, with the sale of the commodity in the market. This imaginary money representation is practically observable in the price at which the producer brings the commodity to the market, it is the offer price of the commodity, which can differ from the actual final sale price. Indeed, it may well happen that the commodity is unsold, and its money representation remains imaginary in the seller's head or in the firm's warehouses. Even more so, the commodities are ideally transformed into imaginary money already during the intermediate stages of the production process within the capitalist firm, when they have not yet reached their final form of the finished product, but are still in their raw state in which, in the event of a stoppage of production, they may remain even until they deteriorate. The internal capitalist accounting, used to evaluate the efficiency of the production process, is in fact drawn up in monetary terms, confirming that the commodity has an imaginary intrinsic value represented in money before its appearance on the final sales market. The progressive increase in the intrinsic value of the processed goods from the initial stage of raw material to the final stage of the finished product, always expressed in monetary terms, can be observed through the firm's internal accounting.[23] Only when the commodity is actually sold does the imaginary intrinsic measure become the real intrinsic measure of the exchange value of the commodity, i.e. the real expression of the abstract labour time objectified in the commodity. However, the fact that this intrinsic value has a purely imaginary form in its ideal representation in money, visible in the tags attached to the product on the sales counter or in the firm's internal accounting reports, does not mean that it is not an expression of a real social process with its own material and concrete existence. The intrinsic value ideally expressed in money is not the extemporaneous and bizarre fruit of the seller's fantasy, a pure individual subjective representation of the producer as can be a desire or a dream, but it is an objective social phenomenon that arises from the actual operation of the law of value within the capitalist production process of the commodity. It is such a concrete and real process that it determines working conditions, fixes times, ways, and forms of the concrete labour of the workers, feeds on the fatigue and sweat of living labour and conveys all the power of capitalist command in the organization of the working process. The failure to transform the intrinsic measure from an imaginary monetary expression into reality produces important social effects because it causes corporate or general economic crises and, in any case, reduces total social labour to a size smaller than that potentially available to satisfy the needs of society. The distinction between imaginary and real monetary expression of the intrinsic measure of exchange value is the visible and practical consequence of the dual nature of the specific form of social labour as abstract labour in capitalism. The imaginary monetary representation of the exchange value occurring before the commodity enters the market, still inside the working process, shows that the commodities are constituted by objectified abstract labour time that can be measured, though ideally, before and independently from the exchange.

Money, as an expression of the intrinsic measure of the exchange value, is the external, material, phenomenal representation of the abstract labour time objectified in the commodities. Money is the mirror in which the abstract labour objectified inside the body of a given commodity is reflected in form of price, since "when other commodities express their prices in gold, this gold is but the money-form of those commodities themselves" (Marx, *MK1*, chap. 3, p. 72). The metaphor of the mirror, to indicate the visible expression, the external appearance of the exchange value of a commodity in the form of another commodity acting as money, is repeatedly used by Marx in the analysis of value form in the first chapter of the first book of *Capital*.[24] It was then resumed by Hilferding comparing the value of paper money with the light of the Moon, which, lacking its own light, merely reflects the rays of the Sun on the Earth[25]. However, another metaphor that was impossible in Marx's time, expresses this function of money even better than the mirror. Money is like an X-ray in which what is hidden inside the human body is represented as a visible image. Thanks to the X-ray, we can compare a healthy human organ with a sick one, but obviously, it is not the radiography that makes the organ what it really is, healthy or sick. It is true that without it one could not compare the organs of living people, but they are comparable not because they are impressed on the X-ray, but because they are constituted by human cells as the common biological material organized in form of that organ, that is, by a common human organic substance. In the case of money, this common substance is abstract labour, and the human organ is the abstract labour time objectified in the commodity. We could go further and, passing from metaphor to homology, say that the biological substance imprinted in the form of a human organ in the X-ray is the result of a genetic code of self-organization and differentiation of human cells that are the result of a biological algorithm spontaneously activated at the moment of conception, in homology to what we have said about value as a social algorithm.

But let us interrupt the homology here and continue with the metaphor by examining the physical material of which X-rays are made. To perform diagnostic functions the physical material of the X-ray image is not important. Before the advent of the electronic age, X-rays were plastic films coated with silver nitrate; today, they are completely dematerialized as digital images visible on a monitor. What was previously a plate of plastic and silver is now immaterial digital information formed by an ordered set of bytes that are processed by a computer allow us to see the X-ray image, but not to touch it as with the plate. The fact that the physical change in the material expression of the X-ray did not change its diagnostic functions in any way seems so obvious that no one questions it. However, this is not always the case for money, whose transformation from the material form of gold to the immaterial form of contemporary state-issued inconvertible money has raised doubts about the current validity or the correctness of Marx's theory.

On this point, two different views can be identified. On the one hand, there are those who claim that the monetary developments of contemporary capitalism make Marx's original value theory anachronistic because it cannot abandon the convertible money hypothesis.[26] On the other hand, there are those who say that, if properly adjusted, Marx's theory would be reinforced by the replacement of gold with credit money, even though it would renounce some of its cornerstones, such as the use of socially necessary labour time in measuring value.[27] Both these visions, while reaching opposite conclusions on the status of value theory, share the belief that Marx's original theory of money is not appropriate to contemporary capitalism and must be abandoned or substantially corrected. Finally, although a minority, there is also the specular opposite opinion of those who believe that in reality, nothing has changed in contemporary capitalism and that gold still continues to be the basis of the international monetary system, to which all national currencies must necessarily refer, albeit only ideally, to perform the function of the measure of values, otherwise impossible with fiat money.[28] In reality, gold is no longer the material form assumed by money, but nevertheless, the dematerialization of money in contemporary capitalism has not changed in any way the meaning and function of money as the measure of values, just as digitalization has not changed the meaning and function of X-rays as a diagnostic tool.

The dematerialization of money concerns the replacement of gold as a means of payment and not as a medium of circulation. The qualitative leap, indeed, has taken place when gold has been replaced by the inconvertible monetary base, issued under monopoly by the central bank, as the instrument for the final extinction of debt and credit obligations in the economy. The circulation of banknotes and credit money were already widely used forms of monetary circulation at the time of the Gold Standard. In this respect, as Marx repeatedly pointed out in polemic with the quantitative theory of money, the quantity of credit money in circulation is endogenously determined by the conditions of demand for money resulting from the periodic fluctuations of the economic cycle. What defines the golden or the inconvertible nature of a monetary system is the way in which the creation of a new monetary base takes place, not the monetary circulation that in both cases results from a substantially similar process of endogenous monetary multiplication implemented through the banking system.[29] In the case of the Gold Standard, the monetary circulation was ultimately ruled by the convertibility to gold of the final balances of debt and credit between banking institutions and between countries, thus determining an external anchorage to the creation of a new monetary base given by the amount of new gold produced in each period. In the case of fiat money, this golden anchorage is replaced by the purchase of financial assets, mainly government debt, by the central bank through the issue of inconvertible legal tender money. This change occurred by virtue of state laws, namely as a compulsory obligation imposed by the legitimate power of the state on all economic subjects under its jurisdiction.[30] It is to indicate this new form of monetary creation that I use the term fiat money or fiduciary money issued by the state. The substantial novelty that characterizes contemporary capitalism is that, all other things being equal, the general price level is ultimately determined by the general market exchange ratio of the fiat money at the time of its issuance by the central bank, while in the Gold Standard, it is by the general market exchange ratio of gold at the time of its production. In fact, all other changes in financial systems between the two epochs concern the scale and degree rather than the essence of the phenomena.

The main origin of the controversy about the present-day relevance of Marx's theory of money lies in the misconception that with the transition from gold to that of fiat money, money is no longer a commodity. In fact, as we discussed previously, fiat money is a commodity as much as gold, because it is an object of use and an object of market exchange, although, unlike gold, it is not a capitalist commodity but rather a non-capitalist commodity produced under a state monopoly. This means that while gold has both the intrinsic and extrinsic measure of its exchange value, fiat money has only the extrinsic measure since it is not at all a product of labour. Therefore, the functions of money that were previously performed by a capitalist commodity are now performed by a non-capitalist commodity. What has changed is the phenomenal material form of the expression of money, not the functions that money performs in the economic system – the same happened with X-rays. This leads us to rule out the argument that the Marxian theory was valid when gold performed the functions of money, while it is no longer valid after the demonetization of gold. Either it is erroneous since it was formulated by Marx, or it was valid then as it is today, albeit in different ways. Let us look at the matter in more detail.

If we suppose, as Marx does in the first book of *Capital*, that all commodities are exchanged according to the relative quantities of abstract labour time objectified in them, intrinsic measure and extrinsic measure of the exchange value correspond perfectly. If the exchange is of a monetary nature, for a given commodity both measures manifest themselves in a given amount of money, that is, in the form of price, whatever material form of expression the money has, be it gold or fiat money. Indeed, it should always be borne in mind that commodities are commensurable with each other as exchange values logically before they are expressed in money. The monetary expression is only the external, material, phenomenal representation of their logically pre-existing ratio of equivalence, that is, of their determined exchange value. Since money acts as an intermediary in trade, once it has entered into circulation it remains in circulation, unlike all other commodities which sooner or later leave the trade cycle to be consumed productively or unproductively. Leaving aside the moment of issue, in the function of measure of values, money measures the exchange value of a commodity relative to the exchange value of all other commodities except the one acting as the medium of circulation, i.e. money itself, because nothing can be a measure of itself. The exchange value of money is determined at the moment of its introduction into circulation. At the moment of issuance, money acquires the exchange value of the commodities it purchases until a new monetary issue can readjust the value of money. If we assume the equivalence of exchanges with the full correspondence between intrinsic and extrinsic measure of the exchange value of the commodities purchased by money at its issuance, once money enters into circulation it correctly expresses both intrinsic and extrinsic measures of the exchange value of all other commodities. This is true for any form of money, be it gold or fiat money. If a pair of shoes sold on the market requires on average two hours of social labour and if it is exchanged on the basis of this labour time because intrinsic and extrinsic measures correspond, it is completely irrelevant how this ratio of equivalence is expressed as a general market exchange ratio by money, if in the form of a gram of gold or in the form of 50 dollars. Both monetary expressions will express the same intrinsic and extrinsic measures of the exchange value of the pair of shoes. The only thing that would change is that the golden gram also requires two hours of social labour like shoes, while the 50 dollars require much less. If the dollars that buy the shoes were already in circulation before the exchange, the buyer and seller will have exchanged a socially equivalent amount of exchange value, because the buyer had previously acquired this sum of money by giving in exchange two hours of abstract labour objectified in the form of commodities. If, on the other hand, it is the central bank or government that buys the shoes, the buyer will have obtained a higher exchange value than the one given in exchange.

In general terms, given the equivalence of the intrinsic and extrinsic measures of value for all commodities, including gold money, assumed by Marx in Book I of *Capital*, with convertible money, every exchange is an equivalent exchange between equal amounts of abstract labour time, while with inconvertible money, the central bank and the government have a power of seigniorage because money is the only commodity produced under monopoly. With fiat money, the state appropriates a part of the total social labour without any equivalent counterpart, but this does not change the operation of the law of value, since the occult state levy is evenly distributed on all commodities in circulation in the form of a change in the value of money. The consequence is that all other conditions being equal, primarily the velocity of circulation of money, in the former case, the market exchange ratio of gold, which determines the general price level, depends on the abstract labour time objectified in a quantity of gold. Instead, in the latter case, the market exchange ratio of fiat money, which equally determines the general price level, depends on the supply of the monetary base issued by the central bank that fixes the amount of seigniorage. If, on the other hand, we suppose that, as in the third book of *Capital*, the extrinsic and intrinsic measure of the exchange value normally do not correspond because commodities are exchanged according to prices of production and there are also monopoly conditions like that on land and mining ownership, in the case of fiat money, there would be no substantial change from the previous situation. By contrast, with gold money, we will no longer have equivalence between the abstract labour time objectified in gold and the relative market exchange ratio of money with all the individual commodities, except in the special and accidental case of an organic composition of capital in the gold industry identical to the social average. The determination of the general level of prices, on the other hand, will not change from the way it was in the previous situation. Finally, by introducing state seigniorage into the coinage of gold money as was historically the case in the Gold Standard, the differences between convertible and inconvertible money become even smaller. They only concern is the form in which the power of state seigniorage is exercised. In the case of gold money, seigniorage occurs through the variation of the gold content of the currency unit. In the case of fiat money, it occurs through the change of the stock of financial assets held by the central bank.

From what we have now seen, the differences between gold and fiat money concern the determination of the general price level and the state seigniorage, but there is nothing in them that prevents fiat money from operating as a measure of values, even if in a form different than gold.[31] A simple numerical example can help to clarify the issue. Let us suppose that there are two commodities A and B. Commodity A is the product of two hours of abstract labour and commodity B of four hours of abstract labour. In a barter economy, the intrinsic and extrinsic measures of the exchange value correspond to each other if one unit of commodity B is exchanged with two units of commodity A. Let us now introduce the monetary exchange, beginning with gold money. Let us suppose that one gram of gold is the product of an hour of abstract labour. In order to maintain the correspondence between the extrinsic and intrinsic measure of the exchange value, it is necessary that the price of commodity A be equal to two grams of gold and that of commodity B to four grams of gold. In this case, as in barter, one unit of commodity B continues indirectly to exchange for two units of commodity A. Let us now suppose that gold money is replaced by fiat money, e.g. dollars, with no intrinsic value of its own, and that commodity A has a price of ten dollars. If commodity B has a price of 20 dollars, there is still a correspondence between the intrinsic and extrinsic measures of the exchange value, and fiat money continues to express the intrinsic measure, albeit indirectly instead of directly as in the case of gold money. As the example illustrates, the specific form of money, whether it is a capitalist commodity like gold or a non-capitalist commodity like fiat money, does not change the function of money as an expression of the exchange value, both in terms of market exchange ratio and in terms of objectified abstract labour time. Even in its function of measure of value, money only acts as an intermediary, as the carrier of a ratio of equivalence in the market exchange of commodities that is determined by the law of value and not by the specific nature of money used.

One might ask at this point where is the greater simplicity invoked by Marx to assume that money is a capitalist commodity like gold. A first reason is that if he had introduced a non-capitalist commodity produced in a monopoly, such as fiat money, he would have contradicted the general hypothesis of the first book of *Capital* that all commodities, including money, are exchanged on the basis of abstract labour time. In this way, however, he would certainly have created confusion in the reader who, unlike us, could know nothing about the prices of production and the possible differences between intrinsic and extrinsic measures of value, developed in the later books of *Capital* published 20 or more years later. A second reason for Marx's simplifying hypothesis lies in the fact that, given the general presupposition of the first book, if the intrinsic measure of the exchange value of gold is known (in the previous example, one gram = one hour of labour), the intrinsic measure of all other individual commodities is also immediately known simply through their extrinsic measure, that is, their market exchange ratio with gold or their price. It is therefore sufficient to know the abstract labour time objectified in gold to immediately determine the abstract labour time objectified in all other individual commodities by observing their price. With fiat money, by contrast, this possibility of directly and immediately converting the extrinsic measure of the exchange value of commodities into the intrinsic measure is no longer possible. In order to realize this conversion, it is necessary to introduce a further step of mediation that allows the transformation of the extrinsic measure, that is, the price, into the intrinsic measure of the exchange value of the commodities. As we will see further on, this mediation link is given by the monetary expression of labour time (MELT).

To sum up, therefore, money is a measure of values in the proper sense in whatever specific commodity form because it can always express the intrinsic measure of the exchange values of the commodities, with the only condition that it is a commodity in general, no matter whether a capitalist commodity like gold or a non-capitalist commodity like fiat money. When money had the form of gold, there was an immediate and direct measure of conversion from abstract labour time to its expression in money given by the labour time socially necessary to produce a given amount of gold. In this way, money entered the circulation already endowed with its own intrinsic value as objectified abstract labour time, which was exchanged with the intrinsic value of the purchased commodities giving them monetary expression. With fiat money this direct and immediate conversion of abstract labour time into money is no longer possible. But this does not mean that abstract labour time ceases to be the intrinsic measure of the exchange value of the commodities or that it can no longer be represented in a visible form through the monetary expression. What has changed is only the form of representation of abstract labour time that has moved from a direct and immediate expression through gold money, to an indirect and mediated expression through fiat money. That this is the case is demonstrated by the fact that if we remove the assumption of gold as a simple capitalist commodity and suppose that its production requires an organic composition of capital different from the social average, as normally happens in reality, this does not mean that gold money loses its functions as a medium of circulation and measure of value. In this case, which is the normal and ordinary case, the difference between gold money and inconvertible money can only be quantitative and not qualitative, in the sense that the discrepancy between price and value of gold will be different than the one existing between price and value of inconvertible money. However, from the conceptual point of view, the two forms are identical, and both are able to perform the functions of money. In conclusion, therefore, money must possess only the general form of commodity in order to perform the functions of medium of circulation and measure of values, without necessarily requiring any specific form of capitalist or non-capitalistic commodity

4.3 The fundamental equivalence of value

As we have seen, the dual nature of abstract labour determines the existence of two distinct measures of the exchange value, the extrinsic measure given by the market exchange ratio and the intrinsic measure given by the abstract labour time objectified in the commodities. Both measures have their visible representation in the form of a given amount of money exchanged on the market, i.e. in the form of price. It now remains to determine which are the units of measurement of the two measures and their mutual ratio of conversion. To do this, we return to the process of the exchange of commodities.

4.3.1 The measurement of exchange value: Labour time and money

The magnitude of the exchange value of a given commodity is determined in the act of exchange, where the commodity in the hands of the producer-seller stands in front of the sum of money in the hands of the consumer-purchaser. But its determination is established not in the accidental act of exchange of an individual commodity, but in the social exchange between the total quantity of commodities of the same kind and the total quantity of money with which they exchange on the market. The social producer and the social consumer, that is, society as producer and society as consumer, are therefore, the parts who confront each other in the act of exchange determining the exchange value of a particular commodity. Here, it is important to point out that the analysis has a purely formal character, and therefore, the commodity in the hands of the seller is not to be regarded as use value, but as exchange value waiting to be realized and transformed into the form of money as general equivalent. The use value of the commodity is already presupposed from the outset, that is, from the moment the commodity enters into the act of exchange as demanded by the purchaser.

The commodity in the hands of the seller is not yet money, but it is already objectified, or crystallized living labour time spent in its production. The total amount of labour used to produce the whole quantity of the commodity, as well as the average amount of labour used to produce a unit of commodity, are given quantities, established before the actual completion of the transaction, as soon as production has ended, and the commodity has not yet entered into the exchange. The total amount of labour time that the society has used in the production of that given commodity, that is, the share of the available total social labour used in its production, as well as the number of pieces, the actual volume of commodity supplied, are known before the sale on the market. Consequently, the social labour used on average, under normal conditions of production, to produce one unit of the commodity is also a datum that already exists before and outside the exchange. The commodity in the hands of the seller enters the exchange having already in dowry a certain amount of normal social labour, which the society assigned to it as its part in the distribution of the total social labour among all the different commodities produced.

The normal, average social labour time objectified in the act of production of the commodity represents the *labour expression of value* (LEV), measured by the ratio between the total direct labour time spent in production and the physical quantity, the total volume of the commodity produced in a given period of time. The inverse of the LEV, i.e. the ratio between the physical quantity of the commodity produced in a given period of time and the total direct labour time used in production, defines the product per unit of universal labour or average normal social labour. As we will see later on, at the level of an individual productive unit, direct labour may differ from universal labour due to a labour intensity different from the social average. In this case, it will be necessary to convert the individual direct labour into universal labour to determine the intrinsic measure of the individual value produced by the single productive unit. At the aggregate level, as we are now considering, direct and universal total labour always coincide. The intrinsic measure of value given by the LEV constitutes a logical prius with respect to the extrinsic measure expressed in the form of money in the act of exchange. The latter can perform its function of external measure of value precisely because it is the visible manifestation of a pre-existing internal measure concealed inside the black box of production.[32] In capitalist society, in fact, what appears on the surface and becomes immediately perceptible is only that which takes place in the sphere of the circulation and exchange of commodities, while what takes place in the sphere of production, within the capitalist firm, remains invisible. In this concealment, the secret of the capitalist exploitation of labour is preserved and reproduced, sheltered from prying eyes.

The objectified labour time, measured by the LEV, represents only one of the two attributes of abstract labour as substance of value. It is socially necessary labour only for one side, that of production, but not yet for the other side of the process of general reproduction, that of consumption, the satisfaction of social needs. This one-sided social labour must be confirmed, validated, and recognized as such by the society through the purchase on the market of the commodities that it has produced. It becomes abstract labour, thus gaining the stigma of socially necessary labour in capitalism, when the act of exchange is actually completed, the commodity passes into the hands of the purchaser and is transformed into money. In the act of exchange, the social character of labour is constituted in its integrity by the social algorithm of value and is made visible in the form of the average price of the commodity. The average price of the commodity as the extrinsic measure of value represents the *monetary expression of value* (MEV), given by the ratio between the total net price and the physical quantity of the exchanged commodity. MEV, therefore, indicates the monetary remuneration received in the form of wages and profits by workers and capitalists for each unit of commodity exchanged on the market, which in capitalist social accountability represents the value added per unit of commodity.

As can be seen from their definitions, both LEV and MEV are measured net of the production cost of constant capital, except depreciation, used in production, i.e. in terms of direct labour and gross value added, respectively. Both expressions, in fact, concern the process of the reproduction of society at an aggregate level, which occurs in the connection between social production and the productive and unproductive social consumption in a given period of time.[33] The circulating part of the constant capital, consisting of raw materials and intermediate goods, is excluded in order to eliminate duplications on an aggregate scale. The fixed part of the constant capital, consisting of the wear and tear, is instead included in that part of the new capital goods replacing obsolete means of production, since we are considering the gross rather than net value added, and therefore, gross rather than net profits. For this reason, from now on, for the sake of brevity and simplicity, with the term exchange value of the commodity we will always refer to the new value created in a given period of time, and with the term price we will always indicate the net price, i.e. the value added of the commodity, unless otherwise indicated.

At this point, we can grasp how behind the appearance of the market exchange between a given commodity and a given quantity of money, an equivalence relation is determined between the social labour required by the production of the commodity, expressed by the intrinsic measure or LEV, and the social labour required by the social need that the particular commodity satisfies, expressed by the extrinsic measure or MEV. In this equivalence relation, abstract labour as substance of value is constituted in a determined and integral form. The two aspects of social labour, the one necessary for production and the one necessary to satisfy social needs, are like the two blades that form a scissor only in their inseparable unit. The first blade, the LEV, is the social labour time objectified in the commodity, representing the value created in production still expressed in the particular form of a physical good, while the second blade, the MEV, is the social labour time that society wants to spend to satisfy a particular need, representing the value realized in circulation of that particular commodity now expressed in the form of general equivalent. Both attributes of abstract labour as socially necessary labour in production and in circulation correspond to a specific measure of the same magnitude of exchange value of the commodity. An attribute, labour time, is immanent and concealed within the merely bodily form of the commodity and the other, money, external and visible in the price of the commodity. At the aggregate social level, the two measures of exchange value are equivalent although expressed in different units of measurement, labor time and money, and therefore it is possible to determine a specific mutual ratio of conversion, the monetary expression of labour time.

4.3.2 The monetary expression of labour time

In the capitalist mode of production, the division of social labour is the result of the social algorithm of value operating in the market exchange, which places the social labour time used in the production of a given commodity in an equivalence relation with the social labour time required to satisfying the social need. This equivalent relation defines the exchange value of the commodity. The dual nature of abstract labour, as socially necessary labour for both the commodity production and the satisfaction of social needs, determines a twofold measure of exchange value given by the objectified abstract labour time, or LEV as intrinsic measure, and money, or MEV as extrinsic measure, respectively. In the process of market exchange, the former measures the exchange value in the hands of the seller in the form of a *physical commodity* and the latter the exchange value in the hands of the buyer in the form of *money*. With the completion of the transaction, the forms of value held by the seller and the buyer reverse and swap hands, thus demonstrating their character of equivalents. After the exchange, the bodily form of the commodity, which before was the exchange value in the hands of the seller, is now the use value in the hands of the buyer, and vice versa the money form of the commodity, which before was exchange value in the hands of the buyer, becomes general use value in the hands of the seller.

In the presence of two different but equivalent measures of the same quantity, it is possible to apply a conversion factor that allows changing the unit of measurement without changing the value of the measured quantity. The conversion factors are commonly used for the transformation of the seven base physical quantities from non-standard units of measurement, such as those of the British Imperial system of units, to international standard units of measurement.[34] Conversion factors are also widely used in economics for international comparisons of income and productivity levels between countries with different national currencies, the most common of which are purchasing power parity (PPP) and unit value ratios.[35] On the basis of the same principle and method, it is possible to define the conversion factor between intrinsic and extrinsic measures of value, which is represented by the monetary expression of labour time or MELT. MELT is defined as the ratio between the quantity of money that society wants to use to satisfy a given social need through the consumption of a given commodity, or value in circulation, and the objectified labour time normally required for the society to produce that given commodity, or value in production, that is, by the ratio between MEV and LEV.

A simple algebraic exposition can help to better describe these relationships in the aggregate. Let us define the following variables: Q is the total physical quantity of the net product considered as an average composite commodity, L the total direct labour used in production, P the net price of one unit of the commodity or unit price, Y the nominal net product, and v the unit value expressed in labour time units. The symbol $\equiv$ indicates a relation of identity, that is, the logical definition of a variable in terms of other variables, and the symbol $\sim$ a relation of equivalence as in previous chapter. We have the following expressions:

$$L \sim Q \sim Y \qquad\qquad (4.1)$$

$$\text{MEV} \equiv \frac{Y}{Q} \equiv \frac{PQ}{Q} \equiv P \tag{4.2}$$

$$\text{LEV} \equiv \frac{L}{Q} \equiv v \tag{4.3}$$

$$\text{MELT} \equiv \frac{\text{MEV}}{\text{LEV}} \equiv \frac{PQ}{L} \equiv \frac{P}{v} \tag{4.4}$$

The expression (4.1) is the *fundamental equivalence* of the social algorithm of value. It indicates the relationship of equivalence, established by the social algorithm of value, between the mass of produced goods and, on the one hand, the socially necessary labour in production expressed in objectified abstract labour time, and, on the other hand, the socially necessary labour in circulation expressed in monetary terms. From this fundamental equivalence, it follows that the same magnitude of value can be alternatively measured in terms of physical units, labour time units, and monetary units, through appropriate equivalent conversion ratios given by MEV and LEV represented in the expressions (4.2) and (4.3), respectively. Finally, in (4.4), MELT specifies the rate of conversion of one unit of average social labour in x units of money by indicating how many units of money are equivalent to one unit of labour time in the act of exchange of the commodity, that is, the amount of monetary revenue obtained by the seller for each unit of labour time expended in the production of the commodity. MELT can also be expressed as the ratio between the unit price, representing value in circulation or in monetary form, and unit value, representing value in production or in labour form.

The notion of MELT derives from the definition of the value of money provided by Hilferding,[36] later resumed in modified form by Foley (1982, 1983, 2000) in the context of the so-called *New Interpretation*[37] of Marx's theory of value, by considering only the new value created in the period rather than the total value. In this case, the MELT represents the inverse of the value of money, and it is defined by the ratio between money value added and total direct labour. The great merit of the *New Interpretation* has been to have replaced the traditional approach to Marx's value theory based on two different systems to be converted, the first visible in terms of prices measured by money and the other hidden in terms of values measured by labour time, with an approach based on a single system.[38] The old traditional interpretation was at the origin of the long debate about the problem of the transformation of values into prices of production that never found a shared solution.[39] In fact, as it was erroneously posed, the transformation problem is insoluble because it is impossible to determine a relationship of equivalence between two systems expressed in different units of measurement without first having independently determined an equivalent ratio of conversion.

The crucial innovation of the *New Interpretation* produced a renewed interest in Marxian political economy, opening the way to new theoretical strands often in dispute between them, however, united by the adhesion to a *Single System Interpretation* (*SSI*) of value theory. Within the *SSI*, the *New Interpretation* confronts the post-structuralist approach, inspired by the Althusserian notion of over-determination, where the labour values of the outputs depend on the exchange values of the inputs, both measured in terms of abstract labour time, rather than in money units.[40]

In spite of their differences, the *SSI* approaches share a conceptually similar notion of MELT that requires the independent derivation of labour values and prices to be logically founded. In this theoretical context, however, MELT is not, as in our case, a conversion factor between two equivalent measures of a given known quantity, but an unknown variable, which can only be determined simultaneously to prices. In this case, it was noted that there is circular reasoning,[41] because MELT simultaneously assumes the role of dependent and independent variable in the same system of equations. Faced with these objections, Foley (2005) acknowledged that his definition of MELT is theoretically incomplete, although useful as an empirical tool. The most systematic attempt to overcome the logical inconsistency of the prevailing interpretations of MELT is that of Moseley (2005b; 2011), who proposes two different solutions differentiating between gold money and fiat money.[42] In the first case, the MELT is determined according to the labour time socially necessary to produce a gold monetary unit, while in the second case, according to a method very similar to the quantitative theory of money. In the case of inconvertible money, however, without an explanation of the velocity of circulation of money independent of the price level, the incompleteness in the determination of MELT remains. The difficulty of a coherent derivation of MELT in the presence of inconvertible money has thus strengthened the opinion that the theory of value, as originally formulated by Marx, is inadequate to describe the reality of contemporary capitalism.

What is missing in the *SSI* notion of MELT is the independent element of mediation between the exchange value measured in labour time units and the exchange value measured in money units, the common denominator that places their ratio as a ratio of equivalence. The limit of the *SSI* approaches consists in the lack of recognition of the dual character of abstract labour, as the specific form of social labour in capitalism, which gives rise to a twofold measure of its form of expression as exchange value. Ultimately, behind this limit, there is a view of value as a substantial concept, rather than processual, in which substance and form of value are unitary logical determinations that dialectically oppose each other. In this view, instead of the two independent systems of traditional interpretation, there is a single unitary system measured alternatively in terms of money or labour time, where the MELT should act as a link between them. However, in the absence of a common and independent element of mediation, one inevitably falls back into the dilemma of interdependence or the unilateral definition of value. In this way, either money or abstract labour time become redundant categories, assuming a secondary and derived role in the explanation of the capitalist economy. In some way, within the *SSI*, the old controversy between productivists and circulationists of the traditional dual system interpretation of Marx's value theory lives again in a new and more theoretically elaborated form. In the different *SSI* approaches, the dualism informing all the Marxian economic categories, deriving from the internal scission of the commodity between use value and value, as a reflection of the private character of capitalist social production and reproduction, at a certain point disappears, and, with a shortcut of thought, they arrive at reconstituting a unitary but partial picture of the reality of the capitalist mode of production.

In essence, the misunderstanding of the prevailing interpretations of the Marxian theory of value consists in considering only the social form of the production and exchange process, without considering the bodily or natural form, consisting of the material physical quantity of objects produced and exchanged, whether tangible or intangible. This is true not just, as is evident, for the circulationist interpretations but also for the productivist interpretations of Marx's value theory, which considers only the process of value production while overlooking the underlying process of material production of goods. As discussed in the previous chapter, the social objectuality of value exists concretely only in the material, bodily form of the object of use, to which it confers the social form. As a consequence, the dualistic determinations of substance, form, and measure of value have concrete existence in the material and objectual form of commodity. The object "commodity" in its concrete and bare materiality is at the same time the bearer of value and use value as the social and private form of its relationship with the human subjectivity, respectively. The value form of the commodity indicates a relation between individuals through a relation between things, while the use value form of the commodity indicates a relation between individuals and things. Outside of these relations, the commodity exists as a bare material object, as a mere thing in its bodily, natural form.

The immediate bourgeois consciousness sees in the economic categories of capitalist exchange only the reflection of the use value form of commodity, ignoring the value form. This immediate view underlies the neoclassical economic theory of value as utility. It constitutes the basis of the fetishistic character of commodity in capitalism, which conceals the social relations of bourgeois production and prevents the real knowledge of the functioning laws of capitalist society. However, in the intent to unveil the fetishistic and alienated character of the bourgeois categories, we should not fall into the specularly opposite error of considering only the value form of the commodity. It is not a question here of considering, together with value, the use value that is a prerequisite of commodity exchange indicating the property of the commodity to satisfy a human need. What should instead be considered is the pure, objective, material corporeity of the thing bearing the social form of commodity in the exchange. In addition to being an object of use and an object of exchange, the commodity is first and foremost a mere object. Every commodity, whether tangible or intangible, is the objectification of human labour and desire, and as such, it is also always an object, a thing regardless of its interaction with human beings. If a great catastrophe suddenly extinguishes humankind, leaving the rest of the world intact, the commodities produced and not yet consumed, even the last sound emitted by a singer at a concert, would continue to exist for a longer or shorter time, no more as commodities, but as simple things. This naked material corporeity of the object "commodity", as well as the concrete labour that produced it, is a fact of reality underlying every social form of production, and in capitalism every determination of value as substance, form, and measure.

All the dualistic determinations of value, therefore, have in the external material objectification of the commodity their common point. The dualism, in fact, is a characteristic proper and exclusive of the capitalist social form, deriving from the private character of the production and reproduction of social life. On the contrary, the matter with which men interact in its purely physical and natural aspect, as it presents itself on the scale of human dimension, is not dualistic but unitary. It is constituted by "things", which are what they are and stand next to us in their indifferent corporeity, as Gertrude Stein poetically reminds us with her famous verse: "A rose is a rose is a rose". This bare material corporeity of the commodity constitutes the common point of the internal dualism of value determinations, to which they can be converted and made equivalent. Social labour in capitalism, besides being abstract labour necessary for the production and satisfaction of human needs, is also concrete social labour producing material objects. The exchange value, besides being market exchange ratio and a quantity of objectified abstract labour time, is also the material object bearing it. The measure of the exchange value, besides being money and abstract labour time, is also the number of material objects exchanged.

In the interpretation of Marx's value theory provided here, the dualism is not between substance and form of value but is inside each of the two moments that constitute the value algorithm. Abstract labour is separated into social labour necessary in production and social labour necessary to satisfy social needs, to which corresponds the separation of the exchange value into value in production and value in circulation, each provided with a specific unit of measurement, abstract labour time and money, respectively. Money is the form of manifestation of both measures of exchange value, the intrinsic and the extrinsic, which can be converted into each other by means of the MELT. All these dualistic determinations of value categories have their common and unitary element in referring to the same physical, material quantity of commodities produced and consumed in a given period of time.

In capitalism, the production process is exclusively directed to the valorization of capital, in search of surplus value and profit, however, through this purpose, it indirectly and unconsciously has also to ensure the material reproduction of society. Underneath and behind the process of capital valorization lies the process of continuous reconstitution and renewal of the material bases of social life. In a system based on private production such as capitalism, social reproduction is marked by permanently dualistic and contradictory relations, but this is not the case for material reproduction that must remain consistent and unitary over time, as for any other mode of production. The social and economic conditions that ensure the coherent material reproduction of the capitalist system are the object of Marx's analysis in the second book of *Capital*. In recurrent periods of capitalist economic crisis, the unresolved contradictions of social reproduction determine inconsistency even in the material reproduction, generating an enormous waste of resources and energies that denote the irrational character of the system. However, these periods of crisis are necessarily temporary, otherwise capitalism would collapse and would necessarily be replaced by another form of social organization, more or less equal and efficient. All this could happen in the future, and probably will happen as the ecological crisis worsens, but so far it has not happened, and capitalism has until now survived its terrible crises. In normal times, the material reproduction of capitalist society is a coherent and unitary process that is realized through dualistic and contradictory social relations based on exploitation and class oppression.

The physical quantity of commodities produced and consumed in a given period represents the common denominator of all dualistic determinations of value, the common mediating element that restores to unity the contradictions within each moment of the value process. It is in this way that social labour necessary to production and consumption, exchange value in production and in circulation, and abstract labour time and money price are necessarily reunited in the commodity as a physical, material object, whether tangible or intangible. It is in this way that the whole Marxian development of the concept of value concludes its cycle returning to the starting point, the immense accumulation of commodities that immediately leaps to the eyes on those who observe capitalist society, this time, however, no longer as an immediate perception of a mass of objects for sale but as a concept full of many determinations.

Returning to the derivation of MELT, the common element that makes possible the equivalent relationship between the two measures of the exchange value is the material, bodily form of the commodity as a product of human labour. The common denominator that links abstract labour time to money in an equivalent conversion ratio is the variable Q of the above formulas, as the product of the concrete social labour, which represents the material basis of the process of social reproduction, the known and visible starting point of all the subsequent formal analysis. In our case, we are not dealing with equations and unknown variables but with logical definitions deriving from the fundamental equivalence established with the expression (4.1). It shows that the physical quantity of commodities, the mass of use values in circulation, is produced by a given amount of labour and purchased on the market by a given amount of money. This is a fact, always necessarily true, that can be ascertained even by "a man fell from the moon on the earth", to use an expression used in Sraffa's *Unpublished Papers* (D3/12/7: 87),[43] not an assumption or a hypothesis. The goods produced and not sold, as well as those desired but not produced (which wonder why they are never considered by those who object to this argument), do not enter into the process of material reproduction of the society, and therefore, do not even matter for the determination of value. The quantities of goods, labour, and money in the fundamental equivalence are absolute objective numerical quantities that do not refer to any other type of relationship to be precisely defined. They can therefore be properly considered as given, known and independent exogenous variables of the economic model.[44] By contrast, price, labour productivity, and value of money are derived quantities coming from the relationships existing between the given absolute quantities of the fundamental equivalence.

In formal terms, the difference between the *SSI* definition of MELT and the one given here is that, in the former, MELT is derived directly from the ratio between net or total price and labour time. By contrast, in the latter, MELT is derived indirectly from the fundamental equivalence between independent exogenous variables, through the mediation of the conversion ratios between Q, on the one hand, and money and labour units, on the other hand, that is, by the ratio of MEV and LEV. The final result is identical since, in the indirect derivation of MELT, the same physical quantity appears to the denominator of the divider and the dividend. The direct derivation, however, omits a fundamental logical passage, that of the equivalence between physical commodity, money, and labour time, and this omission undermines the logical foundation of the discourse. In the direct method, MELT is defined on the basis of the symmetrical property of the equivalence relation, while in the indirect method the transitive property applies. This crucial difference is made clear by the fact that often in the literature, MELT and MEV are used alternatively one to the other as synonyms,[45] or they are differentiated only formally based on the width of the numerator (net or total price, aggregate or sectoral value added[46]), however, both remaining a direct relationship between money and labour time. In the expression (4.2), instead, MEV is a ratio between money quantity and physical quantity, corresponding to the unit price, and, as such, conceptually distinct from MELT.

While the term "monetary expression of labour time" never appears in his work, Marx makes several times use of the term "monetary expression of value" just in the sense here defined, as the unit price of the commodity.[47] Marx moreover explains the reason for which it is not correct to put directly in relation the money price of a commodity with its value expressed in labour time, saying that in such a case it would always be assumed an equivalent exchange, that is, a perfect correspondence between price and value.[48] The definition of MELT as direct ratio between price and labour time, therefore, obscures the difference between the form of price and the form of value, that instead represents an essential character of the capitalistic law of value. This is the reason for which the direct derivation of the MELT ultimately leads to an indetermined expression or to a partial and unilateral determination of value as a result of production only (labour time) or the circulation only (money).

The total labour in production and the total money in circulation both represent, in an equivalent way even if expressed with different units of measurement, the same material object, that is, the total physical volume of the produced and exchanged commodities. This same identical material basis of the exchange value is expressed once in the intrinsic form of labour time and once in the extrinsic form of money. For both measures of exchange value, abstract labour time and money, the material bearer is the same, that is the commodity in its bodily, physical form. The social net product, in its concrete materiality, is the basis of the reproduction of society and it is the product of the concrete social labour as a whole. In capitalist exchange, it is doubled because a purely social form expressed in money is added to its bodily form, but it always remains the product of social labour, now also doubled into concrete and abstract labour. However, at the level of society as a whole, the totality of concrete labour coincides with that of abstract labour, and the totality of material production is equivalent to that of its monetary expression and the total labour time used in its production. The social net product in its physical form is, therefore, the visible and concrete expression, the material connection of equivalence between objectified labour time and money, both measuring the same magnitude of exchange value. The physical social product is the common basis of the ratio of conversion of the two distinct units of measurement, through which it is possible to determine the MELT as the real measure of the exchange value,[49] where money appears as the expression of the objectified abstract labour time in production, and vice versa, the objectified abstract labour time appears as money in the process of circulation.

It is argued that it would be impossible to prove the derivation of surplus value and profit from surplus labour without establishing a causal relationship between exchange value expressed in labour time and exchange value expressed in money, thereby undermining the fundamental pillar of Marxian economics consisting of the exploitation of labour power as the origin of profit.[50] However, this objection does not apply to the argument presented here. In fact, the material basis of the net total physical volume of commodities is entirely produced by the living labour of the workers during the production process and then distributed through the impersonal mechanism of the market according to the law of value operating in capitalism. In this theoretical framework, the notion of exploitation can be clearly defined since surplus value and profit, as different expressions of the same capitalist economic surplus, constitute the residue of the net total physical production that is not appropriated by the real wages of the workers. This surplus product, which is first logically determined in physical terms, results from the surplus labour, and then turns into surplus value and profit when the commodities enter the sphere of circulation. The notion of MELT as a conversion factor between two units of measurement does not present any logical contradiction, in the same way that there is no contradiction in transforming the measurement of the length of a given object from inches to centimetres. The condition for this to be true is obviously that the two units of measurement of the same magnitude, in terms of labour time and money, inches and centimetres, are defined independently of each other. In our case, therefore, we need to see how MEV and LEV are defined independently of each other.

As far as MEV is concerned, its independent definition implies the determination of the absolute price of the net product, that is, its relative price with respect to money, which corresponds to the general price level. In this respect, the answer is straightforward because, at any given period of time, the price level is determined by the ratio between the existing quantity of base money multiplied by its velocity of circulation, and the total quantity of commodities circulating on the market. From this point of view, it makes no difference if the monetary base is constituted by specie money, like gold, or by fiat money, like money issued by the central bank, since the defined relation is a mere accounting identity that is always verified on a synchronic level. As an accounting identity, it cannot be considered true only *ex post* but is always true, because in considering a given moment, we are precisely disregarding the temporal dynamics. In other words, when every possible act of exchange of commodity for money takes place, the general price level is already predetermined independently of the specific form of money. The question would be different if we consider how the price level changes over time. In this case, we need to introduce causal relationships into what we have previously considered as a mere accounting identity and turn it into a theory of price level determination such as the quantitative theory of money or the theory of endogenous money. This issue, however, does not concern our problem, because MEV simply refers to the given general price level existing at the moment of the exchange, which is always determined by the accounting identity defined previously.

With regard to the theory of price level determination, it is known that Marx rejected the quantitative theory of money, according to which the price level is determined by the circulating stock of money, and favoured an endogenous theory of money, according to which it is the quantity of circulating commodities that determines the money supply through variations in the velocity of circulation. In the latter case, the price level changes in the course of time only if the velocity of circulation finds obstacles to its full adjustment to the demand for money, as can happen in the case of a freeze of bank credit following a deflationary economic crisis, or vice versa in the case of inflationary pressures of extra-monetary character originating from distributive struggles. However, this important subject has nothing to do with the determination of the MEV and is addressed by Marx at a much more concrete stage of analysis than the determination of the exchange value of the commodities presented in the first chapters of the first book of *Capital*.

With regard to the other element of the ratio constituting the MELT, the independent definition of the LEV requires a definition of the unit of measurement of the labour time objectified in the production of the commodity. This leads to the problem of the homogenization of the concrete labour actually spent in production, which by its nature is qualitatively heterogeneous and incommensurable between different commodities. Universal labour is given by the labour with *real physical* productivity identical to the average social productivity, as expressed in equation (4.3). Since real physical productivity can only be determined for commodities of the same kind, it must first be calculated at a sectoral level, thus determining the universal labour of each particular industry, which will coincide with the total sectoral direct labour. In aggregate, total universal labour will result from the sum of all the single industries and, obviously, it will coincide with total aggregate direct labour.[51] The issue of universal labour, however, will be discussed in detail later, where we will see that the question of the definition of the unit of universal labour on a world scale constitutes one of the essential modifications of the international law of value with respect to the national one.

4.4 The law of value and unequal exchange

4.4.1 Value transfers and the law of value

Hitherto we have seen that the exchange value has two measures, one intrinsic in labour time and the other extrinsic in money, indicating value in production and value in circulation, respectively, which can be converted into each other on the basis of a universal conversion factor, the MELT. The assumption we have made so far is that these two measures of value are equivalent, and therefore, value in production and value in circulation are quantitatively identical. In this case, the exchange of commodities is an equivalent exchange. However, this is true only at a general level of abstraction when we consider the social process of production and exchange in the aggregate. At the level of the whole society, indeed, total value in production and total value in circulation are necessarily equal, but this is not true at the individual level since the general equivalence is the result of a statistical average.[52] By contrast, we define as unequal exchange a situation in which value in production is different from value in circulation. In the case of equivalent exchange, the individual MELT of both trade partners is identical to the average social MELT, while when they differ from each other there is unequal exchange and value transfers. The unequal exchange implies that an individual unit of universal labour time has a monetary expression different from the social average.

In capitalist society, every single market exchange is normally an unequal exchange, since the general social equivalence of value is obtained through a myriad of individual inequalities, and the overall equilibrium is the product of a chaotic series of particular disequilibria (Farjoun and Machover, 1983). In this sense, the market equilibrium, resulting from the algorithm of value, is an abstraction because what in practice occurs is a constant succession of imbalance conditions, but it is a *real* abstraction because it unconsciously determines and guides the action of the individual subjects in the exchange. This real abstraction is the hidden driving force that produces the social order from the chaos of the incessant individual competition between people, and between capitalist firms, sectors of production, and countries. In this sense, Marx, in a letter to Kugelmann, states that

> actual everyday exchange relations can not be directly identical with the magnitudes of value. The essence of bourgeois society consists precisely in this, that a priori there is no conscious social regulation of production.

The rational and naturally necessary asserts itself only as a blindly working average.

(*MEC*, July 11, 1868)

Our analysis has developed in accordance with the method adopted by Marx in *Capital*, where the order of presentation goes from the most abstract to the most concrete categories of reality. In doing so, we have omitted to consider the action of competition in the process of capitalist social reproduction by supposing that it was achieved in a single act of exchange between the two general moments of production and consumption, supply and demand, of the society as a whole. This allowed us to grasp the essential determinations of the concepts of value, abstract labour, and exchange value in their pure and abstract form. Now we must see how these abstract determinations of capital in general act and transform themselves in the concrete reality of the capitalist mode of production, marked by the presence of many individual capitals in incessant competition with each other. In particular, the analysis will focus on the dimension of international competition between different national capitals, while the other two dimensions of capitalist competition, between firms and between productive sectors, will be examined only in relation to the former.

Marx's investigation deals with the three forms of capitalist competition according to a growing order of complexity. He begins, in book I of *Capital*, with the simplest dimension of national competition between firms, within a branch of production having an average organic composition of capital identical to that of general social capital. He then introduces in book III the more concrete dimensions of competition between sectors of variable organic composition of capital producing commodities of different kinds. Finally, Marx was planning to analyse the case of competition between national social capitals in international trade, which should have been examined in the book about the world capitalist market that he did not have time to write. In each of these successive steps, from the simplest and more abstract to the more complex and concrete dimension of capitalist competition, the law of value undergoes essential modifications.

The intra-industry competition within national industries with an average organic composition of capital leads Marx in book I of *Capital* to the formulation of the law of value in its pure and abstract form, in which the two measures of exchange value in labour form and in money form correspond with each other at the level of aggregate average industry, although they may differ at the level of individual firms with different degrees of efficiency. In this case, the social unit value in production and social unit value in circulation are identical for all commodities, but for individual firms, the unit values in production and circulation may differ, thus giving rise to an intra-industry non-equivalent exchange. In book III of *Capital*, with the transition to inter-industry competition between capitals of different branches of production composing national social capital, the law of value undergoes a first modification with the formation of prices of production diverging from values, due to the national equalization of the profit rate between industries with different organic composition of capital. In this case, social value in production and social value in circulation diverge for every commodity produced with an organic composition of capital different from the national social average. A non-equivalent exchange between industries, deriving from the formation of prices of production, is therefore added to the intra-industry non-equivalent exchange. As we will show in Chapter 5, a second essential modification of the law of value occurs with the international capitalist competition, which will lead to the definition of a third form of unequal exchange between different countries distinct from the first two forms of non-equivalent exchange. And it is only at this final stage of investigation that the law of value reaches the complete logical and historical development as the fundamental engine of the capitalist mode of production with international trade and the formation of the world market, as Marx states very clearly in the following passage of the *Theories of Surplus Value*:

> But it is only foreign trade, the development of the market to a world market, which causes money to develop into world money and abstract labour into social labour. Abstract wealth, value, money, hence abstract labour, develop in the measure that concrete labour becomes a totality of different modes of labour embracing the world market. Capitalist production rests on the value or the transformation of the labour embodied in the product into social labour. But this is only [possible] on the basis of foreign trade and of the world market. This is at once the pre-condition and the result of capitalist production.
>
> (Marx, *MTSV*, chap. XXI, 858)

In all three dimensions of capitalist competition, intra-industry, inter-industry, and international, the individual act of market exchange may incorporate transfers of values arising from the non-equivalence between value in production (or intrinsic measure) and value in circulation (or extrinsic measure), which in aggregate offset each other by giving a total sum equal to zero at the level of individual average industry, national economy, and world economy, respectively. In the case of competition between individual firms within the same industry, value transfers are temporary in nature and tend to disappear over time, as the most efficient production techniques gradually spread throughout the industry. In the other two cases, those of competition between sectors and between countries, on the contrary, the difference between produced and realized value at the level of individual industry or country tends to persist over time. This is due to structural factors that prevent capitalist competition from eliminating the individual difference between value in production and value in circulation. In the case of inter-industry competition, the structural factor is given by the average technical configuration of the different production processes, which requires variable combinations of labour and means of production according to the merchandise category of the produced goods, thus determining different organic compositions of capital. The existence of an inherent structural technological constraint implies that competition establishes conditions of equal profitability for capitals invested in different sectors through the distortion between social values and prices of production, thus giving rise to a discrepancy between value in production and value in circulation for individual industries.

In the case of international competition, as we will see in Chapter 5, the structural factor is given by the different national units of social labour resulting from the degree of economic development of each country, which determines a different value of international money between the various national economies, expressed by the structural real exchange rate misvaluation between national currencies. As with inter-industry national competition, even in the case of the world competition between different national capitals, for a given economy, international value in production normally diverges from international value in circulation, thus giving rise to value transfers between countries.

The divergence between value in production and value in circulation assumes a specific form of expression at the level of individual constituent units (firms, industries, and countries) for each of the three successive formulations of the law of value. In fact, value transfers derive from discrepancies between individual value and social value in the form of a quasi-rent for individual firms of the same industry, value and price of production in the form of non-equivalent exchange for individual sectors of a given national economy, and national value and international value in the form of unequal exchange in the strict sense for individual countries of the world economy, respectively. The beneficiaries of value transfers, deriving from a value realized in circulation greater than that created in production, are the more efficient firms, the sectors with the higher organic composition of capital, and the more developed countries with an higher than world average labour productivity, at the expense of the less efficient firms, the less capital-intensive sectors, and the less developed countries, respectively, where value in circulation is smaller than that in production. In the final and most concrete stage of the analysis of the world market, the three different forms of value transfer coexist at the same time, so that the total unequal exchange between countries in international trade will be the result of the sum and interaction of all of them.

4.4.2 The world market and unequal exchange

There is a formal analogy between the quasi-rent received or transferred within an industry by firms more or less efficient than the average and the unequal exchange between countries in international trade. Both forms of value transfers derive from the difference between the individual value and the social value of the commodity, one on the domestic market and the other on the world market. This analogy was expressly emphasized by Marx in the following passage of the third book of *Capital*, where trade between developed and backwards countries is confronted with competition between firms of the same industry having different labour productivities:

Capitals invested in foreign trade can yield a higher rate of profit, because, in the first place, there is competition with commodities produced in other countries with inferior production facilities, so that the more advanced country sells its goods above their value even though cheaper than the competing countries. In so far as the labour of the more advanced country is here realised as labour of a higher specific weight, the rate of profit rises, because labour which has not been paid as being of a higher quality is sold as such. The same may obtain in relation to the country, to which commodities are exported and to that from which commodities are imported; namely, the latter may offer more materialised labour in kind than it receives, and yet thereby receive commodities cheaper than it could produce them. Just as a manufacturer who employs a new invention before it becomes generally used, undersells his competitors and yet sells his commodity above its individual value, that is, realises the specifically higher productiveness of the labour he employs as surplus-labour. He thus secures a surplus-profit.

(Marx, *MK3*, chap. 14, p. 163)

In this important piece, two aspects deserve special consideration. Firstly, the quasi-rent of the more productive firm within an industry represents a temporary situation, which lasts until innovation spreads and becomes the normal production technique of the sector ("it becomes generally used"). On the contrary, as we will see in Chapter 5, the advantage of the more productive country is a long-lasting phenomenon, which could disappear only when the differences in economic development between countries are eliminated. Since, however, in the global capitalist economy, there are mechanisms of circular and cumulative causation, which continuously reproduce the differences in economic development between countries, the phenomenon of unequal exchange is itself continually reproduced, thus becoming an ordinary and permanent feature of the world market. Secondly, Marx notes that international trade remains mutually beneficial to all participating countries, despite the transfers of value that it involves. This is in accordance with another passage, in which Marx states that the exploited country still benefits from international trade: "(T)he richer country exploits the poorer one, even where the latter gains by the exchange" (Marx, *MTSV*, 803). These observations show how Marx considered unequal exchange as an ordinary phenomenon of international trade between capitalist countries. In fact, unequal exchange results from normal functioning of the law of value at the international level, and, as such, is present in conditions of perfect market competition, where trade derives from the free will of the partners on the basis of a mutual benefit or a state of necessity not otherwise surmountable.

In Marx, the unequal exchange concerns a different and more in-depth level of analysis with respect to that of the classical theory of international trade of Smith's absolute advantages or Ricardo's comparative advantages since it refers to the value dimension and not to the relative prices. It does not, therefore, constitute a

125

refutation of one or the other theory but of both at the same time, since it shows that international trade can contain relationships of exploitation, even though it is advantageous or necessary for all contracting parties. In this way, it is better understood why Marx speaks of "exploitation" of the poorer countries by the richer ones, using a term full of meaning insofar as it is suggestive of the relationship between capital and labour power. As a matter of fact, with regard to unequal international exchange, an analogy can be noted with what is happening in the labour market with the exchange between capitalists and workers, consisting in the payment of a wage by the former to acquire the right to use the labour power of the latter. This exchange is both free exchange of equivalents and the establishment of an exploitative relationship at the same time.[53] Here, too, it can be said that workers gain from the exchange while accepting to submit to a condition of exploitation because if they remain unemployed, as always happens to many of them, they will see their condition worsen by not having access to means of subsistence. Just as workers do not have the opportunity to refuse the sale of their labour power, as they are dispossessed of the means of production necessary to ensure their livelihood, the same can be said about the integration of poor countries into the world capitalist market.

In fact, with the rise of the global capitalist economy, underdeveloped countries are somehow objectively forced to participate in international trade, because they lack the technological, organizational, and social capacity to produce in an autonomous and independent way a wide range of consumer and investment goods necessary for their economic modernization. Unless radically questioning the model of capitalist economic and social development, the alternative poor countries face is between the subordinate access to capitalist modernity through their dependent integration in the global market or remaining in a pre-modern situation of secular economic and social stagnation. The ruling classes of the peripheral countries will enjoy great material incentives to choose the first alternative, because they will be able to access the luxuries and privileges of the phantasmagorical bazaar of the world market, even accepting the subordination to the dictates of international capital. The cost of this choice, in fact, will be paid entirely by the dominated and oppressed classes, which will be subjected to even more intense and brutal exploitation than that existing in pre-modern societies. In short, therefore, the exploitation of the poor countries by the rich countries through trade is an ordinary phenomenon in capitalism produced by the spontaneous operation of the international law of value, from which it is only possible to escape through conscious political and social actions aimed at breaking with the neoliberal logic of free trade, both within peripheral societies and at the level of the global world economy.

In addition to the objective and purely economic action of the international law of value, resulting from the integration into the world market, the condition of subordination and dependence of peripheral economies is enhanced by additional non-economic factors. These are represented by the forms of direct exploitation of a colonial or neo-colonial character imposed by imperialist powers

126

and transnational corporations, based on political and military domination, over-exploitation of indigenous labour power, and monopolistic control of natural, technological, and financial resources, as Marx does not fail to emphasize in the prosecution of the previous passage as follows:

> As concerns capitals invested in colonies, etc., on the other hand, they may yield higher rates of profit for the simple reason that the rate of profit is higher there due to backward development, and likewise the exploitation of labour, because of the use of slaves, coolies, etc. Why should not these higher rates of profit, realised by capitals invested in certain lines and sent home by them, enter into the equalisation of the general rate of profit and thus tend, pro tanto, to raise it, unless it is the monopolies that stand in the way. There is so much less reason for it, since these spheres of investment of capital are subject to the laws of free competition... The favoured country recovers more labour in exchange for less labour, although this difference, this excess is pocketed, as in any exchange between labour and capital, by a certain class.
>
> (Marx, *MK3*, chap. XIV, p. 163)

In the second chapter of this book, we saw how the lack of understanding of the essential modifications undergone by the law of value at the international level often led many Marxist economists to look with scepticism, if not hostility, at the theme of unequal exchange in trade, considered extraneous or at the most marginal with respect to the theoretical core of Marxism. From the above-mentioned texts, it is clear instead that Marx considered this as an essential theme of his never written book on international trade and the world market. He believed that in the capitalist global economy, the poor countries suffered a condition of exploitation by the richer countries, resulting from a twofold order of reasons, distinct from each other. The first reason is inherent in the normal functioning of the law of value on a world scale, from which the unequal exchange automatically arises, and the second reason derives from specific, variable, and potentially reversible historical circumstances, such as political, economic, and financial monopolies. The few theories dealing with unequal exchange in the strict sense, that is, not concerning the international equalization of profit rate, have been based exclusively on the second reason, deriving the condition of dependency of the less developed countries only from the presence of extra-economic factors, unrelated to the normal operation of the capitalist law of value. This is the case of both the monopoly capital and neo-dependency theory and Emmanuel's theory based on the institutional higher wages in richer countries. The unequal exchange, therefore, appeared more as a historical exception to the supposed general rule of equivalent capitalist market exchange, than as the ordinary and structural result of the expansion of the capitalist system on a global scale. Positions in favour of free trade supported by some Marxists, such as Hilferding, have found their justification in this fundamental theoretical error, often paving the way in recent times for active support for neoliberal globalization policies by left-wing political movements, in the name of the fight against monopolies and nationalisms. In reality, unequal exchange and international exploitation, far from being exceptions, represent an essential feature of capitalist globalization, which are reinforced by policies of market liberalization and deregulation too often adopted and supported even by progressive political movements. It is now time to examine in Chapter 5 the changes in the law of value at international level that give rise to unequal exchange as a structural phenomenon of the capitalist world market.

Notes

1 This sentence appears in the draft index drawn up by Marx in June 1858 in preparation for the publication in parts, which did not take place, of his economic work with the German publisher Duncker, as the first paragraph of the chapter on money as money. See Marx (*MECW*, vol. 29, p. 428).

2 The bibliography on this subject is too vast to be exhaustively listed. Therefore, I only indicate some of the recent works, without any pretension of exhaustiveness. One of the earliest and most influential contributions to Marx's theory of money is that of de Brunhoff (1976). An analysis of Marx's elaboration in the different stages of his work can be found in Nelson (1999). The volume edited by Moseley (2005a) provides a broad overview of the debate based on contributions from authors adhering to different approaches. Other meaningful contributions on the subject are that of Jessop (2013) and (2015), Henning (2014), Lapavitsas (2016a), and Campbell (2017).

3 As evidence of this misunderstanding, see, for example, Germer (2005, p. 21): "Marx's theory of money has become a growing subject of debate in recent years. A crucial point in the discussion deals with the physical nature of money: that is, whether or not money must be a commodity within this theory". The author's answer is that the concept of money in Marx is necessarily that of convertible money, gold. Ivanova (2013) shares the same view, albeit limited to the function of world money. For a critique of these positions, see Prado (2016).

4 This last crucial statement radically differentiates my argument from the one put forward by Itoh and Lapavitsas (1998), according to which in Marx's theory money can take any form, but in no case is it related to the intrinsic measure of the value of commodities.

5 "The commodity that functions as a measure of value, and, either in its own person or by a representative, as the medium of circulation, is money" (Marx, *MK1*, chap. 3, p. 84). After dealing with these two properties, Marx concludes the chapter with a third section devoted to money as money representing the unity of the two essential functions of measure of value and medium of circulation. Money as money includes hoarding, means of payment, and world money.

6 Marx, *MK1*, Preface to the first German edition, p. 6.

7 On the logical genesis of money from the general form of commodity in Marx, see Godelier (1977, p. 149–52)

8 "The universal equivalent form is a form of value in general. It can, therefore, be assumed by any commodity... The particular commodity, with whose bodily form the equivalent form is thus socially identified, now becomes the money commodity, or serves as money. It becomes the special social function of that commodity, and consequently its social monopoly, to play within the world of commodities the part of the universal equivalent" (Marx, *MK1*, chap. 1, p.46).

9 On the method of the "presupposition-posit" in Marx's *Capital*, see Bellofiore-Finelli (1998).

10 "In the discussion of the general forms of the circuit and in the entire second book in general, we take money to mean metallic money, with the exception of symbolic money, mere tokens of value, which are designed for specific use in certain states, and of credit-money, which is not yet developed. In the first place, this is the historical order; credit-production plays only a very minor role, or none at all, during the first epoch of capitalist production" (Marx, *MK2*, chap 4, p. 65).

11 Take, for example, the commercial activities of the Phoenicians, Greeks, and Romans in ancient societies, or the trade with India and China of Venetian merchants in the Middle Ages.

12 Marx distinguishes between reproducible commodities and non-reproducible commodities several times, both in the study of the form of commodity in *Capital I* and in the analysis of the rent in *Capital III*.

13 Marx, *MK1*, chap. 3, p. 70.

14 See Sweezy (1942), Meek (1956), and Mandel (1971). For a critic of traditional Marxism on this point, see, for example, Weeks (1981) and Arthur (1996).

15 For an analysis of the different specific forms of commodities in Marx's work, see Murray and Schuler (2017).

16 Jessop (2015), following Polanyi's terminology, uses a similar definition of capitalist commodity, which he also calls real commodity, to designate the commodity form of gold money in capitalism, as opposed to the forms of fictitious commodity, quasi-commodity, and non-commodity, indicating other forms of non-specie money. In my classification of the forms of commodity, the capitalist commodity is opposed to the non-capitalist commodity, to which all Jessop's non-specie forms of money belongs. All these specific forms of commodity, in turn, are included in the category of commodity in general. Unlike Jessop, therefore, in my interpretation, money is always a commodity in general, which in capitalism can take a capitalist or non-capitalist form.

17 This direct connection is explicitly highlighted by Marx in the following passage of the first chapter of *Capital I*: "Gold is now money with reference to all other commodities only because it was previously, with reference to them, a simple commodity… The simple commodity form is therefore the germ of the money form" (Marx, *MK1*, chap. 1, p. 46–7).

18 Marx calls "formal use value" this property of the commodity to act as equivalent in the exchange, see Marx, *MECW*, vol. 29, p. 326.

19 "It *(the commodity, ndr)* must be exchanged against a third thing which is not in turn itself a particular commodity, but is the symbol of the commodity as commodity, of the commodity's exchange value itself; which thus represents, say, labour time as such, say a piece of paper or of leather, which represents a fractional part of labour time. (Such a symbol presupposes general recognition; it can only be a social symbol; it expresses, indeed, nothing more than a social relation.)… (A)s soon as this has happened, it can in turn be replaced by a symbol of itself. It then becomes the conscious sign of exchange value" (Marx, *MG*, p. 74–5).

20 See Marx, *MECW*, vol. 29, p. 486.

21 See Godelier (1977).

22 "Money as a measure of value, is the phenomenal form that must of necessity be assumed by that measure of value which is immanent in commodities, labour time" (Marx, *MK1*, chap. 3, p. 67).

23 For a Marxist analysis of capitalistic accounting, see the works of Bryer (2017 and 2019)

24 "By means, therefore, of the value-relation expressed in our equation, the bodily form of commodity B becomes the value form of commodity A, or the body of commodity B acts as a mirror to the value of commodity A" (*MK1*, chap. 1, p. 36). "The value of a single commodity, the linen, for example, is now expressed in terms of numberless other elements of the world of commodities. Every other commodity now becomes a mirror of the linen's value" (ibid., p. 42).

25 See Hilferding (1981, p. 40).

26 See, for example, Foley (2005, p. 46): "There is something disorienting in the realization that a key part of Marx's theory of money, the derivation of a commodity-money, does not correspond to the historical and institutional realities of contemporary capitalism. Is the theory wrong in some fundamental sense? Or is our reading of capitalist reality defective?" A similar opinion is in Lavoie (1986), Wolfson (1988), and Gansmann (1998). This view is also shared by the French Regulation school. For a discussion on these interpretations, see Evans (1997).

27 See Bellofiore (2004): "it must be recognized that in capitalism the fundamental nature of money is first of all that of bank-credit financing firms' production. This is yet another reason forcing us to find a different ground – more solid than Marx's own – for seeing in commodity values nothing but expressions of labour" (p. 182). A similar view is in Reuten (1988), Bellofiore (1989), and Taylor (2004). This interpretation is typical of the monetary circuit approach as proposed by Graziani (1997).

28 See Germer (1997) and Sandemose (2018).

29 The issue of the circulation of credit money was a widely known and debated topic in political economy well before Marx, who addressed it in many points of his work, in particular, through the examination of the Bullionist Controversy and the quantitative theory of money. On these aspects see Lapavitsas (1991, 1994, 2000).

30 Knapp (1924) was one of the first to analyse the role of the state, rather than the market, in defining the value of money.

31 As Lapavitsas (2017, p. 74) notes: "The true difference between commodity and valueless fiat money, in other words, is not that the latter cannot measure value, which it evidently can in practice. It is, rather, that the real accounting of value (the rendering of value into market price) by valueless money depends also on the quantity of money; by this token, it could even be manipulated by the state".

32 Marx could not have been clearer about the logical priority of the intrinsic measure of value in terms of labour time, over the extrinsic measure in terms of money, than what he wrote in Book I of *Capital*: "It is not money that renders commodities commensurable. Just the contrary. It is because all commodities, as values, are realised human labour, and therefore commensurable, that their values can be measured by one and the same special commodity, and the latter be converted into the common measure of their values, i.e., into money" (Marx, *MK1*, chap. 3, p. 67).

33 This argument is similar, but not identical, to the one proposed by Moseley (2016a) in his macro-monetary interpretation of the Marx value theory in which the whole constant capital cancels out in the determination of the aggregate surplus value.

34 The seven base quantities of the ISI are the second for time, the meter for measurement of length, the kilogram for mass, the ampere for electric current, the kelvin for temperature, the mole for amount of substance, and the candela for luminous intensity.

35 On the theory and methodology of conversion factors in international economics, see O'Mahony (1996).

36 "(T)he value of paper money is determined by the total price of all the commodities in circulation. The value of paper money... reflects directly the value of commodities, in accordance with the law that its total amount represents value equal to the sum of commodity prices divided by the number of monetary units of equal denomination in circulation" (Hilferding, 1981, p. 39).

37 Besides Foley, the *New Interpretation* was independently developed by Dumenil (1983), however, in a non-monetary version. For an analytical presentation of the *New Interpretation*, see also Mohun (1994).

38 This is how Foley and Dumenil (2018, p. 8448) describe this important theoretical and methodological innovation of the *New Interpretation*: "This interpretation is a single-system approach to the LTV (labour theory of value, *ndr*). This property has important analytical consequences. There is only one economy, one system, not two. There is no 'underlying', hidden economy, which operates in 'values' where the distributional realities that structure the functioning of capitalism could be determined".

39 For an overview of the Marxist debate on the transformation problem, see Howard and King (1992), Jorland (1995), Moseley (2016a), and Tsoulfidis and Tsaliki (2019, chap. 3).

40 See Wolff, Callari, and Roberts (1984), Roberts (1997), and Callari, Roberts, and Wolff (1998). A variant of the post-structuralist approach is the so-called "Temporal Single-System Interpretation" (TSSI), which argues for the temporally successive determination of the labour values of outputs with respect to the exchange values of inputs. On TSSI, see Kliman and McGlone (1999) and the essays contained in the volumes edited by Freeman and Carchedi (1996), Freeman, Kliman, and Wells (2004), and Potts and Kliman (2015). My interpretation differs from those existing in literature because it is based on a simultaneous single dualistic system.

41 On the circular reasoning concerning the use of MELT in some interpretations of Marx's value theory see Fine, Lapavitsas, and Saad-Filho (2004), Kim (2010, 2016), and Moseley (2016b). Mavroudeas (2001) observes that in the *New Interpretation*, the definition of the value of money results in a view similar to that of Adam Smith's labour-commanded.

42 Another attempt, limited to the case of gold money, based on a post-structuralist approach that considers total price rather than value added, is in Kristjanson-Gural (2008).

43 Sraffa's *Unpublished Papers* can be consulted online at the following address: https://janus.lib.cam.ac.uk/db/node.xsp?id=EAD%2FGBR%2F0016%2FSRAFFA.

44 The quantities of the fundamental equivalence satisfy the criteria defined by Sraffa to consider as given and known the variables of an economic model, as those quantities that "have an objective, independent existence at every or some instants of the natural (i.e. not interfered with by the experimenter) process of production and distribution; they can therefore be measured physically, with the ordinary instruments of measuring number, weight, time, etc. These are the only quantities which must enter as constants in economic theory, i.e. which can be assumed to be 'known' or 'given'" (Sraffa, Unpublished Papers, D3/12/13: 2, quote taken from Kurz and Salvadori, 2005, p. 426).

45 See, for example, Basu (2017, p. 1361): "Marx implicitly used... a monetary expression of value (MEV) or what later theorists have called a monetary expression of labour time (MELT)".

46 See Rieu (2008) and Dumenil, Foley, and Levy (2009).

47 See, for example, the following passages: "Price, taken by itself, is nothing but the *monetary expression of value*... Looking somewhat closer into the *monetary expression of value*, or what comes to the same, the conversion of value into price, you will find that it is a process by which you give to the *values* of all commodities an *independent* and *homogeneous form*" (Marx, *MVPP*, chap. 6). "When we speak of the prices of commodities, we always assume that the *overall price* of the mass of commodities produced by capital = the *overall value* of this mass of commodities, and therefore that the *price* of the aliquot part, of the individual commodity, = the aliquot part of that overall value. *Price* here is in general only the monetary expression of *value*" (Marx, *MEW*, 441). "(I)f the commodities are to circulate, their exchange-value must first be

converted into a price, i.e., expressed in terms of money... Price here equals monetary expression of value" (Marx, *MTSV*, 575–6).

48 "Therefore, because it is inherent in price that the commodity takes on a converted form, passes through a process of alienation, first ideally then in reality, it lies in the nature of this process that value and price may diverge. E.g., if a yard of linen has a value of 2s. and a price of 1s., the magnitude of its value is not expressed in its price; and its price is not an equivalent, not the adequate monetary expression, of its value. Nevertheless, it remains the monetary expression of its value—the value expression of the yard of linen—in so far as the labour contained in it is represented as general social labour, as money. Owing to this incongruence between price and value it is possible to speak directly of the price of an object, although one cannot speak directly of its value" (Marx, MECW, vol. 34, p. 114).

49 "(T)he real measure of commodity and gold is labour itself, that is commodity and gold are as exchange values equated by direct exchange" (Marx, *MECW*, vol. 29, p. 306).

50 This point is raised by Moseley (2016b).

51 See Ricci (2016) and (2019).

52 As Marx in the *Critique of Gotha Programme* (*MCGP*, Part I) pointed out, "the exchange of equivalents in commodity exchange only exists on the average and not in the individual case", be it that of an individual firm, a specific branch of production or a given country. In capitalist exchange, the equivalence "consists in the fact that measurement is made with an equal standard, labor... But one man is superior to another physically, or mentally, and supplies more labor in the same time, or can labor for a longer time; and labor, to serve as a measure, must be defined by its duration or intensity, otherwise it ceases to be a standard of measurement. This equal right is an unequal right for unequal labor... It is, therefore, a right of inequality, in its content, like every right. Right, by its very nature, can consist only in the application of an equal standard; but unequal individuals (and they would not be different individuals if they were not unequal) are measurable only by an equal standard insofar as they are brought under an equal point of view, are taken from one definite side only".

53 As Screpanti (2017) points out, the employment contract is a free market relationship where one party, the worker, accepts a relationship of subsumtion and subordination to the command of the other party, the capitalist, thus voluntarily establishing a situation of exploitation.

Bibliography

Arthur, C. (1996). Engels as interpreter of Marx's economics. In *Engels Today*. Ed. C. Arthur. London: Palgrave Macmillan, 173–209.

Basu, D. (2017). Quantitative empirical research in Marxist political economy: a selective review. *Journal of Economic Surveys*, *31*(5), 1359–1386.

Bellofiore, R. (1989). A monetary labor theory of value. *Review of Radical Political Economics*, *21*(1–2), 1–25.

Bellofiore, R. (2004). Marx and the macro-monetary foundation of microeconomics. In *The constitution of Capital. Essays on Volume I of Marx's Capital*. Eds. R. Bellofiore, and N. Taylor. London: Palgrave Macmillan, 170–216.

Bellofiore, R., and Finelli, R. (1998). Capital, labour and time: the Marxian monetary labour theory of value as a theory of exploitation. In *Marxian Economics: A Reappraisal*, Vol. 1. Ed. R. Bellofiore. London: Palgrave Macmillan, 48–74.

Brunhoff de, S. (1976). *Marx on Money*. New York: Urizen Books.

Bryer, R. (2017). *Accounting for Value in Marx's Capital: The Invisible Hand.* Washington, DC: Lexington Books.

Bryer, R. (2019). *Accounting for History in Marx's Capital. The Missing Link.* Washington, DC: Lexington Books.

Callari, A., Roberts, B., and Wolff, R. (1998). The transformation trinity: value, value form and price. In *Marxian Economics: A Reappraisal.* Ed. R. Bellofiore. London: Palgrave Macmillan, 43–56.

Campbell, M. (2017). Marx's transition to money with no intrinsic value in capital. *Continental Thoughts and Theory, 1*(4), 207–230.

Duménil, G. (1983). Beyond the transformation riddle: A labor theory of value. *Science and Society, 47*(2), 427–450.

Duménil, G., Foley, D., and Lévy, D. (2009). A note on the formal treatment of exploitation in a model with heterogenous labor. *Metroeconomica, 60*(3), 560–567.

Evans, T. (1997). Marxian theories of credit money and capital. *International Journal of Political Economy, 27*(1), 7–42.

Farjoun, E., and Machover, M. (1983). *Law of Chaos. A Probabilistic Approach to Political Economy.* London:Verso.

Fine, B., Lapavitsas, C., and Saad-Filho, A. (2004). Transforming the transformation problem: why the "new interpretation" is a wrong turning. *Review of Radical Political Economics, 36*(1), 3–19.

Foley, D. K. (1982). The value of money the value of labor power and the Marxian transformation problem. *Review of Radical Political Economics, 14*(2), 37–47.

Foley, D. K. (1983). On Marx's theory of money, *Social Concept, 1*(1), 5–19.

Foley, D. K. (2000). Recent developments in the labor theory of value. *Review of Radical Political Economics, 32*(1), 1–39.

Foley, D. K. (2005). Marx's theory of money in historical perspective. In *Marx's Theory of Money: Modern Reappraisals.* Ed: F. Moseley. London: Palgrave, 36–49.

Foley, D. K., and Duménil, G. (2018). Marxian transformation problem. In The *New Palgrave Dictionary of Economics,* Third edition. Eds: M. Vernengo, E. Perez Caldentey, B.J. Rosser Jr. London: Palgrave Macmillan, 8441–8451.

Freeman, A., and Carchedi, G. (1996). *Marx and Non-Equilibrium Economics.* Cheltenham, UK: Edward Elgar Publishing.

Freeman, A., Kliman, A., and Wells, J. (Eds.). (2004). *The New Value Controversy and the Foundations of Economics.* Cheltenham, UK: Edward Elgar Publishing.

Ganssmann, H. (1998) The Emergence of Credit Money. In *Marxian Economics: A Reappraisal,* Vol 1. Ed. R. Bellofiore. London: Palgrave Macmillan, 145–156.

Germer, C. (1997). Credit money and the functions of money in capitalism. *International Journal of Political Economy, 27*(1), 43–72.

Germer, C. (2005). The commodity nature of money in Marx's theory. In *Marx's Theory of Money: Modern Reappraisals.* Ed: F. Moseley. London: Palgrave, 21–35.

Godelier, M. (1977). *Perspectives in Marxist Anthropology.* Cambridge: Cambridge University Press.

Graziani, A. (1997). The Marxist theory of money. *International Journal of Political Economy, 27*(2), 26–50.

Henning, C. (2014). *Philosophy after Marx: 100 Years of Misreadings and the Normative Turn in Political Philosophy.* Leiden: Brill.

Hilferding, R. (1981). *Finance Capital: A Study of the Latest Phase of Capitalist Development.* London: Routledge and Kegan Paul.

Howard, M. C., and King, J. E. (1992). *A History of Marxian Economics: Volume II*: 1929–1990. London: Macmillan International Higher Education.

Itoh, M., and Lapavitsas, C. (1998). *Political Economy of Money and Finance*. Berlin: Springer.

Ivanova, M. N. (2013). The dollar as world money. *Science & Society*, 77(1), 44–71.

Jessop, B. (2013). Credit money, fiat money and currency pyramids: reflections on the financial crisis and sovereign debt. In *Financial Crises and the Nature of Capitalist Money*. Eds. J. Pixley and G. Harcourt. London: Palgrave Macmillan, 248–272.

Jessop, B. (2015). Hard cash, easy credit, fictitious capital: critical reflections on money as a fetishised social relation. *Finance and Society*, 1(1), 20–37.

Jorland, G. (1995). *Les Paradoxes Du Capital*. Paris: Odile Jacob.

Kim, C. (2010). The recent controversy on Marx's value theory: a critical assessment. *Marxism 21*, 7(2), 282–320.

Kim, C. (2016). Circular reasoning in Freeman and Kliman's (TSSI) interpretation of the MELT. *Marxism 21*, 3(3), 172–209.

Kliman, A. J., and McGlone, T. (1999). A temporal single-system interpretation of Marx's value theory. *Review of Political Economy*, 11(1), 33–59.

Knapp, G. F. (1924). *The State Theory of Money*. London: Macmillan.

Kristjanson-Gural, D. (2008). Money is time: the monetary expression of value in Marx's theory of value. *Rethinking Marxism*, 20(2), 257–272.

Kurz, H. D., and Salvadori, N. (2005). Representing the production and circulation of commodities in material terms: on Sraffa's objectivism. *Review of Political Economy*, 17(3), 413–441.

Lapavitsas, C. (1991). The theory of credit money: a structural analysis. *Science and Society*, 55(3), 291–322.

Lapavitsas, C. (1994). The Banking School and the monetary thought of Karl Marx. *Cambridge Journal of Economics*, 18(5), 447–461.

Lapavitsas, C. (2000). Money and the analysis of capitalism: the significance of commodity money. *Review of Radical Political Economics*, 32(4), 631–656.

Lapavitsas, C. (2016a). *Marxist Monetary Theory: Collected Papers*. Leiden: Brill.

Lapavitsas, C. (2017). Money. In *Routledge Handbook of Marxian Economics*. Eds. Brennan et al. London: Routledge, 69–79.

Lavoie, D. (1986). Marx, the quantity theory, and the theory of value. *History of Political Economy*, 18(1), 155–170.

Mandel, E. (1971). *Marxist Economic Theory*. Volume I. New York: Monthly Review Press.

Mavroudeas, S. (2001). The monetary equivalent of labour and certain issues regarding money and the value of labour-power. *Economie appliquée*, 54(1), 37–74.

Meek, R. L. (1956). *Studies in the Labor Theory of Value*. New York: New York University Press.

Mohun, S. (1994). A re (in) statement of the labour theory of value. *Cambridge Journal of Economics*, 18(4), 391–412.

Moseley, F. (Ed.) (2005a). *Marx's Theory of Money: Modern Reappraisals*. London: Palgrave.

Moseley, F. (2005b). Money has no price: Marx's theory of money and the transformation problem. In *Marx's Theory of Money: Modern Reappraisals*. Ed: F. Moseley. London: Palgrave, 192–206.

Moseley, F. (2011). The determination of the "Monetary Expression of Labor Time" ("MELT") in the case of non-commodity money. *Review of Radical Political Economics, 43*(1), 95–105.

Moseley, F. (2016a). *Money and Totality: A Macro-Monetary Interpretation of Marx's Logic in Capital and the End of the 'Transformation Problem'*. Leiden: Brill.

Moseley, F. (2016b). The MELT and circular reasoning in the New Interpretation and the Temporal Single System Interpretation. *Marxism 21, 13*(2), 172–209.

Murray, P., and Schuler, J. (2017). The commodity spectrum. *Continental Thoughts and Theory, 1*(4), 112–152.

Nelson, A. (1999), *Marx's Concept of Money. The God of Commodities*. London: Routledge.

O'Mahony, M. (1996). Conversion factors in relative productivity calculations: theory and practice. In *Industry Productivity, International Comparison and Measurement Issues*. Paris: Organisation for Economic Cooperation and Developmen.

Potts, N., and Kliman, A. (Eds.). (2015). *Is Marx's Theory of Profit Right: The Simultaneist-Temporalist Debate*. Washington, DC: Lexington Books.

Prado, E. (2016). From gold money to fictitious money. *Brazilian Journal of Political Economy, 36*(1), 14–28.

Reuten, G. (1988). The money expression of value and the credit system: a value-form theoretic outline. *Capital and Class, 12*(2), 121–141.

Ricci, A. (2016). *Unequal Exchange in International Trade: A General Model*. Working Papers Series in Economics, Mathematics and Statistics, 16/05, Urbino: University of Urbino.

Ricci, A. (2019). Unequal exchange in the age of globalization. *Review of Radical Political Economics, 51*(2), 225–245.

Rieu, D.M. (2008). Estimating sectoral rates of surplus value: methodological issues. *Metroeconomica, 59*(4), 557–573.

Roberts, B. (1997). Embodied labor and competitive prices: a physical quantities approach. *Cambridge Journal of Economics, 21*, 483–502.

Sandemose, J. (2018). *Class and Property in Marx's Economic Thought: Exploring the Basis for Capitalism*. London: Routledge.

Screpanti, E. (2017). Karl Marx on wage labor: from natural abstraction to formal subsumption. *Rethinking Marxism, 29*(4), 511–537.

Sraffa, P. (1960). *Production of Commodities by Means of Commodities: Prelude to a Critique of Economic Theory*. Cambridge: Cambridge University Press.

Sweezy, P. M. (1942). *Theory of Capital Development*. Oxford: Oxford University Press.

Taylor, N. (2004). Reconstructing Marx on money and the measurement of value. In *The Constitution of Capital. Essays on Volume I of Marx's Capital*. Eds. R. Bellofiore, and N. Taylor, London: Palgrave Macmillan, 88–116.

Tsoulfidis, L., and Tsaliki, P. (2019). *Classical Political Economics and Modern Capitalism*. Berlin: Springer Books.

Weeks, J. (1981), *Capital and Exploitation*. Princeton: Princeton University Press.

Wolff, R. D., Callari, A., and Roberts, B. (1984). A Marxian alternative to the traditional "transformation problem". *Review of Radical Political Economics, 16*(2-3), 115–135.

Wolfson, M. (1988). Comment: Marx, the quantity theory, and the theory of value. *History of Political Economy, 20*(1), 137–140.

135

5

THE INTERNATIONAL LAW OF VALUE AND MONEY
A general model of unequal exchange

Andrea Ricci

5.1 Why are prices higher in richer countries?

An important and unsolved puzzle in international and development economics is the long-run discrepancy between current and purchasing power parity (PPP) exchange rate, the latter indicating the rate of conversion that equalizes the purchasing power of different currencies. This effect is known in the literature as the "Penn effect", because it derives from the Penn World Table, a set of comparable national account data covering almost all countries in the world for a long historical period from 1950 to the present day.[1] The "Penn effect" shows that in the world economy, the national price level is positively correlated to the level of the national per capita income, so that the price of an identical bundle of goods and services, measured in a common currency, is regularly higher in richer than in poor countries. A popular illustration of this phenomenon is the "Big Mac index", periodically published by *The Economist* since 1986, that compares the selling price of the famous hamburger sandwich, perfectly identical all over the world, by converting the domestic price in dollars by means of the current exchange rate. This index shows that it is much cheaper in terms of dollars to eat the exact same hamburger in poor countries than in rich countries.

Figure 5.1 shows the GDP per capita in PPP and relative domestic price level for 166 countries in the year 2017 derived from the Penn World Table. The less the price level is correlated with the level of per capita income, the more the points would tend to cluster around a vertical line at the unit value on the x-axis. As can be seen from the dotted line, instead, there is a clear positive correlation between the two variables, which confirms that the richer countries normally have a higher domestic price level than the poorer countries, as expected by the "Penn effect". A similar result is obtained by repeating the analysis for all years covered by the Penn World Tables.

The direct implication of the "Penn effect" is that the long-run nominal exchange rate is unsuitable to express the relative purchasing power of two currencies, thus undermining the empirical validity of the PPP hypothesis on the determination of

136

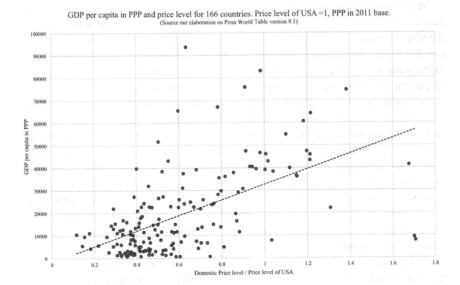

GDP per capita in PPP and price level for 166 countries. Price level of USA =1, PPP in 2011 base.
(Source our elaboration on Penn World Table version 9.1)

Figure 5.1 The Penn effect in 2017. GDP per capita in PPP and price level for 166 countries. Price level of USA = 1, PPP in 2011 base. (Source: Our elaboration on Penn World Table version 9.1.)

the equilibrium exchange rate. In fact, the long-run real exchange rate, measuring the general relative price level expressed in a common currency, is systematically overvalued for the more developed economies and, vice versa, undervalued for the less developed ones. By contrast, under the PPP hypothesis, the equilibrium real exchange rates should be identically equal to one, and in dynamic terms, the logarithms, showing their time variation, should be equal to zero. When these conditions do not hold as with the "Penn effect", the long run movements of the real exchange rates indicate systematic deviations from PPP.[2] As a consequence, the ratio between current and PPP exchange rate, referred to as exchange rate deviation index or ERDI, is itself strictly correlated to the level of the real per capita income.[3]

The "Penn effect" represents a major problem for mainstream economics. This well-established statistical regularity, indeed, deprives the standard neoclassical trade theory of consistent empirical evidence on the supposed long-run equilibrium exchange rate, so undermining one of its conceptual pillars, namely the market mechanism of automatic adjustment of trade imbalances between countries. Moreover, from this empirical evidence, it follows that the terms of trade are systematically distorted in favour of the richest countries in the world economy, suggesting a relationship between the "Penn effect" and the phenomenon of unequal exchange.

More specifically, the real currency misalignment deriving from the "Penn effect", shown by an ERDI different than one, has been proposed as a measure of the size of unequal exchange and imperialist practices in the context of Marxist, neo-Ricardian, and dependency theories of international trade.[4] In this method of investigation, the difference between the value of exports and imports measured in current and PPP exchange rates would reveal the size of the value transfers from poorer to richer countries hidden behind the international market exchange of commodities. This claim, however, has been criticized in the literature for the lack of a solid theoretical basis because it takes real currency misalignments as simple factual data, thus representing merely a calculation method devoid of any explanatory capacity. In particular, the main objections regard the unrealistic assumption of an identical labour intensity and productivity between countries common to most of the ERDI literature, and the lack of a theoretical explanation of the "Penn effect", taken as a mere empirical regularity.[5] In fact, the non-standard trade theory fails to give a consistent account of the "Penn effect" without resorting to extra-economic factors, like monopoly power and market imperfections. Consequently, the use of the gap between current and PPP exchange rate to measure transfers of value in trade, shared by different heterodox approaches on unequal exchange, remains without a solid theoretical basis and it could be easily countered as a meaningless empirical exercise.

This chapter argues that the "Penn effect" arises from the functioning of the international law of value, as sketched by Marx in chapter XXII of the first volume of *Capital*, which is devoted to the differences in national wages between countries. At the international level, the law of value is affected by two essential modifications with respect to the national case which are related to differences in intensity and productivity of labour between countries. The former acts on the unit of measurement of universal labour constituting the intrinsic measure of international value, while the latter acts on the extrinsic measure of international value in determining the comparative value of national money[6] and it gives rise to the "Penn effect". In the presence of different national labour productivities, the international law of value leads to a systematic real overvaluation of exchange rates in more developed countries and, vice versa, undervaluation in less developed countries, thus originating the empirical evidence of the "Penn effect" in the context of perfectly competitive world markets. These real currency misalignments reflect the transfers of value involved in trade between countries at different levels of economic development, as claimed by Marx in commenting on the Ricardian trade theory since they imply a systematic difference between the value produced and the value realized by different countries in the world market. What this analysis shall reveal is the crucial role played by money in Marx's theory, because the distinctive feature of the international law of value ultimately results in the existence of several national monetary expressions of value, expressed by different national currencies linked together by a coherent system of exchange rates converting national money in international money.

Before presenting the theoretical explanation of the "Penn effect" based on Marx's international law of value, however, let us examine in more detail how standard and non-standard trade theories have tried to give an account of this phenomenon.

5.1.1 The "Penn puzzle" in standard trade theory

The persistent and systematic discrepancy between current and PPP exchange rates, even in the long run, is an old and well-known phenomenon in international economics, long before the International Comparison Project provided reliable data on the national price levels at a world scale under the aegis of the United Nations and World Bank.[7] The national price level, that for the purposes of international comparisons can be defined as the ratio of current to PPP exchange rate or ERDI,[8] differs between countries in a non-accidental way since it is positively correlated to the level of the per capita income, as showed by the robust statistical evidence of the "Penn effect", established by a vast empirical literature.[9] This fact infringes the basic prediction of the PPP theory, according to which the real exchange rate should be a random walk over the long run.[10] What actually happens is that the real exchange rate is a non-stationary variable, driven by permanent disturbances leading to a persistent real currency overvaluation for the richer countries and, vice versa, undervaluation for the poorer ones.

The empirical failure of the PPP hypothesis represents a serious problem for the standard neoclassical trade theory, based on the principles of comparative advantages and balanced trade, depriving it of a coherent definition of the long-run equilibrium exchange rate. In standard trade theory, indeed, the adjustment mechanism requires that the real exchange rate automatically adjusts to restore the equilibrium of the trade balance and terms of trade, without the need for additional change in real economic variables. In this context, trade imbalances result from temporary short run deviations of the real exchange rate from its long-term position defined by the PPP theory, which implies that in the long run the net barter terms of trade are equal to one, and the trade balance is in equilibrium.[11] On the basis of these assumptions, the standard theory assesses that free trade is mutually beneficial even though there are different levels of economic development because the adjusting real exchange rate would make all countries equally competitive.[12] In an attempt to reconcile neoclassical theory with empirical evidence, an extensive literature is devoted to explaining the "Penn effect" by adapting the PPP hypothesis without giving up its basic outcomes. In this extended or enhanced PPP theory,[13] two prevalent approaches can be found, both dealing with differences in relative prices of tradable and non-tradable goods between countries with different levels of economic development.

The first is a supply side approach based on the productivity differential model of the exchange rate determination, otherwise known as the "Balassa-Samuelson hypothesis" (BSH), which explains the "Penn effect" by differences in relative sectoral productivity between countries.[14] The antecedents of this model can be traced back to Ricardo (2004, p. 142), who argued that "the prices of home commodities ... are, independently of other causes, higher in those countries where manufactures flourish", so that in two otherwise identical countries, the value of money will be lower in the country with higher productivity, thus determining higher nominal wages and prices. As it is based on the distinction between tradable and non-tradable (home) commodities, Ricardo's argument represents an anticipation of the BSH. Later, it was Angell (1922), who, in arguing against the early doctrine of the PPP theory developed by Cassel (1916), noted that international and domestic prices can move in different directions due to different growths in productivity between industries. According to the BSH, the technological advantage of more developed countries is greater in the production of tradable goods than non-tradable goods. In the absence of any friction in international markets, the law of one price implies an identical price of tradable goods across countries, while the price of non-tradable goods remains different. Under the crucial assumption that national labour markets are homogeneous and wages are equalized across sectors, national wages are determined by the productivity level in the tradable sector.[15] Hence, the relative prices of non-tradable goods, and consequently, the aggregate national price level, will be higher in more developed economies than in less developed ones, from which follows the real currency misalignments described by the "Penn effect". The BSH, originally formulated in terms of a Ricardian trade model with only one factor of production, has subsequently been extended to the case of the neoclassical general equilibrium framework with multiple factors of production without changing the findings.[16]

The second standard explanation of the Penn effect relies on a demand-side approach, deriving from the hypothesis of non-homothetic preferences originally formulated by Linder (1961), according to which rich and poor countries consume identical goods in different proportions of their per capita income. In this case, the differences in relative prices of tradable and non-tradable goods between countries depend on different relative income elasticities of demand in private or public consumption behaviour. In the first case, non-tradable goods are supposed to be superior goods for which private demand is directly correlated to the consumer's wealth,[17] while in the second case, the share of public expenditure on total consumption, largely concentrated on non-tradable services (such as healthcare, education, and public safety), is a positive function of per capita income.[18] The two channels can act simultaneously, thus reinforcing the final effect.[19] In all such cases, the consumption preferences show a bias towards non-tradable commodities as income grows, resulting in higher prices of non-tradable goods in richer countries. With an identical international price of traded commodities, this fact produces the aggregate price level differentials and real currency misalignments between countries at different stages of economic development described by the "Penn effect".

As we saw, therefore, both supply side and demand-side approaches share the hypothesis that in equilibrium the PPP condition holds for tradable goods, even if it does not apply for non-tradable goods. In this way, the adjusted PPP theory maintains the core principles of the standard trade theory pertaining to the constancy of the terms of trade and equilibrium of trade balance for each country in the long run. The empirical evidence, however, does not corroborate this hypothesis by showing that, even in the long run, the PPP condition is not satisfied for traded goods.[20] Moreover, other empirical studies found that relative productivity differentials[21] and relative prices of non-tradable goods[22] are of very limited or null significance on the real exchange rate determination. Finally, the crucial assumption of national wage equalization across tradable and non-tradable sectors does not seem to apply either in the short or in the long run.[23] We can conclude, therefore, that even the adjusted version of the PPP theory is unable to provide a consistent explanation of the observed long-run currency misalignment. The "Penn effect" thus still remains an unsolved puzzle for neoclassical standard trade theory, despite the large amount of research that continues to be dedicated to it.

5.1.2 The "Penn puzzle" in non-standard trade theory

The determination of the long-run equilibrium exchange rate is a neglected issue in modern non-standard trade theory. In this regard, the main contributions have been developed from a classical political economy perspective.[24] The starting point of this approach lies in a mechanism of international competition similar to the national one, in which market prices reflect the production costs of the more productive, or regulating, capitals. In the case of free trade and international capital mobility, the rate of profit will be equalized between regulating capitals of different sectors, but that does not apply to less efficient capitals that gain a lower profit rate. In these circumstances, international trade is based on the principle of absolute cost advantages, which no longer implies long-run trade balance and terms of trade equilibrium between countries, unlike the comparative advantages in the standard trade theory. Following Pasinetti (1973), the regulating production costs are reduced to the vertically integrated real labour costs, representing the major determinant of the relative prices between two commodities. In this framework, the real exchange rate will depend on the vertically integrated real wages and labour input requirements of national productions, adjusted for the non-tradable to tradable goods ratio. Foreign imbalances and terms of trade disequilibria are explained by local structural factors, relating to national income distribution and technological efficiency, and they cannot be removed by changes in real exchange rates, that in fact will act in the opposite direction from restoring trade equilibrium. The real exchange rate, indeed, will tend to move towards depreciation for the more competitive countries, where real unit costs and prices of tradable commodities are lower, and vice versa for the less competitive ones.

Unlike standard trade theory, the classical approach is able to give a cogent account of some persistent external commercial disequilibria and asymmetric trade existing in the actual world economy by pointing out the presence of circular and cumulative processes independent from voluntary policy practices of currency manipulation.[25] This framework, however, is not suitable for analysing the systematic discrepancy between the current and PPP exchange rate as evidenced by the "Penn effect", because the analysis is conducted in terms of relative competitiveness to investigate the temporal dynamic of the exchange rates, not their absolute levels. Furthermore, since an improvement in competitiveness is associated with real currency depreciation, the classical approach involves a negative relation between labour productivity and economic efficiency, on the one hand, and domestic price level, on the other, and not the positive one showed by the "Penn effect".

In a more conventional Marxist approach, the main explanations of the differences in national price levels between countries have been based on particular *ad hoc* assumptions concerning extra-economic forces, such as the presence of monopoly power and a lower level of competition in international markets than national ones.[26] In this regard, two exceptions are worthy of note. Basso (2002) presents a basic Marxist model where the commodities are exchanged in international markets at their national values, derived from the average labour productivities of different countries. The ratio between national values determines the equilibrium real exchange rate that, therefore, would represent by definition a state of equal exchange in trade.[27] In so doing, however, the model restates, in a Marxian way, the PPP theory complemented with productivity differentials, thereby involving a relation between the level of economic development and national price level that is exactly the opposite of the evidence showed by the "Penn effect".

By contrast, Carchedi (1988, 1991) develops an elaborate Marxist framework in which, under the assumption of perfect capital mobility, the commodities are exchanged in international markets at their prices of production expressed in international money, and the equilibrium (or tendential) exchange rate is determined by the conversion in the national currency of the international prices of production. In this case, the tendential exchange rate ensures the international equalization of the profit rate per unit of capital however calculated, in value or in international and national money. This condition implies that in the world capitalist economy there would be a trend towards the equalization of the relative value of the national money between countries, as happens in the PPP theory. This model, therefore, is able to explain better than the standard theory the short-run fluctuations of the current exchange rates around their long-run trend, but it shares the same problems in explaining the systematic divergence of national price levels between countries.

To sum up, therefore, both standard and non-standard trade theories fail to provide a reliable explanation of the "Penn effect". As will be seen, however, a consistent interpretation of Marx's theory of international value is able to solve the puzzle.

5.2 Universal labour and international value in Marx's theory

International trade and the world market were supposed to be the last two books in a plan of six in the critique of political economy, but Marx left his project unfinished.[28] His thoughts on these subjects are spread out on the whole work, and the issue of the internationalization of capital is addressed at all stages of investigation on the capitalist mode of production, from the theoretical analysis to the historical and political writings.[29] In this regard, one of the most important places is chapter XXII of the first volume of *Capital*, in which Marx discusses the causes of the disparities in national wages between countries.[30] If correctly interpreted, this short chapter allows us to outline the backbone of the international law of value. It can therefore shed light on the essential modification mentioned, although not explained, by Marx in the following passage of the *Theories of Surplus Value,* as a possible cause of exploitation of poorer countries by richer ones:

> Loss and gain within a *single* country cancel each other out. But not so with trade between different countries. And even according to Ricardo's theory, three days of labour of one country can be exchanged against one of another country – a point *not* noted by Say. Here the law of value undergoes essential modification. The relationship between labour days of different countries may be similar to that existing between skilled, complex labour and unskilled, simple labour within a country. In this case, the richer country exploits the poorer one, even where the latter gains by the exchange.
>
> (Marx, *MTSV*, chap. 20, 805)

But why should the international comparison of wages bring Marx to address the question of the international law of value? In the analysis of international differences in wages in Chapter XXII, Marx in some ways anticipates the definition of purchasing power parity as a method of comparing economic quantities at the international level, which will be systematically developed only several decades later.

In the chapters preceding XXII, Marx defines the wage as the value of labour power that "is determined by the value of the necessaries of life habitually required by the average labourer" (Marx, *MK1*, chap.17, p. 367). Unlike Ricardo, who considered the wage as physiologically determined in an identical and fixed amount for every place and time, Marx considers the necessary standard of living for the average worker as socially determined and dependent on historical, moral, political, and cultural factors. At any given epoch of a given society, however, the quantity of goods necessary for the reproduction of the life of the workers and their families is known and constant, while its value can change, as it is determined by the labour time socially necessary for the production of the consumption bundle of an average worker. In the sphere of circulation, this value manifests itself in the form of the domestic price of the necessary worker consumption denominated in national money. The international comparison of wages then requires the reduction of the different national monetary expressions of the consumption bundles of workers into a common expression in international value, which as we saw

143

in Chapter 4 has a dual measure, intrinsic and extrinsic. The intrinsic measure is expressed in terms of universal abstract labour time, and the unit of measurement is given by the average unit of universal labour, while the extrinsic measure is expressed in terms of international price with international money as the unit of measurement. The need to express worker consumption bundles in a common measure of value in order to compare wages between different countries leads Marx to make some brief but important considerations on the modifications of the law of value at the international level, which we will now develop in line with the arguments presented in previous chapters.

In chapter XVII, Marx showed that within a country, the wage, at absolute and relative levels, depends on the combination of the following three factors:

> (1) the length of the working day, or the extensive magnitude of labour; (2) the normal intensity of labour, its intensive magnitude, whereby a given quantity of labour is expended in a given time; (3) the productiveness of labour, whereby the same quantum of labour yields, in a given time, a greater or less quantum of product, dependent on the degree of development in the conditions of production.
>
> (Marx, *MK1*, chap. 17, p. 367)

The different combinations of these three factors over time determine wage fluctuations within a country. In chapter XXII, Marx returns to the subject, but this time in a synchronic context, stating that these same factors determine the differences in wage levels between different countries over a given period.[31] He, then, moves on to examine how each of these three factors acts in determining national wages differences.

At the international level, the magnitude of the value of the different national labour powers cannot be compared abruptly by merely calculating the direct labour time embodied in the necessary consumption of workers or their monetary price, but a preliminary operation is needed, namely, the determination of a common unit of universal labour that expresses itself in the world market in the form of international money. Socially necessary labour time, in fact, cannot be merely reduced to the absolute time dimension because its magnitude is a unity of intensive and extensive factors, the former being the value-creating capacity of the living labour or quantum of labour, and the latter, the temporal unit or quantum of time.[32] The unit of labour time measuring the magnitude of value is given by the quantum of labour performed in a quantum of time, depending on the average or normal intensity of labour and the length of the time unit, respectively. Unlike the concept of absolute time, which is a one-dimensional variable defined by always identical regular intervals that are repeated infinitely, the socially necessary labour time is a two-dimensional relative variable, whose magnitude may vary because it varies the intensity, the quantum of labour, although the quantum of time remains unchanged. If the extensive magnitude of labour can be measured in terms of an identical quantum of time in each country, this is not the case for the intensive magnitude because the quantum of labour depends on the specific historical characteristics of the average social worker of each country.

At the national level, the unit of socially necessary labour time is the product of the historical development of the economic and social system on the basis of common laws, customs, and traditions as well as national class struggles, domestic competition, and labour mobility. These particular circumstances lead to the establishment of a normal length of the working day and a normal level of labour intensity in each national industry, thus determining the real quantitative dimension of the average unit of social labour in the form of a given national labour expression of value (LEV), as we saw in Chapter 4. This historical process of reduction of the concrete labour into average social labour within each country brings with it a common unit of the extrinsic measure of value that finds its expression in the national monetary expression of value (MEV) in the form of price denominated in national money. In each country, the national monetary expression of labour time (MELT), defined as the quantity of national money representing one unit of national socially necessary labour time, is the result of the historical process of normalization, synchronization, and homogenization of national labour,[33] spontaneously realized through the free play of market forces, operating within a given institutional national framework in the course of a long period of time. As a consequence, also its inverse, the value of money, that is, the quantity of socially necessary labour time expressed by one monetary unit, is determined on a national basis, since it strictly depends on the historical process of the formation of the average social labour that occurs within each given national society.

What it is important to stress at this point is that international analysis always needs a criterion of differentiation from the national case, allowing us to define its specific and exclusive features deserving of an independent and separate investigation. Usually, in international economics, the peculiarity of the international dimension is of a structural or geographic origin, such as immobility of productive factors, monopolistic markets, barriers to trade, or different resource endowments, deriving from extra-economic factors. In Marx's analysis on differences in national wages between countries, instead, the specific characteristic of the international dimension derives from a historical and institutional origin. In fact, the structural elements of the capitalist mode of production and commodity circulation, set out in the first volume of *Capital*, remain unaffected in chapter XXII, so that we are dealing with perfect competitive markets at the international as well national level. What distinguishes the international from the national case is the existence of a plurality of nation states, each sovereign in its own territory with its own laws and currency and characterized by a peculiar historical development. All this produces different units of intrinsic and extrinsic measures of value for each country, determining a different expression of the exchange value between countries in terms of both homogeneous labour time and monetary units. At the surface of the commodities circulation, this difference manifests itself in the form of different currencies in which national prices are denominated. As we will see, this is not merely a formal aspect because each national currency is marked by its specific monetary expression of international value, or equivalently, the international value of national money is different between countries. With regard to the differences in national units of measurement of socially necessary labour time between countries, on the other hand, they are not immediately visible in international markets.

Unlike the national economy, in the world market, the unit of measure of socially necessary labour time is no longer a matter of fact, owing to the uneven historic development of each country. Capitalism originated and evolved on a national basis, and a world capitalist market begins to form only at advanced stages of development, and so far, this process has not yet fully been accomplished. Over a long period, international economic relations played a decisive role in the primitive accumulation of national capitals, and the forms taken by them were the antagonistic struggles, more or less violent, between imperialistic powers for the hegemony in world trade and financial markets. During this historical phase, the process of labour homogenization has taken place on a national basis, leading to the determination of national social standards of the extensive and intensive magnitude of labour, as the normal length of the working day and average intensity of labour, respectively. Similarly, the level of labour productivity differentiated between countries because of the different national speed of capital accumulation. All of these factors led to different national units of average social labour, that simultaneously coexist in the world market in any given historical period. This is the reason why in the world market, the unit of measure of universal labour is not a historical datum, unlike what happens within domestic boundaries. Instead, it has to be derived from an analytical procedure that, according to Marx, consists of a two-step process of international homogenization of the different national units of socially necessary labour time.

The first step is to define a common quantum of time for all countries, which can be easily addressed by considering the number of daily working hours to remove differences in the average length of the national working day. The extensive magnitude of the different labour time units can be compared in hourly rather than daily terms. The second step relates to the definition of a common quantum of labour allowing to account for differences in the intensive magnitude of different average national social labours, consisting of their respective intensity. According to Marx, this requires that:

> After this reduction to the same terms of the day-wages, time-wage must again be translated into piece-wage, as the latter only can be a measure both of the productivity and the intensity of labour.
>
> (Marx, *MK1*, chap. 22, p. 396)

The international comparison of the value of labour powers between countries should be done, therefore, by taking into consideration piece wages instead of time wages. In the former wage system, workers are paid per unit of produced good, while in the latter, they are paid per unit of time (month, week, day, or hour) spent at work. To better grasp its meaning, this important passage must be read together with another one from the preceding chapter XXI (*Piece Wages*) where, in discussing the differences between the two possible forms of wages, Marx pointed out that:

> Piece-wages do not, in fact, distinctly express any relation of value. It is not, therefore, a question of measuring the value of the piece by the working-time incorporated in it, but on the contrary, of measuring the working-time the labourer has expended by the number of pieces he has produced. In time-wages, the labour is measured by its immediate duration; in piece-wages, by the quantity of products in which the labour has embodied itself during a given time.
>
> (Marx, *MK1*, chap. 21, p. 390)

From the combined reading of these two excerpts, it follows that there are two ways of measuring labour, directly by the working time length corresponding to time wage, or indirectly by the volume of commodities produced in a given interval of time corresponding to piece wage, and only the latter is a real measure of both intensity and productivity of labour. In fact, the working time length can only determine the productivity of labour, that is, the number of goods produced in the unit of time, not the intensity, which is the quantity of labour performed in the unit of time. The direct measurement of working time to compare the wages of different countries, indeed, would arbitrarily assume the same level of labour intensity between all countries.

Time wage and piece wage refer to two different forms of labour time, concrete and abstract time, respectively, to recall the distinction set out by Postone (1993).[34] The first is the clock time spent at work by labourers in the particular production process in which they are employed, on the basis of which duration time wages are paid. The second, instead, is a standardized time resulting from a process of social average and independent from the actual working time of the individual worker, which constitutes the basis of piece wage. The concrete labour time is full of the live events experienced by workers in the course of their concrete working activity. Abstract labour time, on the other hand, is an empty time, independent of the real events that occurred during the individual activity of the real worker. In abstract labour time, the unit of measurement of time is determined by the normal social level of labour intensity, and not by the effective time length of the working period, so that it varies with changing social conditions of production. Therefore, abstract time is constituted by social rather than clock units of time. In contrast to the latter, which are always identical and immutable in magnitude, and measure time in motion, the abstract social units of labour time are constantly changing, and measure time congealed in the production of the commodity. In fact, abstract social units of time measure labour in the very moment when abstract living labour, the substance of value, is transformed into dead labour, social labour objectified in the form of exchange value through the social algorithm of value.

The abstract labour time is remunerated by piece wage that depends on the social unit value of the produced commodity, given the normal rate of surplus value, without any relation with the time experienced by the worker. In piece wage, the real abstraction of the social algorithm of value directly imposes its discipline on the labourers by measuring their social labour time irrespective of their individual concrete time. This is the reason, in the passage quoted previously, Marx speaks of a labour that "has embodied itself during a given period of time", to mean that the subject who creates value is the abstract social labour in its totality, rather than the real and concrete individual labour of workers in flesh and blood. In piece wage, the labour time performed by the individual worker is impersonally determined by the social algorithm of value as part of the total abstract social labour.

Of the two elements constituting the unit of socially necessary labour time, in time wage, the quantum of time is constant and referring to equal clock units of time such as seconds, minutes, and hours, while the quantum of labour is variable depending on the individual intensity of labour performed by each worker. By contrast, in piece wage, the quantum of labour is constant as socially determined by the normal average level of labour intensity, and the quantum of time changes in relation to the individual ability of each worker. In a time wage system, an individual intensity of labour different than normal results in an individual unit value of the produced commodity different than social unit value, thus affecting the individual profit of the employer. In a piece wage system, vice versa, the individual unit value is always identical to the social unit value, and any difference in individual intensity of labour affects the individual wage of the worker rather than the profit of the individual firm.

What do these differences between time and piece wages mean for the measurement of labour time? The direct measurement of labour time by the length of the working time actually performed, corresponding to time wage, measures the quantity of concrete labour spent by the worker in the individual and specific act of production of a particular use value, which is incommensurable in time and space because of its unique quality. Instead, the indirect measurement of labour time by the volume of commodities produced, corresponding to piece wage, measures the magnitude of the abstract labour time socially necessary performed on average by a normal worker. The latter, therefore, is the most appropriate way to compare the magnitude of social value created in the unit of time by different labours. In fact, by using crude direct labour time spent in the production of a given commodity, the implicit assumption would be that all the different concrete labours are of normal quality, thus representing an equivalent quantum of labour. But, in this way, we neglect the individual differences in labour quality to whom the averaging process applies in forming the social value of the commodity, whereas through the indirect measurement we allow for variations of the quantum of labour by keeping fixed the quantum of time. The measurement of labour time through the quantity of a given commodity produced in a unit of time, rather than the length of labour time actually performed, therefore, allows us to consider the different intensities of labour. Consequently, it is this indirect measurement of labour time that has to be used to compare the national wage levels between different countries by a common international measure of abstract labour time. Since national wages are nothing more than the value of the labour power of different countries, the same method should be used in the international comparison of the value of the commodities produced by each individual country. In general terms, therefore, in order to determine the international value of the national productions of the different countries, it is first necessary to define a common unit of measurement of the international quantum of labour on the basis of the average labour intensity at world level, and then proceed to measure the international socially necessary labour on the basis of the indirect measurement of labour time.

When a normal level of labour intensity is commonly established and socially validated, as happens within a national economy, the two measures of labour time tend to be equivalent and interchangeable. This normal social level of labour intensity provides the basis for the monetary expression of labour time in a given national currency. In fact, the concrete labour used to produce a given use value is virtually normalized as average abstract labour in the simple act of expressing the commodity in the form of price denominated in a common currency. At this point, however, Marx goes on by introducing a difference between the national and international case:

> But still, even then, the intensity of labour would be different in different countries, and would modify the international application of the law of value. The more intense working-day of one nation would be represented by a greater sum of money than would the less intense day of another nation.
>
> (Marx, *MK1*, chap.17, p. 370)

Within a country, the different labour intensity between more or less efficient firms affects the individual profit rates without consequences on the national value and its monetary expression, which are determined by the domestic averaging of the individual values of each firm. On the world scale, instead, things are different because the different average intensity of national labour between countries cannot be ignored in the application of the law of value, insofar as they determine different monetary expressions of labour time at the international level. The existence of different monetary expressions of the unit of social labour, resulting from the plurality of national currencies, is the reason international competition is different from national competition, and therefore, requires specific investigative tools to be examined. While at the national level, the elementary components of the economy are the firms, Marx points out that in the world market:

> (the) integral parts are the individual countries. The average intensity of labour changes from country to country; here it is greater, there less.

These national averages form a scale, whose unit of measure is the average unit of universal labour. The more intense national labour, therefore, as compared with the less intense, produces in the same time more value, which expresses itself in more money.

(Marx, *MK1,* chap. 22, p. 396)

According to Marx, the unit of universal labour, expressing itself in international money, results from an average of the different units of national labour, each distinguished by its own normal intensity and expressing itself in a particular national currency. The direct measurement of labour cannot therefore be used to compare different national values between countries. The conversion between national and universal labour shall take place through the indirect measurement by averaging, given the quantum of time, the national quanta of labour into an international quantum of labour, constituting the average unit of universal labour. The homogenization of the different national quanta of labour into an average universal quantum implies that each unit of universal labour produces the same physical quantity of commodities in the unit of time, and consequently, an equivalent amount of international value, represented by an identical sum of international money, independent from its national origin. In this way, what is different between countries is no longer the quantum of labour constituting the unit of national value, but the number of national quanta of labour corresponding to the universal quantum of labour constituting the unit of international value. As a result, for countries with a labour intensity higher than average, one unit of national labour converts to a multiple of units of universal labour, and vice versa for countries with a lower intensity, so that, for example, one hour of more (less) intensive national labour than the world average corresponds to more (less) than one hour of universal labour.[35]

In the end, therefore, given that in a perfectly competitive world market, the international price of a commodity of the same kind is identical for all countries, one hour of more intensive national labour converts itself into more units of international money than one hour of less intensive national labour. In fact, since it produces more goods in the unit of time, the former represents more units of universal labour, and therefore, it creates more international value in a given quantum of time than the latter.

5.3 The value of money and unequal exchange

5.3.1 Intensity and productivity of labour and the value of commodities

So far, the difference in the units of measurement of national and universal labour may appear to be a purely formal rather than essential modification of the law of value, with many similarities with the conversion of skilled into simple labour addressed by Marx at the beginning of *Capital*. But in chapter XXII, Marx continues the discourse by introducing an additional argument as follows:

But the law of value in its international application is yet more modified
by the fact that on the world-market the more productive national labour
reckons also as the more intense, so long as the more productive nation
is not compelled by competition to lower the selling price of its commodities to the level of their value. In proportion as capitalist production
is developed in a country, in the same proportion do the national intensity and productivity of labour there rise above the international level.
The different quantities of commodities of the same kind, produced in
different countries in the same working-time, have, therefore, unequal
international values, which are expressed in different prices, i.e., in sums
of money varying according to international values. The relative value of
money will, therefore, more be less in the nation with developed capitalist mode of production than in the nation with less developed.

(Marx, *MK1,* chap. 22, p. 396)

This passage is the heart of the issue, and it must be recognized that Marx is very
concise in this regard taking for granted a series of logical steps that now we will
retrace. The brevity, however, should not be confused with inaccuracy[36] since,
after the first German edition of the first volume of *Capital* published in 1867,
Marx revised this chapter three times, for the second German edition in 1872, the
French translation in 1872–5, and the third German edition in 1883, by making
merely formal modifications.[37]

As seen previously, the unit of measure of labour time depends on the normal
or average level of labour intensity, but not on the level of labour productivity. In
fact, labour intensity refers to the variable quantum of labour performed in a given
quantum of time, while labour productivity refers to the variable quantity of goods
produced by a given quantum of labour in a given quantum of time. Therefore,
as shown by Marx in chapter XVII, in the former case, the total value created
in a given quantum of time varies in direct proportion to the intensity of labour,
whereas in the latter case, the total value is always the same regardless of the level
of productivity as both components of the unit of value shall remain unchanged.
This is why "(m)ore intense labor produces more use values and more value; more
productive labor produces more use values but the same value" (Emmanuel, 1972,
p. 100). In the case of higher intensity of labour, more commodities having the
same social unit value will be produced in the unit of time, while in the case of
higher labour productivity, more commodities of lower social unit value will be
produced in the unit of time. Hence, the effect on the unit value and market price
of a given commodity is neutral as regards labour intensity, and inversely proportional as regards labour productivity.[38]

The levels of productivity and intensity of labour depend on different and distinct factors. Labour productivity is directly proportional to the organic composition of capital because a greater endowment of means of production per unit
of labour increases the number of goods produced in the unit of time. In fact,
for Marx, technological progress is capital-using and labour-saving with constant

returns of scale, as it was for Smith and Ricardo.[39] Labour intensity, on the other hand, depends on the pace of work of each worker using the same amount of means of production of identical quality. To put it simply, labour productivity depends on the investment choices of the capitalist, while labour intensity depends on the will, ability, and effort of the worker.

Capital is constantly trying to reduce the power of workers on the degree of labour intensity, making it a controlled and pre-determined variable, thus narrowing their autonomy within the labour process through what Marx called the shift from formal to real subsumption of labour under capital (*MEW*, 469-480). As shown by Braverman (1974), this was the goal of Taylorism and the scientific organization of labour that transformed the capitalist labour process at the beginning of the last century. For this reason, within certain limits, labour intensity is indirectly influenced by capital accumulation, as technical progress in capitalism tends to introduce new organizational and technological innovations aimed at constantly increasing the pace of work by eliminating interruptions of the production flow, making work movements more fluid and depriving the worker of knowledge and control over his work process.[40] To this end, capital also uses material and moral incentives that encourage workers to feel part of a common corporate mission, thus obtaining more disciplined and cooperative attitudes of the workforce. Because of this, labour intensity and productivity normally march hand in hand, both increasing with the level of capitalist development. However, the fact remains that they refer to distinct phenomena, producing different effects on the value of commodities.

At an aggregate level, an increase in both average social intensity and productivity of labour leads to an increase in surplus value and in the rate of exploitation of labour, the former by increasing the surplus labour and the latter by reducing the necessary labour.[41] Labour intensity affects absolute surplus value by increasing the capitalist surplus, while labour productivity affects relative surplus value by reducing the value of wages. At the individual firm level, differences in labour intensity and productivity both determine different individual unit profits for a given value of labour power, but this occurs through two distinct mechanisms. In the case of higher labour intensity, the extra-profit derives from a higher-than-normal rate of exploitation[42] without any change in the unit value and market price of the commodity, since the increase in labour intensity acts in the same manner as the lengthening of the working day.[43] Firms with higher labour intensity are more profitable because they produce more social value in the unit of time than the average firms in the sector. On the contrary, in the case of higher productivity, the extra-profit takes the form of a quasi-rent at the expense of less productive firms, by means of an individual unit value lower than social unit value.

At the national level, however, the competitive advantage of the firms with higher labour intensity tends to perpetuate over time, depending on the unique characteristics of their labour force, while the same does not happen to the more productive firms. In fact, the competitive advantage deriving from an individual labour productivity higher than the social average is a temporary phenomenon since intra-industry and inter-industry competition between firms leads to the elimination of the technological rent. Within the industry, indeed, the more productive firms will be induced to fix a selling price lower than the market price, but higher than the individual unit cost plus the normal profit, in order to increase the market share and maximize earnings. Since the higher labour productivity of the most profitable firms is a consequence of their productive innovations, a process of technological and organizational imitation will be established within the industrial sector aimed at adopting the most efficient production techniques. The firms already operating in the sector will tend to copy the techniques introduced by the innovative firms and, at the same time, new firms will be incentivized to enter the sector looking for profits higher than normal. In the absence of monopolistic barriers, this imitative process deriving from intra- and inter-industrial competition will produce over time an increase of the supply and a decline in the market price of the commodity. The less productive firms will be progressively pushed out of the market, as long as the market price further reduces and becomes lower than their individual unit cost. In the face of this competitive pressure, the most efficient techniques of production will tend to spread to a growing number of firms until they become the normal techniques in the industry. The competition between firms, therefore, sets in motion a process of adjustment that ultimately results in the establishing of a new social unit value and market price of the commodity at the level of the more productive firms, leaving the total value of production unchanged.

5.3.2 The essential modification of the international law of value

According to Marx, the levelling of the labour productivity triggered by national competition does not take place at the international level, as evidenced by the ongoing disparities in the productive power of national labours in the capitalist global economy. The reason for that does not depend on a lack of competitiveness in the world market due to the presence of monopolistic conditions,[44] because in such a case, Marx would not have dealt with the subject in the first book of *Capital*, whose premise is that of perfect competition, but eventually in the third book. The assumptions of the analysis are those of free trade, leading to a single international price for a commodity of the same kind in the world market, and perfect intra-industry and inter-industry capital and labour mobility within each national economy. These assumptions are sufficient to ensure a situation of perfect competition at the international level, resulting in an identical remuneration per unit of capital between different countries, regardless of the degree of international mobility of factors of production.[45] The reason for the persistent difference between individual national value and international social value of commodities, produced according to different levels of productivity between countries, therefore, is to be found in structural factors other than world market competitiveness. Let us now clarify the matter by reconstructing the implicit logic underlying Marx's cryptic statement about the further modification of the international law of value caused by differences in labor productivity between countries.

In premise, it should be noted that the international comparison refers to real physical productivity of labour between different countries, and not to nominal labour productivity as is the case for comparison between national firms. In fact, if, at the national level, real and nominal productivity gaps between firms of the same industry coincide given the existence of a common national currency, the same does not happen at an international level because of different national currencies. In empirical analysis, this requires the use of indexes of productivity measured in PPPs rather than by nominal exchange rates. As Marx reminds us in the text mentioned previously, in the analysis of the world market, the individual countries take the place occupied by individual firms in the domestic market, as elementary basic economic units in competition with each other. The difference is not only formal but substantial, because the countries as basic actors of the world market competition are not reducible to the figure of the representative agent of a multitude of national individual capitals, since they are not merely an aggregate of private domestic firms, but they also include nation states, each with their own currency. The existence of many nation states, each independent and sovereign within its own territory, is the crucial feature distinguishing national and international competition. In the previous paragraph, we have seen how this difference results in different national units of the intrinsic measure of exchange value of commodities. Similarly, this peculiar characteristic results in differences in the national units of the extrinsic measure of exchange value, consisting of different national currencies. Unlike the domestic market where the national currency expresses the common unit of national labour for all domestic firms, in the world market there are several national currencies expressing different units of national labour. As a consequence, just as national units of labour should be converted into universal labour units, in the same way, the monetary expression of the universal labour unit is mediated by a coherent system of exchange rates able to convert the different national monetary units in an equivalent common international monetary unit. This latter is a virtual unit of account and measure of values having an identical purchasing power all over the world and represents the monetary expression of universal labour in the international market. When the current exchange rates between national currencies correspond to the relative ratios of conversion in the common PPP international monetary unit, the national units of labour are coherently converted in units of universal labour having an identical monetary expression for all the countries. If this is not the case, a unit of universal labour has a different international monetary expression depending on its national origin, thus giving rise to discrepancies between value created in production and value realized in the circulation of the commodities exchanged on the world market, that is, to unequal exchange in international trade.

The peculiarity of world market competition affects the functioning of the law of value at the international level. As happens with the competitive advantage of an individual firm in the domestic market, in the case of a competitive advantage in the world market deriving from higher national labour productivity, the more productive national capitals will be pushed to lower the international selling price for gaining new market shares and extra-profits to the detriment of less competitive countries. This behaviour arises from an individual national unit value lower than the average international unit value. When normal price elasticity holds, there will be an increase in the volume of exports of more productive countries resulting in a trend towards a structural improvement of their trade balance. In addition, in the presence of a partial or total international mobility of capital, the extra-profits earned by the more productive countries will at the same time attract new capital investments from abroad, thereby generating an inflow of capital and a tendential improvement of the foreign capital account as well.

Starting from real exchange rate equilibrium, these competitive reactions of both national and foreign capitals produce a tendential improvement of the overall balance of payments of the more productive countries, regardless of its initial situation. This will be reflected in a structural increase in the demand for their national currency in the foreign exchange market. Consequently, given the nominal exchange rate, there will be an inflationary pressure in the more productive countries, and vice versa a deflationary pressure in the less productive ones, both caused by the changes in domestic money supply necessary to maintain the stability of the nominal exchange rate. This effect would occur in the case of both a specie monetary system, such as the gold exchange standard, and a system of fixed exchange rates with inconvertible money, such as contemporary ones. Alternatively, in the case of a flexible exchange rate regime, given the domestic price levels, in the foreign exchange market, there will be a movement towards the nominal appreciation of the currencies of the more productive countries that ultimately counterbalances the effect of the reduction of the selling prices of their commodities on the world market, leaving them unchanged in terms of international money. At the end, in both cases of a fixed or flexible exchange rate regime, or even in a combination of them as with floating exchange rates, a new stable equilibrium is established, marked by a persistent real currency overvaluation for the more productive countries, and vice versa, real currency undervaluation for those less productive, leaving the initial balance of the foreign accounts and international prices of the traded commodities unchanged.

Under any regime of exchange rates, therefore, once the adjustment process is completed and in the absence of further variations in labour productivity, the new situation will be characterized by the improvement (worsening) of the terms of trade of the more (less) productive country. Starting from a situation of equivalent exchange in which the terms of trade are equal to one as supposed by PPP, now the new terms of trade will become different than one for the identical foreign account balance, thereby indicating a discrepancy between relative prices and relative values between countries that will result in unequal exchange. In the theoretical framework presented here, the equilibrium of the trade balance can be accompanied by disequilibrium of the terms of trade with respect to the PPP, unlike the standard neoclassical theory. Terms of trade equilibrium and trade balance equilibrium are distinct concepts, determined by independent factors, so that it is possible to have different reciprocal combinations. Countries with favourable terms of trade benefiting from unequal exchange may have a trade balance deficit, as, for example, the United States, and vice versa, countries with a trade balance surplus may have unfavourable terms of trade and experience value outflows deriving from unequal exchange in international trade, as, for example, China. The real exchange rate adjustment required for trade balance equilibrium may be of a different magnitude from that required for terms of trade equilibrium. Only in the presence of similar levels of labour productivity between countries will the two equilibrium real exchange rates tend to coincide. In the absence of factors preventing adjustment on the money and exchange markets, such as the unique role of the dollar as the international reserve currency, in the long run, the real exchange rate will tend to move in the direction of restoring the equilibrium of the trade balance. By contrast, no automatic trend towards rebalancing the terms of trade exists in real and financial world markets. In this second case, only the narrowing of the gaps in economic development between countries can be effective in reducing unfavourable terms of trade and unequal exchange.

In the presence of different levels of labour productivity, the individual unit values of commodities traded in international markets persist lower in more productive countries and higher in less productive, and meanwhile, all of them express themself into an identical international price, due to the real exchange rate adjustments. It is just this formal mediation of the real exchange rate that reflects the essential modification undergone by the international law of value with respect to the national one. In fact, in the case of differences in productivity between firms within the internal market, domestic competition determines a gradual adjustment of unit values and market prices to the levels of the most productive firms, while in the world market the international unit value and price do not change. In the world market, differences in productivity between countries lead to real exchange rate movements that freeze existing development gaps, instead of producing changes in international unit values and prices.

It should be emphasized that these real exchange rate misalignments resulting from productivity differences between countries are independent of the degree of international mobility of capital and labour. As far as the international mobility of capital is concerned, we have already seen that it tends to accentuate the imbalances on the foreign exchange market because capital flows are directed towards the most productive countries in search of extra-profits. Analogously, labour migration in the same direction will produce an increase in labour supply in the more productive countries with a consequent reduction in real wages and an increase in profits that reinforce their competitive advantage. The only way to eliminate real exchange rate misalignments is through the convergence of labour productivity levels across countries. However, since labour productivity depends on capital accumulation in accordance with the classical conception of technical progress, the capital inflows of the more productive countries act in the sense of increasing international productivity gaps rather than reducing them. In short, a typical mechanism of circular and cumulative causation is operating in the world economy, which tends to accentuate rather than reduce existing disparities in development.

5.3.3 The international value of money and unequal exchange

In the previous paragraph, we have seen that differences in the degree of labour intensity between countries result in non-equivalent national units of the intrinsic measure of the exchange value in terms of labour time, while differences in labour productivity result in non-equivalent national units of the extrinsic measure of the exchange value in terms of international money. In the former case, since the universal labour unit is the average of the national labour units, the different individual national unit values of the commodities contribute to determining the international average unit value. By contrast, in the latter case, the international average unit value does not change and differences in productivity determine a difference in the value of national money reflected in the misalignment of real exchange rates. In other words, a different intensity of labour is reflected in a different amount of international value produced by each national unit of labour, while the value produced by every universal unit of labour, in which the national units convert, is identical between countries. By contrast, a different productivity of labour is reflected in a different amount of international value in circulation realized by each universal unit of labour in different countries, although the international value produced by every national unit of labour is identical regardless of the countries of origin. Differences in labour intensity between countries lead to differences in the value produced by each national unit of labour, and differences in labour productivity lead to differences in the value realized in the world market by each universal unit of labour between countries.

Under these circumstances, discrepancies in labour productivity between countries produce the same effects as that of labour intensity on the international monetary expression of a national unit of labour, because the product of one hour of the more productive national labour has an international price higher than the product of one hour of the less productive. In this sense, Marx says that in the world market, "the more productive national labour reckons also as the more intense", even though it is not. There is, however, a fundamental difference between the two conditions.

In the case of different national labour intensities, the international monetary expression of one unit of universal labour is the same for all countries, because there is an exact correspondence between the higher or lower international value created by one unit of more or less intensive national labour, and the higher or lower international price in which it is expressed. Suppose, for example, that a given country A has twice the world average labour intensity and the same labour productivity as the world average. In this case, one unit of national labour produces twice as many goods in the unit of time than the world average and simultaneously converts into two universal labour units on the world market. The real cost of production measured in terms of universal labour units is exactly equal to the world average. The international value produced by a universal labour unit of country A is therefore exactly equal to the world average, and so will be its international monetary expression of labour time. Country A does not enjoy a competitive advantage in terms of the real cost of production over other countries since the unit value and international unit price of its commodities are in line with the world average. The greater than world average amount of international money, into which the product of one unit of A's national labour is converted, results from the fact that a unit of national labour is equivalent to a multiple of the universal labour unit on the world market. The effect of higher labour intensity is exactly the same as a longer working day: the increase in daily working hours does not lead to a gain in international competitiveness but simply increases the degree of exploitation of the labour force.[46] Consequently, differences in labour intensity between countries do not infringe an equal exchange relation in international trade because the more intensive national labour produces, at the same time, a corresponding higher international social value, just as in domestic trade when the individual intensity of labour differs between firms. The real exchange rate remains, therefore, unaffected since the national unit prices of commodities, and consequently the average national price level, do not depend on the degree of labour intensity.

On the contrary, in the case of different labour productivity, the international monetary expression of one unit of universal labour differs depending on its national origin, because it is higher for the more productive countries and lower for the less productive. In fact, for given labour intensity and working time length, in the world market, one unit of more productive national labour expresses itself in a greater amount of international money than the less productive, although the international social value created is the same and both represent an equivalent unit of universal labour. Suppose, for example, a country B that has a labour intensity equal to the world average and a labour productivity twice the world average. In this case, a national labour unit produces twice as many goods as the world average while being equivalent to one universal labour unit. The real cost of production measured in terms of universal labour units is half the world average, and therefore, the national unit value of the commodity also corresponds to half the international unit value. With perfectly competitive world markets, the real exchange rate of country B will undergo an appreciation that leads the international unit price of the commodity of country B to remain identical to the average international price. The competitive advantage of country B, therefore, results in an improvement in its terms of trade that allows the product of one of its units of national labour, which coincides with one universal labour unit, to be converted into a sum of international money twice the world average. In this case, the effects of a greater productivity are similar to those of a greater intensity of labour, with the difference, however, that now the universal labour unit of country B is converted into a sum of international money twice the average of the units of universal labour of the rest of the world.

Since the individual unit value of the commodities produced by the more productive countries is lower than the international social unit value (and vice versa, higher for the less productive), one unit of national labour is expressed in a sum of international money greater (lesser) than what it is really worth in terms of units of universal labour, that is, in terms of the given quantum of labour in a given quantum of time constituting the unit of international value. In other words, this means that in the world market, one unit of universal labour converts itself in a different sum of international money depending on the productivity of the national labour from which it originates. This difference manifests itself in the form of real overvaluation of the currency of the more productive countries.

As a result, differences in labour productivities make the international trade unequal because the same quantity of average universal labour, exchanged in the form of commodities of an equivalent international value, expresses itself in a variable quantity of international money, without involving a proportional different creation of international value between countries.[47] Since the productivity of labour is higher in more capitalist developed countries than in less developed countries, international trade thus gives rise to transfers of value from poorer to richer countries. In this framework, it is important to note that the unequal exchange does not result from market imperfections or monopolistic practices, being the international unit price equivalent to international unit value or price of production for all countries, but it is the spontaneous outcome of the functioning of the international law of value in perfectly competitive world markets when there is uneven economic development between countries. Furthermore, in addition to free trade and competitive world markets, the international mobility of capital and labour operates as a factor that enhances the structural trend towards the real currency misvaluation at the origin of the unequal exchange in trade.

The value transfers implied by this kind of unequal exchange take the form of a higher international purchasing power of the nominal remuneration of capital and labour in more developed countries than in less developed ones. In other words, ceteris paribus, monetary wages and profits of different countries can buy different quantities of the same bundle of physical goods in the world market depending on the specific national currency in which they are denominated, despite their equivalence in terms of the amount of international social value represented. In the world market, therefore, the wages and profits paid in the currency of more developed countries are worth more in real terms than equivalent wages and profits paid in the currency of the less developed countries.

However, this does not mean that real wages are necessarily higher in developed countries than in less developed ones, because the national price level in the former is also higher than in the latter because of the higher prices of non tradeable goods.[48] What this implies for the purchasing power of wages is that in the domestic market of developed countries, tradeable goods will be relatively cheaper than domestic non tradeable goods, and vice versa, in less developed countries. This is precisely the kind of relationship highlighted by the "Penn effect". The only certain benefit is for the part of the wages of the immigrant labour force in rich countries that is sent to the country of origin in the form of migrant remittances. This aspect, resulting from the overvaluation of the real exchange rate of developed countries, contributes to a large extent to explain the incentives for mass migration, despite the precarious and exploitative conditions to which migrant workers are subjected in capitalistically advanced countries. The benefit of the real overvaluation of the exchange rate is certainly much greater for capital where the uses, unlike wages, are not tied to a specific geographical location but spread over the whole world. For example, an overvalued real exchange rate makes it possible to buy the ownership and use of the natural and productive resources of the less developed countries at a real cost lower than the corresponding value they would have on the national market. Similarly, as we will see later, it also allows multinational capital to take advantage of the intermediate commodity trade and relocation of production processes through the global value chains.

The differences in labour productivities have a direct impact on the international value of money, price level, and exchange rate between countries. The international value of money is the inverse of the average world price level, and it represents the quantity of universal labour expressed by one unit of international money in the world market. For each individual country, it is equivalent to the inverse of the national price level denominated in international currency, derived by multiplying the national price level by the current exchange rate with respect to the international currency unit. Since, as seen previously, in the world market, one unit of universal labour of the more productive countries expresses itself into a sum of international money higher than that of the less productive, then in the former, the international value of money will be lower, and the price levels measured in a common unit of account higher, than in the latter. The reason is that at the international level, unlike the domestic market, labour productivity differentials act on the real exchange rates, leaving unchanged the social unit values of the commodities. Consequently, the exchange rate turns out to be necessarily different from the PPP level, just as shown by the "Penn effect", thus originating a persistent real currency overvaluation in more developed countries and undervaluation in less developed.

In perfectly integrated world commodity markets, wherein the law of one price holds as a result of free trade, the real exchange rate is the adjusting variable assuring that in equilibrium the international market price of a commodity of the same kind will be identical for all countries, notwithstanding the differences in individual unit value and value of money between countries. The resulting deviation of the current exchange rate from the PPP, denoted by an ERDI different from one, reflects the difference between national and world average labour productivity in the determination of the international monetary expression of one unit of universal labour of different countries, and it provides a measure of the transfers of value involved in trade between partners at different levels of economic development.

The "essential modification" of the law of value at the international level deriving from different national labour productivities is an example of Marx's typical dialectical method able to solve the logical contradictions by the entry of a new category, representing the real mediation between two apparently antithetical poles. On the one hand, the national unit values, including the value of money, are lower in more productive than less productive countries. On the other hand, in the world market, free competition leads to equal international prices, expressed in a common currency, for all countries. The real exchange rate, or in Marx's terms the value of money on international market, is the mediation between these two apparently antithetical features of the capitalist world market. The mediation, however, does not represent the final solution leading to a reconciled and harmonious state, but rather it opens to an even more radical contradiction of the world capitalist system, the structural antagonism between developed and underdeveloped countries. In fact, the persistent gap between current and PPP exchange rate is the necessary result of the contradiction, and it represents the visible manifestation of the systematic transfer of value from poorer to richer countries hidden under the apparently equivalent exchange of commodities in the capitalist global market. We can consider this form of unequal exchange as the result of a specific form of rent deriving from the currency monopoly, constituted by the existence of a plurality of national currencies, each with its own specific and unequal international purchasing power according to the level of economic development of the country. As will be shown in Chapter 6, this difference in the value of money between countries plays an important role in the reshaping of the international division of labour in the last two decades of economic globalization, resulting from the increasing spread of global value chains as the specific way of organization of production of multinational enterprises.

That way, we saw how Marx's labour theory of value can provide an explanation of the "Penn effect" without incurring the problems encountered by Ricardian and neoclassical theories, and, at the same time, to reveal the unequal character of free trade in the capitalist global economy. Real currency misalignments are no longer a question related to market imperfections and trade frictions, but rather the result of differences in the level of economic development in the presence of several currencies expressing different national units of value in perfectly competitive international markets, unlike monetary integrated national markets. Any obstacles to free trade, as natural and custom barriers or monopolistic practices, only exacerbate an otherwise structural phenomenon, deriving from the specific functioning of the law of value at the international level.

5.3.4 Trade and unequal development in regional and international capitalist space

The systematic divergence in national price levels between countries at different levels of economic development, resulting from the long-run real currency misalignments described in the literature as "Penn effect", still remains unexplained in the standard theory of long-run equilibrium exchange rate determination. The same applies to non-standard theories too, so that the use of the difference between current and PPP exchange rates as a measure of unequal exchange, common to a widespread heterodox literature on international trade, is lacking in solid theoretical foundations and it just relies on extra-economic assumptions such as monopoly power and market imperfections.

In the previous paragraphs, it was shown that both questions can be answered by a consistent interpretation of Marx's international law of value in the general context of perfect integrated and competitive world markets, where the existence of different national monetary units plays a crucial role. The analysis carried out previously showed that, at the international level, the law of value undergoes essential modifications related to differences in national intensity and productivity of labour in determining the unit of universal labour and its international monetary expression, respectively. This results in real currency misalignments and a different value of money between countries at different levels of economic development described by the "Penn effect".

The key factor that distinguishes the international from the national functioning of the law of value is the existence of different units of national value, each one resulting from the different degree of economic development of the country, which is expressed in different national currencies related to each other by a coherent system of exchange rates. The real exchange rate represents the adjusting variable assuring both conditions, the validity of the law of one price in the world market and simultaneously the persistent divergence of the individual unit value of the same commodity between countries. As a consequence, in the capitalist world economy, the monetary expression of a unit of universal labour is higher for more productive countries than less productive when expressed in a common international currency. Hence, one unit of international money expresses a lower quantity of commodities and a higher price in the domestic markets of the more productive countries, and vice versa, higher quantity and lower price in the less productive.

An important corollary of this argument, expressly stated by Marx, involves the possibility of exploitation of poorer countries by the richer ones by means of transfers of value in international trade. The comparative value of money, indicating the real exchange rate in classical political economy, is indeed directly related to the level of economic development, thereby causing unfavourable terms of trade for the less developed countries and, vice versa, favourable for the more developed. In Marx's theory of international values, therefore, both the "Penn effect" and the existence of unequal exchange can find a solid theoretical foundation that justifies the use of the difference between current and PPP exchange rate as a measure of international transfers of value in trade.

In this regard, it is worth noting the distinctive features of the mechanism of uneven capitalist development operating at regional and international level, respectively. In Marx's theory, the differences in levels of labour productivity between firms, as well as between geographical regions, derive from differences in the organic composition of capital. The greater the amount of means of production used for unit of labour, the greater the number of goods produced by an average labourer in the unit of time. The gain in labour productivity is the principal stimulus to capital investment and technical progress in a capitalist economy because it allows firms to reduce the individual selling price below the market price and, at the same time, increase the unit profits because of even lower unit costs. Consequently, the past capital accumulation represents a crucial factor in explaining the structure of capitalist space, characterized by the contemporary presence of different stages of economic development between regions within a country and between countries in the world economy.

As discussed in Chapter 2, in traditional Marxist theory of unequal exchange, differences in sectoral or geographic organic composition of capital involve non-equivalent exchange in trade, resulting in transfers of value in favour of the more capital-intensive industries or areas through the equalization of profit rates. The direction of capital mobility implied in the formation of prices of production is from sectors with higher organic composition of capital towards sectors with lower organic composition of capital until an equal rate of profit is reached. From a geographical perspective, no matter if it is of a regional or international nature, this type of intersectoral capital mobility determines an inflow of capital to the less developed areas, without narrowing the development gap, since the new capital investments reinforce the pre-existing industrial specialization of production marked by a lower organic composition of capital in backwards territories. In Marxist theories of imperialism, capital flows from more to less developed economies in search of new investment outlets by excess capital of central capitalist countries. The case of unequal exchange deriving from different productivities of labour between geographical areas, discussed in this chapter, entails a direction of capital flows different from that of non-equivalent exchange. Furthermore, in such a case, it is possible to highlight some important differences in the dynamic of reproduction of uneven economic development between regions within a given country, or between countries in the world economy.

If a region has a competitive advantage deriving from a higher productivity of labour, the firms localized in its territory make extra-profits because of an individual unit value of the produced commodities lower than the national social value. The resulting higher monetary return per unit of capital, expressed in terms of the common national currency, will attract new investment from other regions, thus originating an agglomerative process marked by the concentration of industrial activities in the more developed regions and deindustrialization of the other less developed regions. When capital competition has eliminated the extra-profits, and new national social values have been established at the level of the more productive capital-intensive techniques, the national economy will be characterized by a dualistic structure typical of the regional configuration of capitalist countries, with a developed industrial centre, the "town", and an underdeveloped periphery, the "country". The direction of capital mobility from the periphery to the centre, involved in this pattern, sets in motion a circular and cumulative process *à la* Myrdal that reproduces the uneven regional development of a national capitalist space. In fact, it accentuates the dualistic productive specialization marked by more productive capital-intensive industries mainly localized in central regions, while the less productive and more labour-intensive industries remain concentrated in peripherical regions. This pattern of industrial specialization, in turn, tends to enhance the non-equivalent exchange in inter-regional trade between "town" and "country" regions. However, in the presence of perfect competitive domestic markets of goods and productive resources, including labour, the inter-regional trade within a dualistic national economy does not involve unequal exchange in the strict sense, because there are no transfers of value besides those relating to the formation of national prices of production. In this situation, therefore, inter-regional trade is certainly asymmetric since it reiterates the structural development gap between regions, but strictly speaking, it is not unequal.

As we saw previously, in the case of international differences in labour productivity, the real exchange rate tends to be overvalued for the more productive countries and, vice versa, undervalued for the less developed ones. When the real exchange rates and terms of trade are adjusted to reflect the structural differences in labour productivity, a long run stable condition is reached in both, the foreign exchange market and trade and financial flows between countries. This condition, empirically observable in the "Penn effect", is marked by systematic transfers of value from poorer to richer countries, deriving from unequal exchange in international trade. It, however, does not imply a clear and definite pattern of international financial flows, since in a situation of stable, long run real exchange rate disequilibrium, the monetary rates of return on national capital are equal between countries. For less developed countries, indeed, the real undervaluation of the currency involves a real depreciation of the national capital when this latter is converted in foreign currency. Other things being equal, the resulting capital depreciation exactly counterbalances the higher real productivity of the foreign investment in a more developed country with an overvalued currency, thus leaving unchanged the monetary return per unit of capital invested. The same result of an identical monetary return per unit of capital is equally true in the reverse case of capital investment from more developed countries to less developed countries.

What is true for the monetary return is not, however, true in terms of the physical return on capital. In fact, since the relative prices measured in a common currency are lower in less developed countries, a given quantity of money invested by capitals of the more developed countries is, ceteris paribus, remunerated through a greater quantity of physical goods in less developed countries than in the domestic market, even if the two remunerations are identical in monetary terms. This advantage in terms of the physical return on capital can help to explain the phenomenon of intra-firm trade and global value chains,[49] which experienced a big boost in the past two decades of economic globalization on the initiative of multinational corporations.

Intra-firm trade, also called arm's length trade as opposed to trade between unrelated parties, consists of international flows of goods and services occurring within multinational enterprises between parent companies and their affiliates or among affiliates of the same corporation, localized in different countries of the world economy.[50] It represents a part of the wider phenomenon of offshoring, which also includes the relocation of production activities abroad to independent suppliers. In this case, the direct investment of multinational corporations, aimed at delocalizing some parts of the internal chain of production towards underdeveloped countries, can take advantage of the different international purchasing power of currencies. In fact, multinational corporations can transform the higher physical return on capital in higher monetary return through the practice of the intra-firm trade, because the cost of production of the intermediate commodities is reduced by the monetary effect of the real currency misvaluation, in addition to the overexploitation of the peripheral workforce and the practice of transfer pricing to avoid taxation. Under these circumstances, therefore, the direction of capital mobility deriving from international differences in productivity can go from more developed countries towards less developed, and it can involve a process of industrialization of the periphery, mainly concentrated in small territorial enclaves by no means integrated with the rest of the domestic economy. This type of peripheral industrialization, however, remains even more dependent on the conditioning of the centre than in past traditional forms of international division of labour between primary and manufacturing producer countries.

5.4 A general model of unequal exchange

In this section, a model of unequal exchange in international trade will be presented in formal terms on the basis of the theoretical foundations previously discussed. The model involves two successive steps. The first step consists of the determination of the exchange rate in accordance with the international law of value presented in the previous paragraphs. It will show that the deviations of the current equilibrium exchange rate from PPP, described by the "Penn effect", derive from different labour productivities between countries affecting the terms of trade. The second step contains a disaggregated model of the world economy able to account for all the different forms of unequal exchange identified in the literature.

5.4.1 A Marxian model of exchange rate determination

Consider a world economy composed of two countries, A and B, producing and trading an average composite commodity (Q) representing the net product, under the assumptions of free trade and perfect competitive markets. The nominal international prices are expressed in terms of the currency of country B. Since we are considering a composite commodity, consisting of the national net output, the exports and imports of the two countries can be considered in terms of shares of the net product, whose product mix can vary between countries while the total size remains the same, so that the trade balance is in long-term equilibrium. In a long run perfect competitive world market equilibrium, the law of one price holds, and consequently, the international prices of the composite commodity of the two countries are equal, as follows:

$$e\, p_A q_A = p_B q_B \qquad (5.1)$$

where:

e = current exchange rate quoted as number of units of international currency per unit of national currency of A;

p = unit price in national currency;

q = unit of composite good.

For simplicity, let us consider the case of flexible nominal exchange rates, which adjust to ensure a single international price of composite goods, and fixed national prices. In this way, changes in the nominal exchange rate correspond to changes in the real exchange rate. In the opposite case of fixed exchange rates, in which the law of one price is ensured by the flexibility of the national prices, the results do not substantially change. The relative price of the composite commodity corresponds to the net barter terms of trade, defined precisely as the ratio between units of imported and exported goods having equal market value in international prices. Therefore, we have the following relation:

$$\frac{e\, p_A}{p_B} = \frac{q_B}{q_A} \qquad (5.2)$$

The standard neoclassical theory of international trade states that, under free trade and competitive market conditions, the real exchange rate defined by (5.2) should be equal to one, thus resulting in balanced terms of trade and the nominal exchange rate equal to the ratio between national price levels. The equilibrium nominal exchange rate, assuring a real exchange rate equal to one, is defined as the PPP exchange rate (e^p), as follows:

$$e^p = \frac{p_B}{p_A} = e \qquad (5.3)$$

The implicit assumption underlying equation (5.3) is that two price equivalent goods always represent the same identical value in perfectly competitive markets. Since in neoclassical economic theory there is no other dimension of value outside the one expressed by the market price, visible in the sphere of circulation, two exchanged commodities always represent the same value independently from the efficiency of their production. In other words, the individual value of the commodities always and necessarily coincides with their market price. Equation (5.3) represents the tautological conclusion deriving from this initial implicit premise. The problem, however, is that the empirical evidence shows a systematic long-run divergence of the current exchange rate with respect to the PPP exchange rate so that national price levels are directly related to the level of development of countries. As we saw, this is the "Penn effect" to which the standard neoclassical theory fails to provide a cogent explanation without removing the hypothesis of perfect competition. Let us see how it can be explained in Marx's international law of value. In order to distinguish the different effect of labour intensity and productivity on the international law of value, we will examine two cases. The first case assumes identical labour intensity and different labour productivity between the two countries. The second case, vice versa, has identical labour productivity and different labour intensity.

Case (a): Identical labour intensity and different labour productivity.
The production of Q requires a given quantity of national labour (L) in A and B. Since the two national labours have identical intensity, the unit of measurement of each national labour is the same and coincides with the unit of universal labour. As we have seen in Chapter 4, the social algorithm of value determines a relation of equivalence between the socially necessary labour in production or unit value (v), the unit of physical commodity produced, and the monetary expression of the socially necessary labour in circulation or national unit price. Unit value and unit price of the commodity correspond to the expressions of LEV and MEV, respectively, as defined in Chapter 4. We have, therefore, the following equivalences:

$$v_A \sim q_A \sim p_A \tag{5.4}$$

$$v_B \sim q_B \sim p_B \tag{5.5}$$

The international price equivalence of the two composite commodities (q_A and q_B) does not imply that the respective national unit values (v_A and v_B) are also identical, as the neoclassical theory postulates. The equivalence of commodities in the sphere of circulation, which is expressed by the same international market price, does not mean that they are also equivalent in the sphere of national production. On the contrary, they will be different if there are differences in labour productivity between countries. The unit values of the composite good produced in A and B, defined as the units of universal labour necessary to produce one physical unit of the composite good, are the following:

$$v_A = \frac{L_A}{Q_A} \tag{5.6}$$

$$v_B = \frac{L_B}{Q_B} \tag{5.7}$$

Assuming, as before, that the law of one price holds in a perfectly competitive world market, by replacing in (5.1) the physical units with the respective equivalent unit values of the two commodities, from (5.6) and (5.7) we can derive the following expression for the real exchange rate:

$$\frac{e\,p_A}{p_B} = \frac{\dfrac{L_B}{Q_B}}{\dfrac{L_A}{Q_A}} \tag{5.8}$$

Denoting with the symbol φ the real labour productivity, defined as the ratio between the quantity of net product and the universal labour used in its production, we have the following:

$$\frac{e\,p_A}{p_B} = \frac{\varphi_A}{\varphi_B} \tag{5.9}$$

Given the definition of purchasing power parity exchange rate shown in (5.3), we can then rewrite expression (5.9) as follows:

$$e = \frac{\varphi_A}{\varphi_B} e^p \tag{5.10}$$

Or alternatively, by defining with $ERDI_A$ the exchange rate deviation index given by the ratio between current and PPP exchange rate, we have the following:

$$ERDI_A = \frac{\varphi_A}{\varphi_B} \tag{5.11}$$

Equation (5.10) shows that the current exchange rate is systematically different from the PPP rate in accordance with the different labour productivities of the two countries. In fact, the current exchange rate is equal to the PPP exchange rate only in the case of identical labour productivity between the two countries. When, on the other hand, labour productivity is higher (lower) in A than B, the real exchange rate of A will be overvalued (undervalued) compared with that of PPP. As can be seen from (5.6) and (5.7), in the latter case, the individual value of country A is lower (higher) than the corresponding world value. The divergence between current and PPP exchange rate is necessary to ensure that the international prices of the two commodities denominated in a common currency are equal, as is the case with perfectly competitive markets, despite the different individual unit values between countries. In other words, the validity of the law of one price necessarily requires that the equilibrium nominal exchange rate is different from the PPP exchange rate when the labour productivities are different. The exchange rate adjusts to the differences in the individual value of the commodities of the different countries, deviating from the PPP, precisely to maintain the validity of the law of the one price in competitive markets. Let us summarize the causal links that determine this result: 1) for each country, the algorithm of value determines a relationship of equivalence between the national unit price and unit value of commodities; 2) the perfectly competitive world market determines that the price of commodities expressed in a common currency is identical; 3) if labour productivity is different in the two countries, the national unit prices will be equivalent to different quantities of universal labour; and 4) in order to guarantee the same international price of the commodity, the nominal exchange rate must differ from that of PPP. Therefore, far from being an exception or an oddity, on the basis of the international law of value, the "Penn effect" is the product of the ordinary functioning of the world market in a regime of free competition in the presence of different labour productivities between countries.

As a result of the real misalignment of the exchange rate from the PPP, the international monetary expression of a universal labour unit is different between the two countries. Recalling the definition given in Chapter 4, the international monetary expressions of labour time of the two countries, indicated by MELT*, are defined as follows:

$$MELT_A^* = \frac{e\,p_A Q_A}{L_A} = e\,p_A \varphi_A \tag{5.12}$$

$$MELT_B^* = \frac{p_B Q_B}{L_B} = p_B \varphi_B \tag{5.13}$$

From (5.12) and (5.13), we can derive the following expressions:

$$ep_A = \frac{MELT_A^*}{\varphi_A} \tag{5.14}$$

$$p_B = \frac{MELT_B^*}{\varphi_B} \tag{5.15}$$

By substituting (5.14) and (5.15) in (5.1), we can obtain the following:

$$\frac{MELT_A^*}{\varphi_A}\,q_A = \frac{MELT_B^*}{\varphi_B}\,q_B \tag{5.16}$$

Since q_A and q_B both represent one unit of the traded commodity, we can rewrite (5.16) as the following:

$$\frac{MELT_A^*}{MELT_B^*} = \frac{\varphi_A}{\varphi_B} \tag{5.17}$$

By substituting (5.11) in (5.17), therefore, we have the following:

$$\frac{MELT_A^*}{MELT_B^*} = ERDI_A \tag{5.18}$$

From (5.18), we can observe that if ERDI is different from one, there is no correspondence between the expressions of value in international money and labour units. In particular, if country A has a higher labour productivity, which implies an ERDI greater than one, a unit of universal labour will be expressed on the world market with a greater quantity of international money than a unit of universal labour of country B, and vice versa, in the case of a lower productivity of labour in country A. In this context, international trade is characterized by unequal exchange with transfers of value from the less productive country to the more productive country.

Case (b): Different labour intensity and identical labour productivity.
When labour intensities are different between countries, international comparison requires that direct national labour is first converted into a common unit of universal labour with average labour intensity (L_i^u). The conversion establishes that each universal labour unit of the two countries produces the same quantity of goods in the unit of time. To this end, it is necessary to redistribute total world universal labour (L_w) between the two countries on the basis of their respective national shares of physical production over world production. Total labour and total quantity of commodities in the world economy is the sum of labour and production, respectively, of the two countries A and B, as follows:

$$L_w = L_A + L_B \tag{5.19}$$

$$Q_W = Q_A + Q_B \tag{5.20}$$

Therefore, we have the following:

$$L_w = \frac{Q_A}{Q_W} L_w + \frac{Q_B}{Q_W} L_w \tag{5.21}$$

We define the universal labour of countries A and B as the share of total universal labour corresponding to the share of their production in world production, as follows:

$$L_A^u = \frac{Q_A}{Q_W} L_w \tag{5.22}$$

$$L_B^u = \frac{Q_B}{Q_W} L_w \tag{5.23}$$

From (5.22) and (5.23) it follows that:

$$\frac{L_A^u}{Q_A} = \frac{L_B^u}{Q_B} = \frac{L_w}{Q_W} \tag{5.24}$$

Remembering the definition of the unit values given in (5.6) and (5.7), after the conversion of national labour in universal labour, we can see that the international unit values of the two countries are equal to the world average unit value. In that case, the real exchange rate as defined in (5.8) is equal to one, and from (5.10), the current exchange rate coincides with the PPP exchange rate. For example, let us assume that A has a greater intensity of labour than B. The individual national unit value of A measured in the national labour unit is lower than that measured in the universal labour unit. This means that the conversion from national into international value implicitly determines that one hour of national labour exchanges with more than one hour of universal labour in the world market. This difference, however, does not affect the real exchange rate and terms of trade. The reason is that the real exchange rate is the expression of relative individual international values between countries, and not individual national values. Consequently, since national labour of A produces more international value than the average universal labour in the unit of time, the real exchange rate expresses an equal relation between the international values exchanged in trade, even if A obtains more in terms of its national measure of value. We have thus proven that differences in labour intensity do not lead to distortions in nominal and real exchange rates with respect to PPP levels, which can, therefore, only result from differences in labour productivity between countries.

5.4.2 A disaggregated general model of unequal exchange[51]

Consider a world economy with n countries and m non-specific[52] commodities, freely traded in integrated international markets. Subscript letters j, w, and i indicate industry, world, and country, respectively. Each national industry uses direct labour, working with given intensity and means of production, to produce a unit of the good. No prior assumptions are made on capital and labour mobility. Each country has its currency, and international values are expressed in dollars that represent the international currency. At the level of the world economy, total net real output, consisting of the total amount of new goods produced and exchanged in a given period, can be equivalently expressed in terms of units of international money, as the world aggregate value added, and units of necessary universal labour time, as the aggregate world direct labour, in accordance with the fundamental equivalence resulting from the operation of the social algorithm of value as discussed in Chapters 3 and 4.

Universal labour is defined as labour with world industry average productivity.[53] At the world level, this normalization leads to the identity between aggregate direct labour (L_w) and aggregate universal labour (L_w^u):

$$L_w^u \equiv \sum_j L_{wj}^u \equiv \sum_j L_{wj} \equiv L_w \tag{5.25}$$

The ratio between world aggregate value added ($Y_w^\$$) and world aggregate direct labour is defined as the monetary expression of labour time (*MELT*), representing the international monetary value equivalent to one unit of universal labour in the world economy, which coincides with the aggregate world value added per unit of world direct labour:

$$MELT = \frac{Y_w^\$}{L_w} \tag{5.26}$$

Things are different in converting national direct labour into universal labour units. For national industries more efficient than the world industry average, universal labour is a multiple of the national direct labour, and vice versa, universal labour is smaller than national direct labour in the case of lower efficiency. The difference between the two different units of labour, universal labour unit and national direct labour unit, derives from the different degree of both intensity and productivity of labour in different countries. In fact, as discussed in the previous paragraph, at the international level, differences in labour productivity produce the same effects as differences in labour intensity on the conversion of national labour units into the universal unit of labour, although they do not result in different amounts of international value produced in the unit of time by a unit of national labour. This peculiarity of labour productivity on the international law of value is reflected in the divergence between nominal exchange rate and PPP exchange rate, i.e. in an ERDI different from one.

For each national industry, the quantity of universal labour corresponding to the quantity of national direct labour used in production is an aliquot part of world industry direct labour, equivalent to the aliquot part of national industry production on total world industry production.[54] In order to measure the real industry productivity of each country, we use the purchasing power parity exchange rate to convert national nominal industry production into real industry production. Normalizing PPP with the world as 1, national industry universal labour is determined by the following expression:

$$L_{ij}^u = \left(\frac{e_{ij}^p Y_{ij}^{nc}}{Y_{wj}^\$} \right) L_{wj} \tag{5.27}$$

where:

Y_{ij}^{nc} = national value added expressed in national currency;

$Y_{wj}^{\$}$ = world industry value added in dollars;

$$e_{ij}^{p} = e_i^{p} \frac{\sum_i (e_i^{\$} Y_{ij})}{\sum_i (e_i^{p} Y_{ij})} = \text{industry PPP exchange rate}[55];$$

$e_i^{\$}$ = current exchange rate.

The monetary expression of total international value (*TMV*) of a national production, representing the monetary equivalent of the total product of the national industry on the world market, is given by the sum of the *MELT*, multiplied for the units of universal labour used in national production, and constant capital (*C*):

$$TMV_{ij} = \left(MELT + \frac{e_i^{\$} C_{ij}^{nc}}{L_{ij}^{u}} \right) L_{ij}^{u} \tag{5.28}$$

The total international market price of a national production (*TMP*), representing the total monetary value captured by the national industry on the world market, is given by the sum of national value added in dollars and constant capital:

$$TMP_{ij} = \left(\frac{e_i^{\$} Y_{ij}^{nc} + e_i^{\$} C_{ij}^{nc}}{L_{ij}^{u}} \right) L_{ij}^{u} \tag{5.29}$$

Under the usual assumption in sectoral analysis of identical input coefficients for all final uses of product, the difference between total international market price and total international monetary value determines the value transfer (t_{ij}) in exports of a national production:

$$TMP_{ij} - TMV_{ij} = \left[\left(\frac{e_i^{\$} Y_{ij}^{nc}}{L_{ij}^{u}} \right) - MELT \right] \left(\frac{X_{ij}}{Q_{ij}} \right) L_{ij}^{u} = t_{ij} \tag{5.30}$$

where Q_{ij} and X_{ij} indicate the value in dollars of total output and gross exports, respectively.

By substituting (5.27) in (5.30), after some algebraic manipulations, inter-industry transfer (t_{ij}^{B}) can be distinguished from intra-industry transfer (t_{ij}^{W}), both measured per unit of exported universal labour, as follows:

$$t_{ij} = \left(t_{ij}^{B} + t_{ij}^{W} \right) \left(\frac{X_{ij}}{Q_{ij}} \right) L_{ij}^{u} \tag{5.31}$$

where:

$$t_{ij}^B = \left(\frac{Y_{wj}^\$}{L_{wj}}\right) - MELT \tag{5.32}$$

$$t_{ij}^W = \left(ERDI_{ij} - 1\right)\left(\frac{Y_{wj}^\$}{L_{wj}}\right) \tag{5.33}$$

with: $ERDI_{ij} = \dfrac{e_i^\$}{e_{ij}^P}$

Decomposing value added in different categories of revenue (wages and profits, both expressed in international currency), and defining organic composition of capital (OCC) as the ratio between constant capital and universal labour, with the hypothesis of wages paid *ex post*, inter-industry and intra-industry transfer can be rewritten as follows:

$$t_{ij}^B = \left(w_{wj} - w_w\right) + \left(r_{wj}OCC_{wj} - r_w OCC_w\right) \tag{5.34}$$

$$t_{ij}^W = \left(e_i^\$ w_{ij} - w_{wj}\right) + \left(r_{ij} - r_{wj}\right)OCC_{wj} \tag{5.35}$$

where:
r = rate of profit;
w = wage per unit of universal labour.

In expression (5.34), value transfers deriving from differences in inter-industry profit rates and capital intensities are merged together. In order to separate these two different components of unequal exchange, we need to add and subtract $r_w OCC_{wj}$ to obtain the following expression:

$$t_{ij}^B = \left(w_{wj} - w_w\right) + \left(r_{wj} - r_w\right)OCC_{wj} + r_w\left(OCC_{wj} - OCC_w\right) \tag{5.36}$$

Finally, net national transfer in industry j results from the difference between exports and imports of commodity j, as shown in the following expression[56]:

$$T_{ij} = \left(t_{ij}^B + t_{ij}^W\right)\left(\frac{X_{ij}}{Q_{ij}}\right)L_{ij}^u - \sum_{n \neq i}\left(t_{nj}^B + t_{nj}^W\right)\left(\frac{M_{inj}}{Q_{nj}}\right)L_{nj}^u \tag{5.37}$$

where:
T_{ij} = transfers of value of national industry;
M_{inj} = value of imports of country i from country n in current dollars.

174

From equations (5.32), it can be seen that inter-industry transfer of value does not depend on specifically national factors, but on the deviation of world industry value added per unit of universal labour from the world aggregate average constituting the *MELT*, and it therefore results from the particular productive structure of the domestic economy. This difference can result from a plurality of causes. Specifically, it depends on three factors shown in Equation (5.36): (a) a difference in monetary wages per unit of universal labour between world industries, corresponding to Lewis's type of unequal exchange; (b) a difference in profit rates between world industries, corresponding to the Prebisch–Singer thesis on unequal exchange; and (c) equalization of profit rates between world industries with different organic compositions of capital, corresponding to broad unequal exchange of classical Marxist theory. The first two sources, arising from different remunerations of labour and capital between world industries, derive from barriers to the inter-industry mobility of factors of production within each country, and not from their international mobility between different countries. In fact, assuming perfect mobility of labour and capital between different branches of production within each national economy and competitive international trade, inter-industry transfers of value at the international level would be cancelled even in the presence of an imperfect international mobility of factors of production. Therefore, given that inter-industry transfers of value do not depend on specific features of the world market but on limitations of competition within individual national economies, it is inappropriate to consider them as an expression of unequal exchange in the strict sense at the international level. Rather, they should be classified in the category of unequal exchange in the broad sense, or asymmetric trade, together with value transfers resulting from differences in the organic composition of capital. All these three forms of broad unequal exchange are the simple reflection at the international level of the functioning of the national law of value.

On the other hand, unequal exchange in the strict sense, deriving exclusively from the essential modifications undertaken by the law of value at the international level, is represented by value transfers between countries within the same industry, as defined in equations (5.33) and (5.35). The latter shows that intra-industry value transfers depend on two factors: (a) a difference between national industry monetary wages per unit of universal labour and world industry monetary wages; and (b) a difference between national and world industry rates of profit. These two factors correspond to the types of unequal exchange described in the literature by Emmanuel, adjusted for differences in labour productivity, and the theory of monopoly capital, respectively. However, unlike these two approaches, in the model illustrated in this chapter, the unequal exchange in the strict sense does not depend on the presence of monopolistic barriers to competition in the input market but is the ordinary consequence of the functioning of the international law of value with perfectly competitive markets. As we have seen in the previous paragraphs, the international transfers of value within the same industry originates from the development gap between countries, which are reflected on national units of labour and the relative value of national currencies.

Table 5.1 The law of value and unequal exchange

Cause	Difference in	Type
National law of value: Industrial structure of national economy	Intersectoral wages Intersectoral profit rates Organic composition of capital	Unequal exchange in a broad sense or inter-industry unequal exchange
International law of value: National unit of value and value of money	International wages International profit rates	Unequal exchange in a strict sense or international unequal exchange

The divergence of the current exchange rate from the PPP exchange rate, denoted by an ERDI other than one, is, therefore, an indicator of the presence of unequal exchange in the strict sense, and it results from the essential modification of the law of value at the international level deriving from different labour productivity between countries.

Table 5.1 summarizes the forms of unequal exchange derived from the model, which includes all the various forms identified in the previous literature.

Notes

1 The Penn World Table dataset is available at the website of the Groningen Growth and Development Centre, see www.rug.nl/ggdc/productivity/pwt/. It was originally developed by Summers and Heston (1988).
2 On the relation between PPP and real exchange rates, see Taylor (2006).
3 On the correlation between the ERDI and real per capita income, see Yotopoulos (1996).
4 There is a vast literature on this argument, as evidenced by the following contributions: Sau (1993), Kolher and Tausch (2002), Boles (2002), Somel (2003), Chaves (2006), Bond (2006), Elmas (2009), Kohler (2015), Reich (2000, 2007, 2014), Smith (2012), Cope (2012, 2019), and Kellogg (2019).
5 See Raffer (1987, 2006), Thirlwall (1994), and Subasat (2013).
6 In classical political economy, the comparative value of national money stands for the real exchange rate, see Wu (2013).
7 This phenomenon was already noticed by Harrod (1933), Gilbert and Kravis (1954), and Balassa (1961). On the ICP, see Kravis (1986).
8 See Officer (1989).
9 The empirical validity of the "Penn effect" has been extensively proved by several authors. See, among others, Kravis, Heston, and Summers (1978, 1982), Kravis and Lipsey (1982, 1987), Rogoff (1996), Bergin Glick and Taylor (2006), Gala (2008), Deaton and Heston (2010), Ravallion (2010), Fujii (2015), and Cheung, Chinn, and Nong (2017).
10 See Froot and Rogoff (1995).
11 On the significance of long run equilibrium exchange rate in standard trade theory, see Humphrey (1979) and Devarajan, Lewis, and Robinson (1993).
12 For a critical analysis of these aspects of neoclassical trade theory, see Shaikh (1996).
13 On the extended or enhanced PPP theory, see Dunaway, Leigh, and Li (2009) and Cline and Williamson (2008), respectively.

14 See Balassa (1964) and Samuelson (1964, 1994).

15 See Strauss (1997).

16 On neoclassical versions of BSH, see Bhagwati (1984), Asea and Corden (1994), and Cravino and Haltenhof (2020).

17 See Neary (1988) and Bergstrand (1991).

18 See Froot and Rogoff (1991), De Gregorio, Giovannini, and Wolf (1994), and Chinn (1999).

19 See Balvers and Bergstrand (2002).

20 See Canzoneri et al. (1999), Betts and Kehoe (2006), and Zhang (2017).

21 See Lothian and Taylor (2008), Chong et al. (2012), and Bordo et al. (2017).

22 See Asea and Mendoza (1994), Engel (1999, 2000), and Eleftheriou and Müller-Plantenberg (2018).

23 See Lee (2005), Schmillen (2013), and Cardi and Restout (2015).

24 See Shaikh and Antonopoulos (1998), Antonopoulos (1999), Ruiz-Napoles (2004), and Martínez-Hernández (2017).

25 This approach has been used to analyse the trade imbalances between Germany and Greece by Tsaliki, Paraskevopoulou, and Tsoulfidis (2017), and the US and China by Weber and Shaikh (2020).

26 See Matsui (1971).

27 This hypothesis was previously advanced by the Marxist "Berliner Schule" of the early 1970s, on which, see Carchedi (1988) for a critical examination.

28 See Marx's letter to Lassalle on February 22, 1858 (Marx, *MECW*, vol. 40, p. 270) and the *Preface* to *A Contribution to the Critique of Political Economy* (Marx, *MECW*, vol. 29, p. 261). On Marx original outline of *Capital*, see Rosdolsky (1977, chap. 2).

29 On Marx's writings on the world market, see Bryan (1995), Pradella (2015).

30 This chapter has not received a great deal of attention in recent Marxist literature because at first glance it may seem "obvious enough" (Rockmore, 2002, p. 150) and not further developed towards a thorough examination of the Ricardian law of comparative advantage in foreign trade (Harvey, 2010, p. 243). It was not so in the 1970s, when its proper interpretation was an important theme in the debate on unequal exchange in international trade, in particular, among East German Marxist economists, see Siegel (1984) and Mandel (1975).

31 In addition to these factors, national historical and social peculiarities of each country also play a role in the definition of wage levels, among which Marx specifically mentions "the extent of the prime necessaries of life as naturally and historically developed, the cost of training the labourers, the part played by the labour of women and children" (Marx, *MK1*, chap. 22, p. 396).

32 On the concepts of magnitude and measure in Marx's theory, see Hanzel (2015).

33 On the process of normalization, synchronization, and homogenization of value in Marx's *Capital*, see Saad-Filho (2002, chap. 5).

34 On the different concepts of labour time in Marx, see also Tombazos (2014) and Martineau (2015, chap. 3), both influenced by Postone's work.

35 In this sense, Marx (Marx, *MECW*, vol. 34, p. 347), in the fragments of the third rough draft of Book I of *Capital*, subsequently published in *Economic Manuscripts of 1861–63*, thus wrote: "When one considers a number of countries, one finds that... intensity matters as much as does the length of the working day. The more intensive working day in a given country = the less intensive + x... (It) will stand higher not only from the point of view of use value, but also from that of exchange value, and therefore in its monetary expression as well".

36 This is, for example, the case of Siegel (1984, p. 145), who claims that in chapter XXII, "Marx does indeed create a lot of confusion".

37 The comparison between the different versions of the first volume of *Capital*, edited by Marx itself, can be found in the Italian critical edition, see Marx, *MEOC*.

38 On the relation between intensity and productivity of labour in Marx's theory, see Mavroudeas and Ioannides (2011). For a reconstruction of the link between the degree of labour intensity and the magnitude of value in Marx's *Capital*, see Reuten (2004).

39 On Marx's view on technological progress, see Kurz (1998) and Roth (2010).

40 On the relation between the command of capital over labour within the production process, technological progress and the increase of the organic composition of capital in Marx's thought, see the considerations made in the 1960s by the Italian Marxist Raniero Panzieri (1980).

41 On the relation between intensity of labour and rate of exploitation in Marx's analysis, see Joosung (1999).

42 This holds true at the international level too, and it is the reason Marx states that the rate of surplus labour is lower and the wage share on total income higher in less developed countries than more developed countries.

43 On this point, see Harvey (1983).

44 This is what Sandleben (2016) claims, in attributing the persistence of international differences in labour productivity to specific natural conditions of production that distinguish a country from the rest of the world, such as the greater availability of low-cost energy sources. In addition to not complying with the theoretical and methodological context of the first book of *Capital*, this explanation is also contradicted by reality, since in the history of capitalism the countries producing raw materials are usually backwards in terms of labour productivity and economic development.

45 On this point, see Feng (2018).

46 Empirical confirmation of this is given by the inverse relationship existing between working hours and level of development both historically and geographically. Over the course of the 20th century, annual working hours in capitalist countries fell steadily as income levels increased. Similarly, in today's world, average weekly working hours are much higher in backwards countries than in more developed countries. On this point, recent empirical evidence is provided by Messenger (2018).

47 For this reason, there is unequal exchange in international trade even in the presence of double factorial terms of trade equal to one, contrary to Samir Amin's thesis presented in the second chapter.

48 "It follows, then, that the nominal wages, the equivalent of labour-power expressed in money, will also be higher in the first (more developed, *ndr*) nation than in the second (less developed, *ndr*); which does not at all prove that this holds also for the real wages, i.e., for the means of subsistence placed at the disposal of the labourer" (Marx, *MKI*, chap. 22, p. 396).

49 On the relevance of intra-firm trade within the global value chains, see Lanz and Miroudot (2011), who estimates the size of this phenomenon in about one-third of the total imports and exports for the OECD countries.

50 See OECD (2005).

51 The model presented here is a modified version of that presented in Ricci (2016, 2019).

52 Non-specific commodities indicate that, contrary to the hypotheses of the classical theory of international trade, there is no complete productive specialization of a country. As commonly happens in the reality of modern economies, each country imports and exports commodities of the same kind, and therefore, there is intra-industry trade.

53 In Marxist disaggregated models, the problem of determining homogeneous labour at the level of individual industries arises (Rieu, 2009; Meng, 2015). In the macro framework of the *New Interpretation*, for example, homogeneous labour is defined as labour with average aggregate productivity, and the issue of sectoral homogeneous labour is addressed in terms of redistributing homogeneous labour among various industries (Rieu, Lee, and Ahn, 2014). In a disaggregated framework, however, the appropriate

procedure should be from industries to the whole economy, and not the reverse. In fact, for each individual commodity, homogeneous labour is determined by the average technical conditions of production, which can be defined only on an industry level because of the heterogeneity of the production processes.

54 On the "aliquot part" reasoning in Marx's LTV see Roberts (2004, 2005).

55 We have to apply e_{ij}^p and not simply e_i^p because the PPP exchange rate is different for each branch. This transformation assures the equivalence between world value added measured in current dollars and in PPP international dollars.

56 Ricci (2019) presents an empirical estimation of this disaggregated model of unequal exchange by using data from WIOD tables for 40 countries of the world economy. Baiman (2020) applies a similar methodology to domestic intra-industry transfers of value by analysing the case of Facebook and the US advertising and market research sector.

Bibliography

Angell, J. W. (1922). International trade under inconvertible paper. *The Quarterly Journal of Economics, 36*(3), 359–412.

Antonopoulos, R. (1999). A classical approach to real exchange rate determination with an application for the case of Greece. *Review of Radical Political Economics, 31*(3), 53–65.

Asea, P. K. and Corden, W. M. (1994). The Balassa-Samuelson model: An overview. *Review of International Economics, 2*(3), 191–200.

Asea, P. K. and Mendoza, E. G. (1994). The Balassa-Samuelson model: A general-equilibrium appraisal. *Review of International Economics, 2*(3), 244–267.

Baiman, R. (2020). The impact of rent from unequal exchange on Shaikh's classical-Keynesian political economic analysis: The example of Facebook. *Review of Radical Political Economics, 52*(2), 239–258.

Balassa, B. (1961). Patterns of industrial growth: Comment. *The American Economic Review, 51*(3), 394–397.

Balassa, B. (1964). The purchasing-power parity doctrine: Reappraisal. *Journal of Political Economy, 72*(6), 584–596.

Balvers, R. J. and Bergstrand, J. H. (2002). Government expenditure and equilibrium real exchange rates. *Journal of International Money and Finance, 21*(5), 667–692.

Basso, L. C. (2002). An alternative theory for exchange rate determination. *Revista Mexicana de Economía y Finanzas, 1*(2), 143–151.

Bergin, P. R., Glick, R. and Taylor, A. M. (2006). Productivity, tradability, and the long-run price puzzle. *Journal of Monetary Economics, 53*(8), 2041–2066.

Bergstrand, J. H. (1991). Structural determinants of real exchange rates and national price levels: Some empirical evidence. *The American Economic Review, 81*(1), 325–334.

Betts, C. M. and Kehoe, T. J. (2006). US real exchange rate fluctuations and relative price fluctuations. *Journal of Monetary Economics, 53*(7), 1297–1326.

Bhagwati, J. N. (1984). Why are services cheaper in the poor countries?. *The Economic Journal, 94*(374), 279–286.

Boles, E. E. (2002). Critiques of world-systems analysis and alternatives: Unequal exchange and three forms of class and struggle in the Japan US silk network, 1880–1890. *Journal of World-Systems Research, 8*(2), 150–212.

Bond, P. (2006). *Looting Africa: The economics of exploitation.* London: Zed books.

Bordo, M. D., Choudhri, E. U., Fazio, G. and MacDonald, R. (2017). The real exchange rate in the long run: Balassa-Samuelson effects reconsidered. *Journal of International Money and Finance*, *75*, 69–92.

Braverman, H. (1974). *Labor and monopoly capital: The degradation of work in the twentieth century*. New York: New York University Press.

Bryan, D. (1995). The internationalisation of capital and Marxian value theory. *Cambridge Journal of Economics*, *19*, 421–421.

Canzoneri, M. B., Cumby, R. E. and Diba, B. (1999). Relative labor productivity and the real exchange rate in the long run: Evidence for a panel of OECD countries. *Journal of International Economics*, *47*(2), 245–266.

Carchedi, G. (1988). Marxian price theory and modern capitalism. *International Journal of Political Economy*, *18*(3), 1–112.

Carchedi, G. (1991). Technological innovation, international production prices and exchange rates. *Cambridge Journal of Economics*, *15*(1), 45–60.

Cardi, O. and Restout, R. (2015). Imperfect mobility of labor across sectors: A reappraisal of the Balassa–Samuelson effect. *Journal of International Economics*, *97*(2), 249–265.

Cassel, G. (1916). The present situation of the foreign exchanges. *The Economic Journal*, *26*(101), 62–65.

Chaves, E. (2006). Intercambio desigual y tasa de cambio:¿ saqueo o explotación, *Entelequia: revista interdisciplinar*, *2*, 175–195.

Cheung, Y. W., Chinn, M. and Nong, X. (2017). Estimating currency misalignment using the Penn effect: It is not as simple as it looks. *International Finance*, *20*(3), 222–242.

Chinn, M. D. (1999). Productivity, government spending and the real exchange rate: Evidence for OECD Countries. In *Equilibrium exchange rates*. Eds. R. MacDonald and J. L. Stein. Berlin: Springer, 163–190.

Chong, Y., Jordà, Ò. and Taylor, A. M. (2012). The Harrod–Balassa–Samuelson hypothesis: Real exchange rates and their long-run equilibrium. *International Economic Review*, *53*(2), 609–634.

Cline, W. R. and Williamson, J. (2008). Estimates of the equilibrium exchange rate of the renminbi: Is there a consensus and, if not, why not?. In *Debating China's exchange rate policy*. Ed. M. Goldstein. Washington, DC: Peterson Institute, 131–154.

Cope, Z. (2012). *Divided world, divided class: Global political economy and the stratification of labour under capitalism*. Montreal: Kersplebedeb.

Cope, Z. (2019). *The wealth of (some) nations. Imperialism and the Mechanics of Value Transfer*. London: Pluto Press.

Cravino, J. and Haltenhof, S. (2020). Real exchange rates, income per capita, and sectoral input shares. *Review of Economics and Statistics*, *102*(1), 180–194.

De Gregorio, J., Giovannini, A. and Wolf, H. C. (1994). International evidence on tradables and nontradables inflation, *European Economic Review*, *38*(6), 1225–1244.

Deaton, A. and Heston, A. (2010). Understanding PPPs and PPP-based national accounts. *American Economic Journal: Macroeconomics*, *2*(4), 1–35.

Devarajan, S., Lewis, J. D. and Robinson, S. (1993). External shocks, purchasing power parity, and the equilibrium real exchange rate. *The World Bank Economic Review*, *7*(1), 45–63.

Dunaway, S., Leigh, L. and Li, X. (2009). How robust are estimates of equilibrium real exchange rates: The case of China. *Pacific Economic Review*, *14*(3), 361–375.

Eleftheriou, M. and Müller-Plantenberg, N. A. (2018). The purchasing power parity fallacy: Time to reconsider the PPP hypothesis. *Open Economies Review*, *29*(3), 481–515.

Elmas, F. (2009). World-systems analysis and unequal exchange: The Turkish economy during the trade and financial liberalization process. *International Journal of Economic Perspectives*, *3*(3), 159–165.

Emmanuel, A. (1972). *Unequal exchange: A study of the imperialism of trade*. New York: Monthly Review Press.

Engel, C. (1999). Accounting for US real exchange rate changes. *Journal of Political Economy*, *107*(3), 507–538.

Engel, C. (2000). Long-run PPP may not hold after all. *Journal of International Economics*, *51*(2), 243–273.

Feng, Z. (2018). International value, international production price and unequal exchange. In *Economic growth and transition of industrial structure in East Asia*. Eds: T. Kinugasa, L. Yu, Q. Chen, Z. Feng. Berlin: Springer, 73–96.

Froot, K. A. and Rogoff, K. (1991). The EMS, the EMU, and the transition to a common currency. *NBER Macroeconomics Annual*, *6*, 269–317.

Froot, K. A. and Rogoff, K. (1995). Perspectives on PPP and long-run real exchange rates. In *Handbook of international economics*, Vol. 3. Eds. G. M. Grossman and K. Rogoff. Amsterdam: North Holland, 1647–1688.

Fujii, E. (2015). Reconsidering the price–income relationship across countries. *Pacific Economic Review*, *20*(5), 733–760.

Gala, P. (2008). Real exchange rate levels and economic development: Theoretical analysis and econometric evidence. *Cambridge Journal of Economics*, *32*(2), 273–288.

Gilbert, M. and Kravis, I. B. (1954). *An international comparison of national products and purchasing power of currencies: A study of the United States, the United Kingdom, France, Germany, and Italy*. Paris: Organization for European Economic Cooperation.

Hanzel, I. (2015). Marx''s methods of theory construction: Categories, magnitudes, and variations of sizes of magnitudes under certain idealizations. *International Critical Thought*, *5*(4), 413–438.

Harrod, R. F. (1933). *International economics*. Chicago: Chicago University Press.

Harvey, D. (2010). *A companion to Marx''s capital*. London: Verso Books.

Harvey, P. (1983). Marx''s theory of the value of labor power: An assessment. *Social Research*, *50*(2), 305–344.

Humphrey, T. M. (1979). The purchasing power parity doctrine. *FRB Richmond Economic Review*, *65*(3), 3–13.

Joosung, R. (1999). Labour intensity and surplus value in Karl Marx-A Note. *History of Economic Ideas*, *7*(3), 181–191.

Kellogg, P. (2019). Alternatives. Finding the axis of solidarity: Populist protectionism and the end of the North American Free Trade Agreement. *Studies in Political Economy*, *100*(1), 65–81.

Kohler, G. (2015). The structure of global money and world tables of unequal exchange. *Journal of World-Systems Research*, *4*(2), 145–168.

Köhler, G. and Tausch, A. (2002). *Global Keynesianism: Unequal exchange and global exploitation*. New York: Nova Science.

Kravis, I. B. (1986). The three faces of the international comparison project. *The World Bank Research Observer*, *1*(1), 3–26.

Kravis, I. B., Heston, A. and Summers, R. (1978). Real GDP per capita for more than one hundred countries. *The Economic Journal*, *88*(350), 215–242.

Kravis, I. B., Heston, A. and Summers, R. (1982). *World product and income: International comparisons of real gross product*. Washington: The World Bank.

Kravis, I. B. and Lipsey, R. E. (1982). Towards an explanation of national price levels. *NBER Working Paper*, 1034.

Kravis, I. B. and Lipsey, R. E. (1987). The assessment of national price levels. In *Real-Financial linkages among open economies*. Eds. S. W. Arndt and J. D. Richardson. Cambridge (MA): MIT Press, 97–134.

Kurz, H. D. (1998). Marx on technological change: The Ricardian heritage. In *Marxian economics: A reappraisal*, Vol. 2. Ed. R. Bellofiore. London: Palgrave Macmillan, 119–138.

Lanz, R. and Miroudot, S. (2011). Intra-Firm trade: Patterns, determinants and policy implications. OECD Trade Policy Papers, *114*.

Lee, J. J. (2005). Persistent wage differential and its implications on the Balassa–Samuelson hypothesis. *Applied Economics Letters*, *12*(10), 643–648.

Linder, S. B. (1961). *An essay on trade and transformation*. Stockholm: Almqvist and Wiksell.

Lothian, J. R. and Taylor, M. P. (2008). Real exchange rates over the past two centuries: How important is the Harrod-Balassa-Samuelson effect?. *The Economic Journal*, *118*(53), 1742–1763.

Mandel, E. (1975). *Late capitalism*. London: New Left Books.

Martineau, J. (2015). *Time, capitalism and alienation: A socio-historical inquiry into the making of modern time*. Leiden: Brill.

Martínez-Hernández, F. A. (2017). The political economy of real exchange rate behavior: Theory and empirical evidence for developed and developing countries, 1960–2010. *Review of Political Economy*, *29*(4), 566–596.

Matsui, K. (1971). The Marxian theory of international value. *The Kyoto University Economic Review*, *40*(2), 1–17.

Mavroudeas, S. and Ioannides, A. (2011). Duration, intensity and productivity of labour and the distinction between absolute and relative surplus-value. *Review of Political Economy*, *23*(3), 421–437.

Meng, J. (2015). Two kinds of MELT and their determinations: Critical notes on Moseley and the New Interpretation. *Review of Radical Political Economics*, *47*(2), 309–316.

Messenger, J. (2018). *Working time and the future of work*. Genève: International Labour Organization.

Neary, P. (1988). Determinants of the equilibrium real exchange rate. *The American Economic Review*, *78*(1), 210–215.

OECD. (2005), *Measuring globalisation: OECD handbook on economic globalisation indicators*. Paris: OECD.

Officer, L. H. (1989). The national price level: Theory and estimation. *Journal of Macroeconomics*, *11*(3), 351–373.

Panzieri, R. (1980). The Capitalist Use of Machinery: Marx Versus the 'Objectivists'. In *Outlines of a Critique of Technology*. Ed: P. Slater. London: Ink Links, 44-68.

Pasinetti, L. L. (1973). The notion of vertical integration in economic analysis. *Metroeconomica*, *25*(1), 1–29.

Postone, M. (1993). *Time, labor, and social domination: A reinterpretation of Marx''s critical theory*. Cambridge: Cambridge University Press.

Pradella, L. (2015). *Globalization and the critique of political economy: New insights from Marx's writings*. London: Routledge.

Raffer, K. (1987). *Unequal Exchange and the evolution of the World System: Reconsidering the impact of trade on North-South relations*. London: Macmillan.

Raffer, K. (2006). Differences between inequalities and unequal exchange: Comments on the papers by Chaves and Köhler. *Entelequia: revista interdisciplinar, 2*, 197–200.

Ravallion, M. (2010). Understanding PPPs and PPP-based national accounts: Comment. *American Economic Journal: Macroeconomics, 2*(4), 46–52.

Reich, U. P. (2000). Inequality of value in international trade: An input-output approach. *Szigma, 31*(3–4), 107–119.

Reich, U. P. (2007). Inequality in exchange: The use of a World Trade Flow Table for analyzing the international economy. *Economic Systems Research, 19*(4), 375–395.

Reich, U. P. (2014). *Inequality in global production and trade: A proposal for measurement.* IARIW 33rd General Conference, Rotterdam, The Netherlands.

Reuten, G. (2004). Productive force and the degree of intensity of labour: Marx's concepts and formalizations in the middle part of Capital I. In *The constitution of capital: Essays on volume I of Marx's 'Capital'.* Eds. R. Bellofiore and N. Taylor. London: Palgrave-Macmillan, 117–145.

Ricardo, D. (2004). *The Works and Correspondence of David Ricardo. Vol. 1: On the Principles of Political Economy and Taxation.* Ed. Piero Sraffa. Indianapolis: Liberty Fund.

Ricci, A. (2016). *Unequal exchange in international trade: A general model.* Working Papers Series in Economics, Mathematics and Statistics, 16/05, Urbino: University of Urbino.

Ricci, A. (2019). Unequal exchange in the age of globalization. *Review of Radical Political Economics, 51*(2), 225–245.

Rieu, D. M. (2009). The 'New Interpretation': Questions answered and unanswered. *Metroeconomica, 60*(3), 568–570.

Rieu, D. M., Lee, K. and Ahn, H. H. (2014). The determination of the monetary expression of concrete labor time under the inconvertible credit money system. *Review of Radical Political Economics, 46*(2), 190–198.

Roberts, B. (2004). Value, abstract labor, and exchange equivalence. In *The New Value Controversy and the Foundations of Economics.* Eds: A. Freeman, A. Kliman, and J. Wells Cheltenham, UK: Edward Elgar Publishing, 107–134.

Roberts, B. (2005). Quantifying abstract labor: "Aliquot part" reasoning in Marx's value theory. *Research in Political Economy, 22*, 137–170.

Rockmore, T. (2002). *Marx after Marxism.* Oxford: Blackwell.

Rogoff, K. (1996). The purchasing power parity puzzle. *Journal of Economic Literature, 34*(2), 647–668.

Rosdolsky, R. (1977). *The making of Marx's "Capital".* London: Pluto Press.

Roth, R. (2010). Marx on technical change in the critical edition. *The European Journal of the History of Economic Thought, 17*(5), 1223–1251.

Ruiz-Nápoles, P. (2004). The Purchasing Power Parity theory and Ricardo's theory of value. *Contributions to Political economy, 23*(1), 65–80.

Saad Filho, A. (2002). *The value of Marx: Political economy for contemporary capitalism.* London: Routledge.

Samuelson, P. A. (1964). Theoretical notes on trade problems. *The Review of Economics and Statistics, 23*, 145–154.

Samuelson, P. A. (1994). Facets of Balassa-Samuelson thirty years later. *Review of International Economics, 2*(3), 201–226.

Sandleben, G. (2016). Unequal exchange? Marx' solution to the value problem on the world market. *Theoretical Economics Letters, 6*(4), 621.

Sau, R. (1993). Purchasing Power Parity, unequal exchange and foreign direct investment. *Economic and Political Weekly*, *28*(37), 1927–1930.

Schmillen, A. (2013). Are wages equal across sectors of production? A panel data analysis for tradable and non-tradable goods. *Economics of Transition*, *21*(4), 655–682.

Shaikh, A. (1996). Free trade, unemployment and economic policy. In *Global Unemployment: Loss of Jobs in the 90s*. Ed. J. Eatwell. Armonk, NY: ME Sharpe, 59–78.

Shaikh, A. and Antonopoulos, R. (1998). Explaining long-term exchange rate behavior in the United States and Japan. In *Alternative theories of competition: Challenges to the orthodoxy*. J. K, Moudud, C. Bina and P. L. Mason. London: Routledge, 201–228.

Siegel, T. (1984). Politics and economics in the capitalist world market: Methodological problems of Marxist analysis. *International Journal of Sociology*, *14*(1), 1–154.

Smith, J. (2012). The GDP illusion. *Monthly Review*, *64*(3), 86–102.

Somel, C. (2003). Estimating the surplus in the periphery: An application to Turkey. *Cambridge Journal of Economics*, *27*(6), 919–933.

Strauss, J. (1997). The influence of traded and nontraded wages on relative prices and real exchange rates. *Economics Letters*, *55*(3), 391–395.

Subasat, T. (2013). Can differences in international prices measure unequal exchange in international trade? *Competition and Change*, *17*(4), 372–379.

Summers, R. and Heston, A. (1988). A new set of international comparisons of real product and price levels estimates for 130 countries, 1950–1985. *Review of Income and Wealth*, *34*(1), 1–25.

Taylor, M. (2006). Real exchange rates and purchasing power parity: Mean-reversion in economic thought. *Applied Financial Economics*, *16*(1–2), 1–17.

Thirlwall, A. P. (1994). *Growth and development: With special reference to developing economies*, London: Macmillan.

Tombazos, S. (2014). *Time in Marx: The categories of time in Marx's Capital*. Leiden: Brill.

Tsaliki, P., Paraskevopoulou, C. and Tsoulfidis, L. (2017). Unequal exchange and absolute cost advantage: Evidence from the trade between Greece and Germany. *Cambridge Journal of Economics*, *42*(4), 1043–1086.

Weber, I. and Shaikh, A. (2020). The US–China trade imbalance and the theory of free trade: Debunking the currency manipulation argument. *International Review of Applied Economics*, DOI: 10.1080/02692171.2020.1814221, 1–24.

Wu, C. Y. (2013). *An outline of international price theories*. London: Routledge.

Yotopoulos, P. A. (1996). *Exchange rate parity for trade and development: Theory, tests, and case studies*. Cambridge: Cambridge University Press.

Zhang, Q. (2017). The Balassa–Samuelson relationship: Services, manufacturing and product quality. *Journal of International Economics*, *106*, 55–82.

6

THE GEOGRAPHY OF GLOBAL EXPLOITATION

Measuring unequal exchange over the last 30 years

Andrea Ricci

6.1 Global value chains and the new international division of labour

In the 1970s and 1980s, during the debate on unequal exchange following the publication of Arghiri Emmanuel's important and provocative book, a great deal of research was devoted to estimating the dimension of value transfers in international and interregional trade.[1] The theoretical framework underlying most of this research was the traditional interpretation of Marx's value theory, based on a Ricardian approach that immediately identified value with the labour embodied in production and considered the monetary aspects of circulation of commodities as mere superficial reflections. Given their theoretical basis, these empirical investigations on unequal exchange proved inadequate to counter the criticism and objections arising from the debate on the transformation problem that in the same years led traditional Marxist theory to an irreversible crisis. Moreover, they lacked a proper elaboration of the peculiar characteristics undertaken by the law of value at the world level, concerning, in particular, the definition of a universal unit of labour between different countries and its relationship with the value of money. Consequently, the quantitative determination of international value transfers often resulted from an arbitrary comparison of heterogeneous national values. In more recent years, new estimates of unequal exchange have been produced on the basis of the difference between the value of international trade measured in terms of the current exchange rate and purchasing power parity (PPP). The main limitation of this line of research was identified in the absence of an adequate theoretical explanation that could justify the proposed method of calculation of value transfers in trade. The theoretical reconstruction of the international law of value made in the previous chapters now provides a solid conceptual foundation to this methodology.

The empirical analysis of unequal exchange that will be presented in this chapter also has other important features that allow us to investigate the new structure of the international division of labour, established in recent decades as a result of the rise of neoliberal globalization worldwide. In fact, empirical analyses of unequal exchange have so far been performed taking into account traditional total gross trade flows,[2] as they are recorded in the national balance of payments. Traditional measures of exports and imports record the monetary value of goods and services every time they cross a border, including on each occasion the cost of inputs and the value added by each country. This method is appropriate when countries are rigidly specialized in the production of primary products and raw materials, on the one hand, and manufacturing intermediate and final goods, on the other hand, as trade was normally structured in the period before the recent capitalist globalization. When, however, different stages of production of a given final good are regularly distributed among a multitude of different countries, intermediate goods cross the borders several times for further partial processing before reaching the stage for final consumption. In this case, the traditional export and import measures lead to double counting, and official trade statistics become increasingly less reliable in indicating the actual contribution of each country to the formation of the value of the final commodity. This is what occurred over the last three decades, thus radically transforming the former international division of labour between manufacturing Centre and agricultural Periphery, which remained almost intact throughout the previous two centuries.

Since the early 1990s, the world economy has undergone a dramatic process of change, commonly referred to as economic globalization, indicating the increasing integration and interdependence of national, regional, and local economies into a unified global capitalist space. The main drivers of this process have been the widening of the capitalist market worldwide after the collapse of the Soviet Union, the neoliberal policies of deregulation and liberalization imposed on a global scale by Western powers and international economic organizations, and new digital technologies enabling faster material, financial, and information flows between formerly remote geographical locations. Those developments have affected the sphere of production, not just circulation.

Manufacturing activity, once spatially and vertically integrated, has now become fragmented in several different countries and firms around the world. This process is driven by multinational corporations, implementing the delocalization of production in pursuit of increasing profits, through the combination of two basic practices: outsourcing and offshoring. The former consists in entrusting to other formally independent firms some stages of the production process, and the latter in shifting production plants abroad. The resulting cross-border production networks allow multinational corporations to exploit cost advantages of different locations at each stage of production, up to the final assembly. In this way, the new value realized from the final sell of the commodity is created in varying proportions at all stages/locations of the production process, in what has been called the global value chain (GVC).[3] The growth of GVCs has significantly affected the pattern of global production and trade both geographically and structurally.

On the spatial level, the international division of labour, once characterized by a marked dualism between the Periphery specializing in agriculture and mining and the Centre specializing in manufacturing, has profoundly changed. Now the picture is much more varied, with a select group of emerging peripheral countries that have undergone a rapid process of industrialization gaining a significant share of global manufacturing production, and the rest of the Periphery, relegated to the margins of the global economy, experiencing increasing levels of underdevelopment and social poverty. The economies of the Centre, for their part, have become increasingly service-intensive, particularly in the strategic sectors of finance, communication, marketing, product innovation, and research and development, and mainly limiting manufacturing to technology-based industries. Peripheral industrial development, however, has not become self-centred and continues to be highly dependent on the strategic choices of the Centre, which determines the unequal distribution of the value produced in the "global factory", through the technological, financial, and communication monopoly of its multinational industrial and banking corporations.[4]

On a structural level, the previous product-based international division of labour between primary and secondary industries has been replaced by a division by stages of the same individual production process, from design to final sale passing through the material fabrication of the product. The total value added of the whole global manufacturing cycle is not evenly distributed along the chain but is highly concentrated in the initial and final stages compared with the intermediate one, thus giving rise to what has been called the "smiley curve" of value capture between different locations.[5] The knowledge-intensive stages of production with the highest profitability, concerning the ideation and design of the product upstream and the marketing, brand management, and final distribution downstream are localized in the Centre, while the Periphery specializes in the middle stages, concerning the activities of material fabrication of intermediate goods and final assembly, with the lowest profitability. A direct effect of this phenomenon has been the significant growth in trade of intermediate commodities.

The new organization of global labour has led to a change in the scale of wages both nationally and internationally. In the previous international division of labour, wage differences were mainly determined by the branch of employment, manufacturing, or agriculture, and were therefore distributed according to a nationality criterion deriving from the country's specialization, providing the basis for the phenomenon of the national aristocracy of labour.[6] Now, instead, wage differences are mainly between "knowledge workers" and manual workers within the same production process. This, together with the deregulation of labour markets and massive migration flows, has given rise to wage segmentation within each country, both in the Centre and in the Periphery, determined by whether or not the worker possesses the skills favoured by the new capitalist organization of labour. The old national aristocracy of labour has thus been replaced by a narrow global aristocracy of labour present, albeit with different dimensions, both in the Centre and in the Periphery, and accompanied by a vast mass of working poor even within the more developed economies. The result of this process is reflected in the statistics on income inequalities at the global level, which show both a reduction in inequalities between countries and a marked increase in inequalities within each country.[7] The end result, however, is an increase in total inequality, with a sharp reduction in the share of wages in total income to the benefit of capital returns both nationally and globally.[8] In summary, the new international division of labour resulting from GVCs has allowed global capital to greatly expand the basis for the extraction of surplus labour, both intensively with over-exploitation, and extensively with dependent peripheral industrialization.

A large part of the vast academic and institutional literature on the subject underlines the importance of the participation in GVCs by less developed countries, as a vehicle for their rapid industrialization and modernization by the adoption of an export-led growth strategy.[9] In this research, the focus is mainly on microeconomic and organizational aspects relating to the process of firm's upgrading and industrial governance within individual GVCs, with special reference to the functions of cooperation and control in production, and of marketing in distribution. In particular, the economic development strategies that are recommended to peripheral countries are based on the promotion of industrial microeconomic policies aimed at shifting the productive position of the domestic firms upstream or downstream of the product cycle, within a framework of global market integration and intra-peripheral competition for the most remunerative positions in GVCs.[10] The fierce competition between peripheral economies within GVCs should trigger a process of natural selection that allows some emerging countries to catch up with more advanced economies. In this theoretical framework, therefore, underdevelopment is the consequence of the inability of backward countries to seize the opportunities offered by global production networks.

The predominantly microeconomic and entrepreneurial perspective of mainstream research prevents grasping the structural constraints placed on peripheral economies by their participation in GVCs resulting from the global functioning of the world capitalist economy. Little or no attention is devoted to the monetary and macroeconomic conditions that may affect the spatial distribution of value within GVCs so that the latter always looks consistent with the spatial production of value. This view, however, completely obscures the fact that the status of each national location within GVCs does not only depend on competitive factors within individual production processes but is instead strongly influenced by the hierarchical structure of the global capitalist economy on the political, monetary, financial, and technological levels. In fact, the different position occupied by each individual country within the hierarchical scale of global capitalism results in the decoupling of value captured from the value produced among different geographical locations of the same integrated process of production. When this decoupling occurs, however, GVCs can strengthen the reproduction of unequal development by means of the new international division of labour, rather than the reverse.

This chapter contributes to a still little explored line of research which, on the basis of a heterodox or more specifically Marxist approach, intends to highlight the role of GVCs in the reproduction of unequal development in the current global capitalist economy.[11] It aims to analyze how the hierarchical structure of the international monetary system, deriving from the functioning of the international law of value previously discussed, influences the distribution of the value created outside and within GVCs. As shown in previous chapters, a structural feature of the international monetary system is the systematic difference between current and PPP exchange rates of national currencies according to the level of economic development of countries. This phenomenon, which has long been known in the literature as the "Penn effect", derives from a persistently lower domestic price level in less developed countries than in more developed ones. As a result, the real exchange rates of the first group of countries are systematically undervalued in the face of a persistent overvaluation of the currencies of the second group, with a consequent imbalance in the terms of trade to the benefit of the richer countries.[12] As we have seen in the previous chapter, this phenomenon can find a consistent explanation in the context of Marx's theory of value, as a result of the ordinary functioning of the international law of value, even in the presence of perfectly competitive world markets.

The model presented in the following paragraph, and the empirical results from its application to the world economy, will show that behind the "Penn effect" there are substantial transfers of value from peripheral to central countries hidden within GVCs, in addition to those resulting from traditional export and import flows of final goods and services. In order to take account of the important changes in the international division of labour in recent decades, unequal exchange will be measured by using value added trade statistics, in which country's exports and imports are measured in terms of contribution to the final value added of commodities regardless of their border crossing. In this way, it will be possible to distinguish value transfers originating within GVCs from those present in traditional export and import flows.

6.2 An aggregate model of unequal exchange in value added trade with GVCs

An aggregated version of the general model presented in Chapter 5 will be used for the empirical estimation of the unequal exchange in value added trade. Due to its aggregated nature, the model only captures the unequal exchange in the strict sense resulting from intra-industry value transfers. Similarly to the disaggregated model in the previous chapter, the fundamental equivalence of value discussed in Chapters 3 and 4 applies here, according to which at the aggregate world level total net product can be expressed equivalently in terms of units of international money and units of necessary universal labor time.

Consider a world economy with n countries producing and trading one composite commodity, the net product (Q_i), where the suffix i denotes a national economy.[13] Each country uses direct labour, working with given intensity and means of production, to produce one unit of Q_i. The monetary value of Q_i represents the value added in national currency (Y_i^{nc}), constituted by the sum of wages and gross profits derived from the market sale of Q_i at a national price P_i:

$$Y_i^{nc} = P_i Q_i \tag{6.1}$$

Because each country has its own national currency, it occurs a common unit of account to internationally compare the nominal value of Q_i. Hence, for each country, a value added in dollars ($Y_i^{\$}$) is calculated by multiplying value added in national currency by the current exchange rate between national currency and dollar ($e_i^{\$}$), where the current dollar represents the reference currency unit measuring nominal values in the world economy. Expressing exchange rates according to the volume-quotation system as units of foreign currency per one unit of national currency, we have the following:

$$Y_i^{\$} = e_i^{\$} Y_i^{nc} \tag{6.2}$$

Due to possible differences in price levels between countries, however, value added in dollars does not necessarily correspond to the volume of net product produced by each country. In other words, the volume of Q_i expressed by one dollar could differ between countries in the world economy. Consequently, for each country, the equivalent international monetary expression of the net product is measured by a PPP conversion factor, or PPP exchange rate (e_i^{p}), defined as the units of national currency necessary to buy in the domestic market the same volume of net product as one dollar buys on weighted average in the world economy. The PPP dollar represents the artificial reference unit measuring the equivalent quantity of net product in the world economy. Due to normalization, the actual international price in dollars corresponds to the PPP international price, both placed equal to one in such a way that one unit of net product corresponds to one unit of the PPP dollar. The PPP dollar thus represents the equivalent international monetary expression of one unit of Q, that is, the unit value of Q expressed in international currency. The PPP exchange rate assures that the price of one unit of Q is equal for each country of the world economy, being determined as follows:

$$e_i^{p} = \frac{P_w}{P_i} = \frac{1}{P_i} \tag{6.3}$$

As a result of the PPP definition, the average world price level (P_w) is set equal to one, and the equivalent monetary expression of the world net product coincides with the world value added in dollars ($Y_w^{\$}$):

$$Q_w = \sum_i^n Y_i^{\$} = Y_w^{\$} \tag{6.4}$$

By substituting expressions (6.3) in (6.1), we have the national net product given by the following:

$$Q_i = e_i^P Y_i^{nc} \qquad (6.5)$$

Unlike in an aggregate world economy, for each individual country, the equivalent international monetary expression of the net product could differ from the value added in dollars, as we can see by substituting (6.5) in (6.2):

$$\frac{Y_i^\$}{Q_i} = ERDI_i \qquad (6.6)$$

where $ERDI_i = \dfrac{e_i^\$}{e_i^P}$

The exchange rate deviation index ($ERDI_i$) measures the gap between dollar and PPP exchange rates of a currency. When $ERDI_i$ is greater than 1 there is real overvaluation of the currency because the value added in dollars of country i is greater than the equivalent international monetary expression of the net product. Vice versa there is real undervaluation in the case of $ERDI_i$ smaller than one. With $ERDI_i$ equal to one, real and nominal values are identical.

Universal labour is defined as labour with world average productivity, so that total world direct labour (L_w) is equal to total world universal labour (L_w^u):

$$L_w = L_w^u \qquad (6.7)$$

This definition implies that one unit of universal labour has the same real productivity in every country of the world economy, as follows:

$$\frac{Q_w}{L_w} = \frac{Q_i}{L_i^u} \qquad (6.8)$$

Rearranging (6.8), we can see that world universal labour is distributed between countries according to the corresponding aliquot parts of their net product in the total world net product as follows:

$$L_i^u = \frac{Q_i}{Q_w} L_w \qquad (6.9)$$

By using universal labour rather than direct labour, the quantity of direct labour used in production is adjusted to differences in intensity and productivity of labour between countries, deriving from differences in skills and technology. Countries with intensity and productivity higher than the world average will have a rate of conversion between direct and universal labour greater than one, and vice versa in the opposite case. In the former case, one unit of direct labour translates into more than one unit of universal labour, while in the latter case less.

International value (IV) is defined as the quantity of Q produced by a unit of universal labour in the world economy, corresponding to the real productivity of universal labour. It indicates the quantity of net product *produced* by one unit of universal labour, or value in production, and from equation (6.8), the result is identical to the world average labour productivity:

$$IV_i = \frac{Q_i}{L_i^u} = \frac{Q_w}{L_w} = IV_w = IV \qquad (6.10)$$

International value, as expressed in (6.10), represents the equivalent physical expression of one unit of universal labour in the world economy. It is the inverse of the labour expression of universal labour (LEV) as defined in Chapter 4. In fact, given the fundamental equivalence between total direct labour, total net product, and total net price established by the social algorithm of value, at aggregate world level, the magnitude of value can be indifferently expressed in terms of units of universal labour time, units of physical product, or units of money through the equivalent conversion ratio that relates monetary expression of value (MEV), LEV, and monetary expression of labour time ($MELT$), as discussed in Chapter 4. Since in our system the world price level is equal to one because of PPP normalization, we have that the monetary and physical expression of value coincides, that is, one unit of net product is equal to one unit of the PPP dollar. As a consequence, at the aggregate level, the physical expression of universal labour is identical to the PPP expression of universal labour, and international value coincides with PPP labour productivity. Finally, remembering that at an aggregate level, the price in PPP coincides with the price in current dollars, we have that in the world economy real productivity coincides with nominal productivity, and therefore, the monetary expression of universal labour is identical to its physical and PPP expressions.

All these equivalent relations between the different expressions of the magnitude of value derive from the equivalence that exists at the aggregate level between the two measures of exchange value in labour time and money. In formal terms, they are represented by the definition of $MELT$ in the world economy. The $MELT$ is defined as the number of dollars exchangeable with the net product produced by a unit of universal labour. It indicates the value *captured* by a unit of universal labour in the world economy, corresponding to the nominal labour productivity, and represents the value in circulation realized by a unit of universal labour. Given the fundamental equivalence of value, in the aggregate world economy, the $MELT$ is identical to the value in production created by a unit of universal labour. Consequently, from (6.4) and (6.7), at the aggregate world level, it results that international value coincides with both the monetary and physical expression of universal labour, and value in production is identical to value in circulation, as follows:

$$MELT = \frac{Y_w^\$}{L_w^u} = \frac{Q_w}{L_w} = IV_w \tag{6.11}$$

The fundamental equivalence between the different expressions of the magnitude of value of the net product is verified only at the aggregate level of the whole world economy since it results from the average between the individual units that compose it. It is not valid at the level of the individual units of the economic system, which in our case are the individual countries. The individual monetary expression of the net product produced by a unit of universal labour for each country in the world economy ($MELT_i$) is given as follows:

$$MELT_i = \frac{Y_i^\$}{L_i^u} \tag{6.12}$$

$MELT_i$ represents the value captured by one unit of universal labour of a given country i in the world economy. Unlike in the aggregate world level, for a national economy, the international value produced could differ from the value captured, as we can see by substituting (6.6) in (6.12):

$$MELT_i = ERDI_i\, IV \tag{6.13}$$

From (6.13), it results that for national economies values produced and captured by a unit of universal labour are equal only if $ERDI_i$ is equal to one, that is when the current exchange rate is identical to the PPP exchange rate. On the contrary, when $ERDI_i$ is different from one, the net product produced by country i exchanges with a quantity of dollars expressing a different quantity of world net product. In this case, produced and captured value differs for country i.

In particular, when $ERDI_i$ is less than one, the quantity of value captured by a country is less than that produced, and vice versa when $ERDI_i$ is greater than one. In international trade, these situations originate unequal exchange, defined as the difference between international value captured by selling exports (or buying imports) in the world market and the international value of produced exports (or imports), regardless of labour intensity and productivity differences between countries since both are expressed in terms of identical universal labour units. In fact, in the former case, there is an outflow transfer of value to the rest of the world embedded in exports of country i, while in the latter there is an inflow transfer of value from the rest of the world achieved through exports. At the world level, inflows and outflows transfers offset each other, and value produced is equal to the value captured in the total world economy.

For each country, domestic value added in total exports is given by the sum of domestic value added in national exports and domestic value added in foreign exports. Domestic value added in national exports can be derived by subtracting foreign value added in national exports from total value added in national exports. Therefore, we have the following relations:

$$Y_i^{\$x_i} = Y^{\$x_i} - \sum_{j \neq i}^{n} Y_j^{\$x_i} \tag{6.14}$$

$$Y_i^{\$x} = Y_i^{\$x_i} + \sum_{j \neq i}^{n} Y_i^{\$x_j} \tag{6.15}$$

where:
$Y_i^{\$x_i}$ = domestic value added in national exports in current dollars;
$Y^{\$x_i}$ = total value added in national exports in current dollars;
$Y_j^{\$x_i}$ = foreign value added in national exports in current dollars;
$Y_i^{\$x}$ = domestic value added in total exports in current dollars;
$Y_i^{\$x_j}$ = domestic value added in foreign exports in current dollars.

For each country, we can derive the quantity of universal labour used in the exported net product by dividing the domestic value added in total exports in current dollars by the individual monetary expression of labour time, as follows:

$$L_{x_i}^u = \frac{Y_i^{\$x}}{MELT_i} \tag{6.16}$$

Afterwards, the international value of total exports (Q_i^x) is determined by multiplying the homogeneous universal labour in exports by the international value of exports, as follows:

$$Q_i^x = L_{x_i}^u IV^x \tag{6.17}$$

where: $IV^x = \dfrac{\sum_i^n Y_i^{\$x}}{\sum_i^n L_{x_i}^h}$

Total transfers of value in trade ($T_i^\$$), measured in current dollars, are given by the difference between captured and produced value added in trade, as follows:

$$T_i^\$ = Y_i^{\$x} - Q_i^x \tag{6.18}$$

By substituting (6.15), (6.16), and (6.17) in (6.18), after some simple algebraic manipulations, we obtain the following formula:

$$T_i^\$ = \left(1 - \frac{IV}{MELT_i}\right)\left[\left(Y_i^{\$x_i} + \sum_{j\neq i}^{n} Y_j^{\$x_i}\right) + \left(\sum_{j\neq i}^{n} Y_i^{\$x_j} - \sum_{j\neq i}^{n} Y_j^{\$x_i}\right)\right] \qquad (6.19)$$

Recalling the equation (6.13), we can write (6.19) in the following way:

$$T_i^\$ = \left(1 - \frac{1}{ERDI_i}\right)\left[\left(Y_i^{\$x_i} + \sum_{j\neq i}^{n} Y_j^{\$x_i}\right) + \left(\sum_{j\neq i}^{n} Y_i^{\$x_j} - \sum_{j\neq i}^{n} Y_j^{\$x_i}\right)\right] \qquad (6.20)$$

As can be seen from (6.20), when the real exchange rate is overvalued with respect to PPP and therefore ERDI is greater than one, the country has a positive inflow transfer of value, while when the real exchange rate is undervalued with an ERDI less than one, the country has, vice versa, a negative outflow transfer of value. The unequal exchange, therefore, benefits countries with a price level higher than the world average and penalizes countries with a price level lower than the world average. As we have seen in Chapter 5, the "Penn effect" shows that the former are more developed countries with a higher per capita income, and the latter are less developed countries with a per capita income below the world average.

The first expression in the bracket square of equation (6.20) represents the traditional notion of unequal exchange deriving from the final exports of a country ($UE_i^{x_i}$), constituted by two components referring to the value of national final exports and imported input embedded in national final exports, respectively. A country can capture more value than that produced by both acquiring a monetary value higher than the real value of its exports and by ceding a monetary value lower than the real value of its imported input. The second expression in the bracket square of equation (6.20), instead, represents the unequal exchange deriving from GVCs involving a country (UE_i^{GVC}). In this case, the two components refer to the value of national input embedded in foreign exports and foreign input used in national exports, respectively. The net balance of these two factors constitutes the value transfer coming from the GVC participation of a country.

Expression (6.20), therefore, may be shortened as follows:

$$T_i^\$ = UE_i^{x_i} + UE_i^{GVC} \qquad (6.21)$$

where:

$$UE_i^{x_i} = \left(1 - \frac{1}{ERDI_i}\right)\left(Y_i^{\$x_i} + \sum_{j\neq i}^{n} Y_j^{\$x_i}\right) \qquad (6.22)$$

$$UE_i^{GVC} = \left(1 - \frac{1}{ERDI_i}\right)\left(\sum_{j\neq i}^{n} Y_i^{\$x_j} - \sum_{j\neq i}^{n} Y_j^{\$x_i}\right) \qquad (6.23)$$

Expressions (6.20), (6.22), and (6.23) will be used in the next paragraph to empirically calculate total net value transfers, net value transfers in final exports, and net total value transfers in GVCs, respectively.

6.3 International value transfers from 1990 to 2019

The model set up in the previous paragraph has been the basis for the empirical measurement of trade value transfers in the world economy over the last three decades. The period under consideration goes from 1990, the year immediately following the fall of the Berlin Wall, which marked the end of the Cold War with the dissolution of the Soviet political-economic bloc, to 2019, the year before the outbreak of the Covid-19 pandemic, which has hindered the expansion of neoliberal globalization. The statistical sources of data are the International Monetary Fund (IMF) for gross domestic product (GDP) in current dollars and in PPP, the World Bank (WB) and the International Labour Organization (ILO) for employment data, and the UNCTAD-EORA Global Value Chains database for trade in value added generated from EORA Multi-Region Input-Output tables (MRIOs).[14] The key indicators of the UNCTAD-EORA database are domestic value added embedded in a country's exports corresponding to traditional net exports flows, foreign value added embedded in a country's exports, and domestic value added embedded in other countries' exports, the last two corresponding to the value added embedded in GVC internal flows. Complete data have been available for 175 countries, clustered in 16 regions of the world economy according to World Bank geographical criteria, as shown in Appendix 6.1.

Table 6.1 shows GDP per capita in current dollars and in PPP, the relative price level, and the regional world share of GDP and population of the 16 regions in 2019, the final year of the period.

As can be seen, there is a sharp division between the five richest regions (North America, European Monetary Union – EMU, Western Europe, East Asia, Oceania), constituting of the group of the Centre that includes the most developed capitalist countries with GDP per capita in current dollars more than three to five times the world average, and the remaining 11 regions of the Periphery. Within the latter, in turn, there is a clear differentiation between a group of six emerging regions, the Emerging Periphery, with per capita income levels close to the world average (China, Russia, Eastern Europe, South America, Central America, Middle East), and another group of five extremely poor regions, the Poor Periphery, with very low per capita incomes less than half the world average (South Asia, Southeast Asia, Central Asia, North Africa, Sub-Saharan Africa). The inequalities in the distribution of world income are dramatically highlighted by the comparison between the world shares of GDP in dollars and the population of the different regions: the Centre with 13.5% of the world population gets 58.1% of world income, the Emerging Periphery with 34.4% of the population has 30.4% of world income, and finally the Poor Periphery with 52.1% of the population and only 11.5% of world income. Comparing the two opposite extremes of

Table 6.1 GDP per capita in current dollars ($) and in purchasing power parity (PPP), relative price level, and population of world regions in 2019

Geographic areas		GDP per capita		Price level (world=1)	World share		
Groups	Regions	GDP in $	GDP in PPP	Domestic price level	GDP in $	GDP in PPP	Population
Centre	North America	63,320	41,757	1.52	26.9	17.7	4.8
	Western Europe	49,731	34,682	1.43	5.6	3.9	1.3
	Oceania	40,349	25,710	1.57	1.9	1.2	0.5
	EMU	38,926	32,051	1.21	15.5	12.7	4.5
	East Asia	38,634	29,650	1.3	8.2	6.3	2.4
	Total	**48,616**	**35,070**	**1.39**	**58.1**	**41.9**	**13.5**
Emerging Periphery	Eastern Europe	14,175	20,349	0.7	1.7	2.5	1.4
	China	10,738	11,144	0.96	17.8	18.5	18.8
	Russia and CSI	9,601	16,019	0.6	2.2	3.7	2.6
	Middle East	9,415	10,653	0.88	2.8	3.1	3.3
	Central America	8,281	11,196	0.74	2	2.6	2.7
	South America	7,899	9,860	0.8	3.9	4.9	5.6
	Total	**10,006**	**11,633**	**0.86**	**30.4**	**35.3**	**34.4**
Poor Periphery	Central Asia	5,211	11,089	0.47	1.3	2.8	2.8
	Southeast Asia	4,277	7,866	0.54	3.3	6	8.6
	North Africa	3,442	7,476	0.46	0.8	1.7	2.6
	South Asia	1,989	4,326	0.46	4.2	9	23.6
	Sub-Saharan Africa	1,571	2,545	0.62	2	3.2	14.5
	Total	**2,498**	**4,941**	**0.51**	**11.5**	**22.7**	**52.1**
World	**Total average**	**11,317**	**11,317**	**1**	**100**	**100**	**100**

Source: Our elaborations on IMF and World Bank data.

the distribution scale, it can be seen that on average a North American citizen has an income in current dollars about 40 times higher than a citizen of Sub-Saharan Africa. In terms of PPP, the difference is reduced, but it is still very large since on average a North American citizen has a real income equal to that of more than 16 sub-Saharan African citizens. An important point to note in Table 6.1 is the relative regional price level with respect to the world average price level. When the former is higher than the latter, there is a real overvaluation of the current exchange rate compared with the PPP level, and vice versa, a real undervaluation in the opposite case. As can be seen, only the regions of the Centre are in a situation of real overvaluation, while all the peripheral regions are in the opposite situation of real undervaluation. This is the "Penn effect" that shows that the average domestic level of price is directly proportional to the level of development of the countries.

6.3.1 The total size of value transfers in the global economy

International value transfers in total and GVC trade in value added are calculated according to equations (6.20) and (6.23), respectively. The difference between the two measures is given by the value transfers in traditional net export flows, this latter consisting of the domestic value added embedded in gross exports. Figure 6.1 shows the amount in current dollars of world value transfers over the whole period 1990–2019.

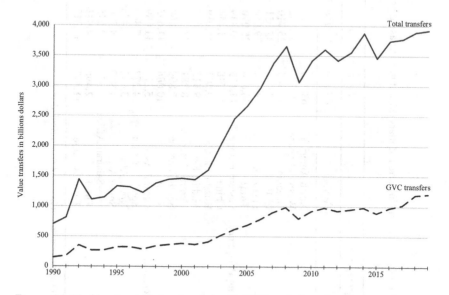

Figure 6.1 World value transfers in total and GVC trade in value added. Billions of dollars, 1990–2019. (*Source*: Own elaborations on UNCTAD-EORA, IMF, WB, and ILO data.)

In nominal terms, world value transfers in total trade have increased more than fivefold over the last 30 years, from $704 billion in 1990 to $3,924 billion in 2019. Even more marked was the increase in value transfers within GVCs from $150 billion to $1,209 billion, with a multiplication factor greater than eight times the initial value, demonstrating the emergence of a new international division of labour increasingly focused on transnational chains of value production. The difference between the value produced and captured by the different locations within the global integrated process of production of the individual commodities goes to fuel the profits of the multinational firms and the over-remuneration of the privileged strata of the Centre's workers. These data show that the absolute dimension of unequal exchange in the world economy is of primary importance. Suffice it to say that in the same period the total worldwide amount of net official development assistance received by developing countries was, according to data provided by the OECD, $165.8 billion in 2018 ($59.3 billion in 1990), about one-twentieth of the value transfers leaving developing countries with international trade.

The growth rate of value transfers was particularly high during the first decade of the new century, which begins with the birth of the euro and China's entry into the World Trade Organization. Following the outbreak of the global financial crisis in 2008, there has been a sharp contraction in absolute terms in value transfers due to two distinct factors: the shrinking of world trade resulting from the global recession and the relative structural upgrading of some of the peripheral economies, first and foremost China. It was only at the end of the following decade that the absolute size of the unequal exchange reached levels that were steadily higher than before the great crisis.

Since there has been significant growth in world GDP and trade over the period, the real size of value transfers in the global economy can be better captured in Figure 6.2, which shows the value transfers as a percentage of world GDP.

During the period, the relative size of value transfers to world GDP increased, both in total and GVC terms, from 3.1% and 0.7% in 1990 to 4.5% and 1.4% in 2019, respectively. Apart from the isolated peak in 1992, resulting from the effects of the collapse of the Soviet Union, the unequal exchange reached its highest expansion during the 2000s, with an all-time high of 5.7% in total and 1.5% in GVC transfers on world GDP in 2007. After the global spread of the financial crisis in 2008, the reduction in the weight of value transfers on world GDP was mainly due to the traditional export component returning to the levels of the 1990s, while the GVC component essentially stabilized, thus increasing its relative importance.

Aggregate world data on the magnitude of unequal exchange in international trade, however significant, do not give an exact picture of the extent of the phenomenon and its decisive importance in defining the allocation of income between the Centre and the Periphery of the global capitalist economy. To this end, a disaggregated analysis for the different regions of the world economy is much more meaningful. In this way, we can also see the existence of a widely differentiated situation within each of the three major groups (Centre, Emerging Periphery, and Poor Periphery) into which the global economy has been divided.

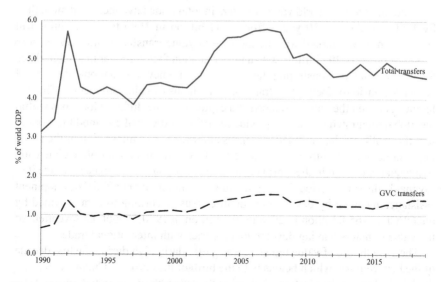

Figure 6.2 World value transfers in total and GVC trade in value added. Percentage of
world GDP, 1990–2019. (*Source*: Own elaborations on UNCTAD-EORA, IMF,
WB, and ILO data.)

6.3.2 The receivers: Inflow value transfers in Centre regions

During the whole period considered, central capitalist regions are the only beneficiaries of unequal exchange, all receiving significant inflows of value from
peripheral regions, whether emerging or poor. Table 6.2 and Figure 6.3 show the
decomposition of total and GVC value inflows in billions of dollars for each of
the five central regions.

The region that is the largest absorber in absolute terms of value transfers is
the European Monetary Union, followed by North America and Western Europe.
During the 1990s, the order of magnitude of value inflows among these three
regions, along with East Asia, was on a comparable scale. After the creation of
the single European currency, during the first decade of the new century, the EMU
took the lion's share in allocating the benefits of unequal exchange, appropriating about half of all value transfers in global international trade. This performance shows that the replacement of individual national currencies by the euro
has greatly increased the power of European countries in the appropriation of the
global currency rent, thus constituting a decisive factor in strengthening European
capital vis-à-vis that of the United States and Japan. First, the great crisis of 2008,
and then the difficulties of the euro following the Greek crisis, weakened the position of the Eurozone in appropriating value flows, although remaining by far in
first place as the absolute beneficiary of the unequal exchange. North America,
Western Europe, and Oceania show a more regular and steady growth in value
inflows in contrast to the stagnation of East Asian capitalism, which instead
has seen a substantial impasse in value inflows as a result of the long Japanese

Table 6.2 Centre regions: Inflow value transfers in total and GVC trade in value added. Billions of current dollars, 1990–2019

	North America		EMU		Western Europe		East Asia		Oceania		Centre	
	TOT	GVC	TOT	GVC	TOT	GVC	TOT	GVC	TOT	GVC	TOT	GVC
1990	136	30	277	48	145	28	134	41	11	3	704	150
1991	153	34	318	62	162	31	168	47	11	3	812	176
1992	281	55	636	175	243	50	260	70	21	3	1,441	353
1993	240	47	419	113	165	32	274	74	14	2	1,113	268
1994	241	51	419	100	170	32	302	84	16	3	1,148	270
1995	225	53	546	125	203	38	345	101	15	3	1,319	321
1996	249	61	538	121	209	41	302	98	21	4	1,334	326
1997	297	63	449	102	218	46	241	71	22	4	1,228	287
1998	350	81	555	116	245	51	219	91	13	3	1,382	342
1999	382	87	518	123	249	55	283	97	16	3	1,447	365
2000	465	104	377	101	249	61	360	111	13	3	1,465	379
2001	478	106	414	106	244	59	298	96	9	2	1,443	368
2002	485	110	533	128	282	65	286	103	15	3	1,600	409
2003	476	114	852	194	351	78	330	130	30	7	2,039	524
2004	523	127	1,044	228	450	106	389	147	45	11	2,451	618
2005	576	138	1,174	252	474	111	382	176	60	15	2,666	691
2006	654	159	1,325	288	559	139	362	185	65	17	2,965	787
2007	657	165	1,643	350	667	168	320	197	87	23	3,374	903
2008	625	161	1,921	408	698	174	308	215	105	29	3,657	988
2009	573	148	1,576	339	524	119	311	176	79	19	3,063	801
2010	670	164	1,536	347	632	158	443	220	140	35	3,421	924
2011	648	158	1,583	346	700	182	490	248	183	47	3,604	980
2012	697	166	1,353	296	692	185	497	237	183	45	3,422	928
2013	731	187	1,610	339	725	186	314	198	176	44	3,556	954
2014	796	205	1,756	364	835	217	308	153	180	44	3,875	983
2015	881	210	1,339	302	768	201	319	144	154	35	3,461	892
2016	922	223	1,487	353	746	188	423	176	167	36	3,745	976
2017	942	227	1,539	356	721	182	397	221	180	40	3,778	1,025
2018	912	254	1,701	452	683	182	448	267	151	38	3,894	1,192
2019	980	278	1,657	444	673	182	466	268	147	37	3,924	1,209

Source: Own elaborations on UNCTAD-EORA, IMF, WB, and ILO data.

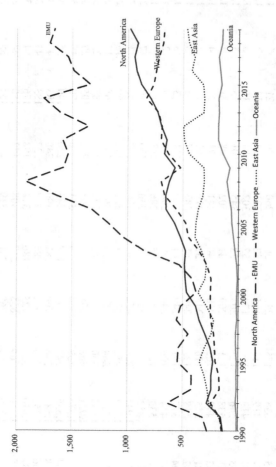

Figure 6.3 Centre regions: Inflow total value transfers. Billions of dollars, 1990–2019. (*Source:* Own elaborations on UNCTAD-EORA, IMF, WB, and ILO data.)

recession begun in the 1990s, and the Asian Tigers crisis of 1997–1998 that heavily affected the South Korean economy.

.The decisive role of unequal exchange for the prosperity of central capitalist regions can be better grasped by looking at inward total and GVC value transfers as a share of GDP, shown in Table 6.3 and Figures 6.4 and 6.5.

On average, the annual contribution of the total unequal exchange in international trade to the aggregate GDP of the regions of the Centre has steadily increased over the last 30 years from 5.3% in the 1990s, to 7.1% in the 2000s, and 8% in 2010s. An even more pronounced upward trend characterizes the value transfers through GVCs. These value inflows are far higher than the average Centre's real GDP annual growth rates in the same years and show that unequal exchange plays a significant role in the mechanism of capitalist accumulation in the central regions of the world economy. This is particularly true for the central European regions, EMU and Western Europe, and Oceania, for which the contribution of unequal exchange reaches more than 10% of GDP. These three regions result to be much more dependent on the neoliberal trade liberalization developed since the 1990s, from which they have profited to an increasing extent, compared with North American and Japanese capitalism, which, in particular the U.S., have arguably benefited most instead from international financial liberalization.[15] It is, therefore, to be expected that, following the economic effects of the recent Covid-19 pandemic, a prospective trade flows reduction will produce greater repercussions in the medium term in the former three regions of the capitalist Centre than in the latter two regions. Looking at the composition of the value transfers, for East Asia, and Japanese capitalism, in particular, GVC flows constitute the main source of drainage of value from the peripheral countries, as a reflection of its specific model of organization of labour strongly focused on the delocalization of intermediate stages of manufacturing towards the backward regions of the area.

6.3.3 *The donors: Outflow value transfers in the Emerging Periphery*

All 11 regions belonging to both the Emerging and Poor Periphery were net donors of value over the whole period considered. However, the share of the value outflows of the two groups has reversed over time.

As Figure 6.6 shows, during the first two decades, the Emerging Periphery has been the principal contributor to the total unequal exchange in the world economy. The proportion has reversed over the last decade, during which the poorest countries are responsible for most of the outward value transfers to the Centre. The restructuring of the global economy in the aftermath of the great crisis of 2008 has, therefore, resulted in a competitive strengthening of the emerging economies vis-à-vis the Centre, progressively offset by an even heavier exploitation suffered by poorer economies.

Table 6.4 and Figure 6.7 show the transfers of value in billions of dollars from the Emerging Periphery to the Centre.

Table 6.3 Centre regions: Inflow value transfers in total and GVC trade in value added. Percentage of GDP, 1990–2019

	North America		EMU		Western Europe		East Asia		Oceania		Centre	
	TOT	GVC	TOT	GVC	TOT	GVC	TOT	GVC	TOT	GVC	TOT	GVC
1990	2.1	0.5	4.9	0.9	7.4	1.4	3.9	1.2	3.0	0.7	3.9	0.8
1991	2.3	0.5	5.3	1.0	7.9	1.5	4.3	1.2	3.0	0.7	4.2	0.9
1992	3.9	0.8	9.5	2.6	11.4	2.4	6.0	1.6	5.8	0.9	7.0	1.7
1993	3.2	0.6	6.8	1.8	8.7	1.7	5.6	1.5	3.8	0.6	5.4	1.3
1994	3.0	0.6	6.5	1.5	8.3	1.6	5.6	1.6	3.8	0.8	5.1	1.2
1995	2.7	0.6	7.3	1.7	8.9	1.7	5.7	1.7	3.3	0.7	5.4	1.3
1996	2.8	0.7	7.1	1.6	8.8	1.7	5.5	1.8	4.1	0.8	5.3	1.3
1997	3.2	0.7	6.5	1.5	8.9	1.9	4.8	1.4	4.4	0.8	5.1	1.2
1998	3.6	0.8	7.8	1.6	9.6	2.0	4.9	2.0	2.8	0.7	5.7	1.4
1999	3.7	0.8	7.3	1.7	9.7	2.1	5.5	1.9	3.3	0.7	5.6	1.4
2000	4.2	0.9	5.8	1.5	9.8	2.4	6.5	2.0	2.9	0.7	5.6	1.5
2001	4.2	0.9	6.3	1.6	9.8	2.4	6.0	1.9	1.9	0.4	5.6	1.4
2002	4.1	0.9	7.4	1.8	10.4	2.4	5.9	2.1	3.0	0.6	5.9	1.5
2003	3.8	0.9	9.6	2.2	11.0	2.4	6.3	2.5	4.8	1.1	6.7	1.7
2004	3.9	1.0	10.3	2.2	12.1	2.9	6.8	2.6	5.8	1.4	7.3	1.8
2005	4.0	1.0	11.1	2.4	12.1	2.8	6.6	3.0	7.0	1.7	7.5	2.0
2006	4.3	1.0	11.8	2.6	13.3	3.3	6.4	3.2	7.2	1.9	8.0	2.1
2007	4.1	1.0	12.7	2.7	13.9	3.5	5.5	3.4	7.9	2.1	8.3	2.2
2008	3.8	1.0	13.5	2.9	14.4	3.6	4.9	3.4	8.7	2.4	8.5	2.3
2009	3.6	0.9	12.2	2.6	12.8	2.9	4.9	2.8	7.0	1.7	7.6	2.0
2010	4.0	1.0	12.1	2.7	14.7	3.7	6.3	3.1	9.9	2.5	8.1	2.2
2011	3.7	0.9	11.6	2.5	14.7	3.8	6.4	3.2	10.8	2.8	8.0	2.2
2012	3.8	0.9	10.7	2.3	14.6	3.9	6.4	3.1	10.3	2.5	7.6	2.1
2013	3.9	1.0	12.2	2.6	14.8	3.8	4.6	2.9	10.2	2.5	7.8	2.1
2014	4.1	1.1	13.0	2.7	16.1	4.2	4.7	2.3	10.7	2.6	8.4	2.1
2015	4.4	1.1	11.5	2.6	16.1	4.2	5.2	2.4	10.7	2.4	7.9	2.0
2016	4.5	1.1	12.4	3.0	16.4	4.1	6.3	2.6	11.3	2.4	8.3	2.2
2017	4.4	1.1	12.2	2.8	15.7	4.0	5.9	3.3	11.2	2.5	8.1	2.2
2018	4.1	1.1	12.5	3.3	13.9	3.7	6.3	3.8	9.1	2.3	7.9	2.4
2019	4.2	1.2	12.4	3.3	14.1	3.8	6.5	3.7	9.1	2.3	7.8	2.4

Source: Own elaborations on UNCTAD-EORA, IMF, WB, and ILO data.

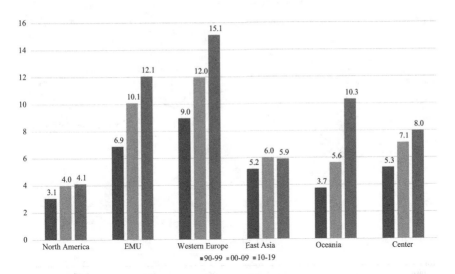

Figure 6.4 Centre regions: Inflow total value transfers. Percentage of GDP, ten-year average, 1990–2019. (*Source*: own elaborations on UNCTAD-EORA, IMF, WB, and ILO data.)

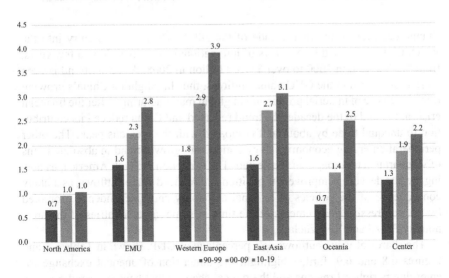

Figure 6.5 Centre regions: Inflow GVC value transfers. Percentage of GDP, ten-year average, 1990–2019. (*Source*: Own elaborations on UNCTAD-EORA, IMF, WB, and ILO data.)

As can be seen, in the first part of the period considered until the early 2000s, the six peripheral regions contributed almost equally to the unequal exchange. The exception was Russia in the early 1990s, when the collapse of the Soviet Union led to a real plundering of resources characterized by the sale of the country's industrial, mining, and land wealth at derisory prices abroad. A radical

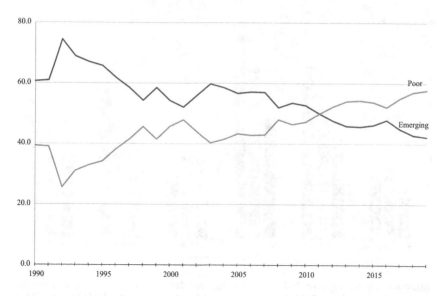

Figure 6.6 Share of outflow value transfer from Emerging and Poor Periphery regions. (*Source*: Own elaborations on UNCTAD-EORA, IMF, WB, and ILO data.)

change occurred in the first decade of the 2000s when, after its entry into the WTO, China increased its outflows of international value fivefold in a few years, from $257 billion in 2000 to over $1,100 billion in 2008. A similar trend is even more pronounced in the GVC value outflows, thus highlighting China's growing role as the core of material production in global manufacturing. After the financial crisis at the end of the decade, the trend reversed and China reduced its contribution to unequal trade by about half compared with the previous peak. The other peripheral emerging economies show a moderate growth trend in absolute terms of value transfers throughout the period. The exception is South America, as during the last decade, it improved its position and reduced value outflows, as a likely consequence of the policies of national autonomy and independence promoted by the progressive governments of the time in some large countries of the area, notably Brazil and Venezuela.

The shares of value outflows as a percentage of GDP, shown in Table 6.5 and Figures 6.8 and 6.9, further highlight the dimension of unequal exchange for emerging peripheral regions and the radical changes that have occurred over the last three decades.

The burden of unequal exchange on the emerging peripheral economies is considerable, especially in the first two decades when it exceeded 15% of GDP on average. In the last decade, value transfers from this group have been halved on average compared with the previous two decades, reflecting a dramatic change in the global economic and trade hierarchy. This improvement is almost entirely due to China's changed position within the group from the first to the last net

Table 6.4 Emerging Periphery: Outflow value transfers in total and GVC trade in value added. Billions of current dollars, 1990–2019

	China		Russia CSI		Eastern Europe		South America		Central America		Middle East		Emerging Periphery	
	TOT	GVC	TOT	GVC	TOT	GVC	TOT	GVC	TOT	GVC	TOT	GVC	TOT	GVC
1990	−103	−15	nd	nd	−94	−25	−87	−16	−40	−6	−103	−27	−427	−89
1991	−98	−16	nd	nd	−143	−36	−100	−19	−41	−7	−113	−29	−495	−106
1992	−32	−10	−711	−183	−73	−16	−68	−14	−18	−7	−172	−45	−1074	−275
1993	−76	−16	−304	−78	−83	−21	−86	−17	−17	−6	−199	−51	−767	−189
1994	−202	−37	−165	−43	−74	−21	−96	−19	−24	−7	−209	−54	−770	−181
1995	−242	−46	−163	−47	−101	−30	−87	−18	−68	−14	−217	−57	−878	−211
1996	−228	−47	−123	−36	−104	−32	−95	−20	−69	−14	−196	−52	−816	−201
1997	−205	−37	−125	−36	−102	−31	−77	−15	−52	−12	−157	−37	−719	−169
1998	−223	−39	−165	−50	−79	−25	−59	−12	−46	−14	−179	−50	−751	−190
1999	−242	−48	−243	−74	−89	−26	−82	−17	−38	−13	−153	−41	−847	−219
2000	−257	−56	−220	−68	−102	−30	−73	−16	−21	−14	−121	−32	−794	−216
2001	−246	−51	−203	−63	−87	−26	−80	−17	−6	−11	−129	−34	−752	−203
2002	−290	−60	−193	−59	−76	−24	−128	−26	−7	−11	−202	−54	−896	−234
2003	−437	−93	−228	−71	−79	−28	−173	−36	−35	−13	−267	−74	−1218	−315
2004	−584	−126	−244	−77	−78	−31	−197	−42	−48	−15	−284	−82	−1435	−373
2005	−719	−157	−228	−73	−71	−30	−177	−38	−43	−14	−273	−79	−1511	−391
2006	−904	−203	−220	−72	−82	−36	−170	−38	−48	−16	−271	−81	−1694	−446
2007	−1092	−251	−224	−74	−66	−36	−179	−40	−66	−17	−296	−91	−1923	−509
2008	−1128	−261	−215	−72	−37	−29	−168	−39	−82	−18	−271	−83	−1902	−503
2009	−798	−176	−262	−84	−66	−34	−149	−33	−94	−21	−271	−79	−1640	−426
2010	−965	−227	−257	−82	−110	−49	−97	−21	−97	−23	−278	−82	−1804	−484
2011	−1023	−246	−219	−70	−118	−55	−76	−17	−107	−24	−261	−77	−1804	−488
2012	−826	−195	−175	−55	−160	−67	−77	−19	−106	−25	−287	−83	−1631	−444
2013	−762	−169	−173	−55	−147	−68	−166	−41	−87	−22	−298	−85	−1633	−440
2014	−726	−156	−295	−93	−156	−69	−198	−50	−90	−24	−305	−87	−1770	−478
2015	−360	−71	−503	−157	−171	−60	−133	−34	−86	−26	−348	−102	−1600	−450
2016	−488	−111	−521	−157	−170	−60	−89	−22	−118	−32	−406	−116	−1793	−496
2017	−599	−138	−397	−121	−163	−59	−48	−14	−121	−33	−372	−108	−1700	−472
2018	−624	−186	−368	−111	−119	−47	−176	−39	−111	−25	−275	−80	−1672	−488
2019	−609	−183	−372	−113	−137	−53	−209	−60	−93	−24	−239	−75	−1659	−508

Source: Own elaborations on UNCTAD-EORA, IMF, WB, and ILO data.

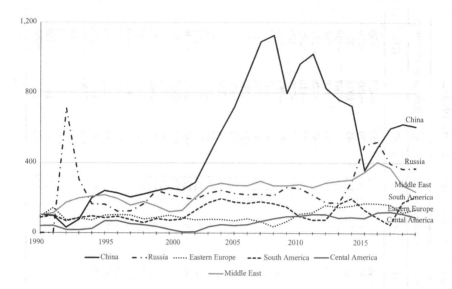

Figure 6.7 Emerging Periphery regions: Outflow total value transfers. Billions of dollars, 1990–2019. (*Source*: Own elaborations on UNCTAD-EORA, IMF, WB, and ILO data.)

contributor of value transfers. Looking at the data for GVCs, a downward trend in value outflows in proportion to GDP can be seen throughout the period, which has been accentuated over the last decade. Again, much of this trend is explained by the upgrading of the Chinese economy, reflecting an increasing ability to capture the value produced within GVCs. For Russia, Eastern Europe, and the Middle East, the burden on GDP of total and within GVC value outflows is significant and above average throughout the period, albeit with a moderate downward trend, thus showing a slower release from a position of economic subordination to central economies. This situation reflects the asymmetric structure of the European integration process and the dependent inclusion of the former socialist countries in the global capitalist market. Finally, for the countries of Latin America, the burden of unequal exchange on the domestic economy takes on smaller dimensions, even if still remarkable, indicating a lower involvement in the mechanisms of global commercial exploitation compared with other peripheral areas.

It is interesting to note that the financial crises of the 1990s and early 2000s played a key role in accentuating the mechanism of unequal exchange. With the exception of China, which has always maintained a high degree of financial and banking protectionism, all other regions of the Emerging Periphery experienced serious financial crises in those years, marked by the collapse of the national banking system, capital flight abroad, and massive currency devaluations. First Mexico in 1994, then Russia in 1998, and Brazil, Ecuador, and other South American countries in 1999–2002 experienced this situation. All these countries, together with those of India in 1991 and Southeast Asia in 1997–1998, which we will

Table 6.5 Emerging Periphery: Outflow value transfers in total and GVC trade in value added. Percentage of GDP, 1990–2019

	China		Russia CSI		Eastern Europe		South America		Central America		Middle East		Emerging Periphery	
	TOT	GVC	TOT	GVC	TOT	GVC	TOT	GVC	TOT	GVC	TOT	GVC	TOT	GVC
1990	-16.1	-2.4	nd	nd	-59.7	-15.6	-10.8	-2.0	-11.5	-1.9	-11.7	-3.1	-15.1	-3.2
1991	-14.2	-2.3	nd	nd	-96.6	-24.3	-12.1	-2.3	-9.9	-1.7	-18.1	-4.6	-18.3	-3.9
1992	-3.8	-1.2	-557.9	-143.9	-42.5	-9.1	-7.7	-1.6	-3.8	-1.4	-43.1	-11.3	-37.3	-9.5
1993	-7.8	-1.7	-124.3	-31.7	-46.7	-11.8	-9.1	-1.8	-3.0	-1.0	-46.9	-12.0	-22.8	-5.6
1994	-21.0	-3.8	-46.8	-12.4	-35.3	-9.9	-8.5	-1.7	-3.9	-1.1	-44.6	-11.5	-20.6	-4.8
1995	-20.8	-3.9	-42.2	-12.0	-31.2	-9.4	-6.0	-1.2	-15.0	-3.0	-41.3	-10.8	-20.4	-4.9
1996	-17.3	-3.5	-25.5	-7.5	-29.8	-9.2	-6.2	-1.3	-13.5	-2.8	-32.5	-8.6	-17.0	-4.2
1997	-14.2	-2.6	-24.9	-7.1	-27.6	-8.4	-4.7	-0.9	-8.5	-2.0	-24.1	-5.7	-13.8	-3.2
1998	-15.0	-2.7	-47.0	-14.3	-20.0	-6.3	-3.7	-0.7	-7.2	-2.1	-27.0	-7.5	-14.6	-3.7
1999	-15.4	-3.0	-94.8	-29.0	-23.5	-7.0	-6.3	-1.3	-5.2	-1.8	-19.8	-5.3	-17.0	-4.4
2000	-15.0	-3.3	-67.6	-20.8	-26.9	-7.9	-5.3	-1.2	-2.5	-1.7	-12.7	-3.4	-14.2	-3.9
2001	-13.5	-2.8	-53.1	-16.4	-20.8	-6.3	-6.3	-1.4	-0.7	-1.3	-14.2	-3.8	-13.2	-3.6
2002	-14.8	-3.0	-44.7	-13.6	-16.1	-5.0	-12.9	-2.6	-0.8	-1.2	-28.1	-7.6	-16.3	-4.3
2003	-20.3	-4.3	-42.6	-13.2	-14.0	-5.0	-16.1	-3.3	-4.0	-1.5	-33.2	-9.3	-20.3	-5.2
2004	-23.4	-5.1	-33.5	-10.6	-11.5	-4.6	-15.1	-3.2	-5.1	-1.6	-29.4	-8.5	-20.2	-5.3
2005	-25.0	-5.5	-24.1	-7.7	-9.1	-3.8	-10.7	-2.3	-4.0	-1.4	-23.1	-6.7	-17.7	-4.6
2006	-26.8	-6.0	-18.1	-5.9	-9.3	-4.1	-8.4	-1.9	-4.1	-1.3	-19.4	-5.8	-16.8	-4.4
2007	-25.9	-6.0	-14.0	-4.6	-5.9	-3.2	-7.2	-1.6	-5.1	-1.3	-17.9	-5.5	-15.6	-4.1
2008	-21.4	-5.0	-10.5	-3.5	-2.7	-2.1	-5.6	-1.3	-6.0	-1.3	-13.1	-4.0	-12.6	-3.3
2009	-13.9	-3.1	-17.5	-5.6	-5.7	-2.9	-5.1	-1.1	-8.2	-1.8	-14.8	-4.3	-11.5	-3.0
2010	-14.3	-3.4	-14.0	-4.5	-9.3	-4.1	-2.6	-0.6	-7.3	-1.7	-12.9	-3.8	-10.6	-2.8
2011	-12.3	-3.0	-9.6	-3.1	-9.1	-4.2	-1.7	-0.4	-7.2	-1.6	-10.2	-3.0	-8.9	-2.4
2012	-8.8	-2.1	-7.1	-2.2	-13.2	-5.6	-1.7	-0.4	-6.9	-1.6	-11.2	-3.2	-7.6	-2.1
2013	-7.3	-1.6	-6.7	-2.1	-11.6	-5.3	-3.8	-0.9	-5.4	-1.4	-11.2	-3.2	-7.1	-1.9
2014	-6.4	-1.4	-12.9	-4.1	-11.9	-5.3	-4.6	-1.2	-5.4	-1.4	-11.1	-3.2	-7.5	-2.0
2015	-3.0	-0.6	-33.0	-10.3	-14.8	-5.3	-3.6	-0.9	-5.6	-1.7	-14.7	-4.3	-7.2	-2.0
2016	-4.0	-0.9	-36.3	-10.9	-14.5	-5.1	-2.5	-0.6	-8.1	-2.2	-17.0	-4.9	-8.1	-2.2
2017	-4.6	-1.1	-22.6	-6.9	-12.5	-4.5	-1.2	-0.4	-7.8	-2.1	-14.5	-4.2	-7.1	-2.0
2018	-4.3	-1.3	-19.8	-6.0	-8.1	-3.2	-4.9	-1.1	-6.7	-1.5	-9.7	-2.8	-6.5	-1.9
2019	-4.0	-1.2	-20.0	-6.1	-9.4	-3.6	-6.0	-1.7	-5.4	-1.4	-8.5	-2.6	-6.3	-1.9

Source: Own elaborations on UNCTAD-EORA, IMF, WB, and ILO data.

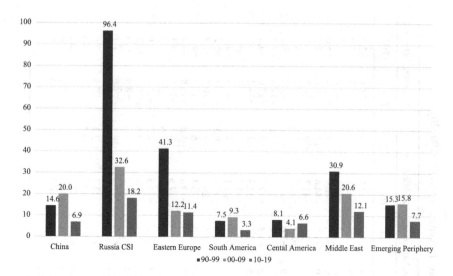

Figure 6.8 Emerging Periphery regions: Outflow total value transfers. Percentage of GDP, ten-year average, 1990–2019. (*Source*: Own elaborations on UNCTAD-EORA, IMF, WB, and ILO data.)

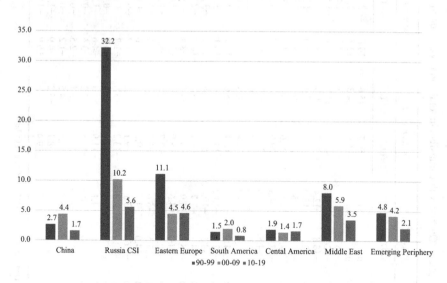

Figure 6.9 Emerging Periphery regions: Outflow GVC value transfers. Percentage of GDP, ten-year average, 1990–2019. (*Source*: Own elaborations on UNCTAD-EORA, IMF, WB, and ILO data.)

analyse later, accepted the conditions of economic and financial liberalization imposed by the International Monetary Fund in return for international loans. The consequence for each of them has been a drastic worsening of the international terms of trade and a huge increase in value outflows through unequal exchange that have far exceeded the number of financial resources received from abroad, sometimes definitively interrupting a process of progressive upgrading previously started. The data presented on unequal exchange show that neoliberal solutions, imposed by international economic organizations in those years as a counterpart to international financial aid, have had the effect of reaffirming and accentuating the position of productive and commercial dependence of these countries on multi-national capital, and also playing a non-secondary role for the implementation of GVCs on an increasingly larger scale.

6.3.4 The donors: Outflow value transfers in the Poor Periphery

The picture that emerges from Table 6.6 and Figure 6.10, concerning the transfers of value in billions of dollars from the poorest regions of the planet to the richest countries, is impressive.

During the last 30 years of neoliberal globalization, transfers of value from the Poor Periphery to the Centre have continuously increased more than eight times, reaching $2,265 billion in 2019, a value only slightly less than the total annual GDP of countries like the United Kingdom or France. Even faster has been the increase in value transfers within GVCs, which have increased almost 12 times from 1990 to 2019, reaching over $700 billion at the end of the period. Looking at the individual regions, the impetuous increase in outward value transfers in Southeast Asia and Indian South Asia is striking. Over the last decade, after the 2008 crisis, this part of Asia has become by far the centre of gravity of unequal global trade, more than offsetting the Chinese upgrading in global production and trade.

Data on value transfers as a share of GDP, shown in Table 6.7 and Figures 6.11 and 6.12, reveal that unequal trade is a decisive factor in the economic underde-velopment of the poorest regions of the global economy.

On overall average, the burden of unequal exchange over the three decades has fluctuated between one-third and one-fifth of the total GDP of the Poor Periphery, peaking in the first decade of the century. As had already happened on a smaller scale for India following the crisis of 1991, in Southeast Asia, the percentage rose dramatically after the crisis of the Asian Tigers in 1998, which involved the whole area, causing the collapse of the regional banking system, a prolonged recession, and massive currency devaluations. It was from that moment that this region became the main protagonist of unequal exchange and also within GVCs became the main reservoir of a qualified and low-cost labour force for the delocal-ized production of multinational corporations. For South Asia, on the other hand, the increase in outward value transfers, both total and within GVCs, is particu-larly concentrated after the great crisis of 2008, when India and other countries

Table 6.6 Poor Periphery: Outflow value transfers in total and GVC trade in value added. Billions of current dollars, 1990–2019

	South Asia		Southeast Asia		Central Asia		North Africa		Sub-Saharan Africa		Poor Periphery	
	TOT	GVC	TOT	GVC	TOT	GVC	TOT	GVC	TOT	GVC	TOT	GVC
1990	−41	−8	−165	−34	−12	−2	−27	−8	−33	−8	−278	−60
1991	−56	−11	−173	−37	−15	−2	−40	−12	−33	−8	−317	−70
1992	−43	−8	−113	−33	−162	−23	−29	−9	−20	−5	−367	−78
1993	−60	−12	−142	−36	−83	−14	−33	−10	−28	−7	−346	−79
1994	−71	−14	−172	−42	−52	−10	−45	−14	−38	−9	−378	−89
1995	−96	−20	−223	−53	−43	−8	−56	−18	−38	−10	−456	−109
1996	−105	−23	−248	−61	−46	−9	−61	−20	−43	−11	−503	−125
1997	−103	−21	−267	−60	−44	−9	−57	−18	−38	−9	−509	−118
1998	−105	−22	−397	−95	−37	−8	−52	−17	−39	−10	−631	−153
1999	−110	−23	−328	−79	−44	−9	−56	−18	−64	−16	−601	−146
2000	−127	−28	−367	−86	−45	−10	−64	−21	−67	−18	−671	−163
2001	−125	−28	−377	−84	−53	−12	−65	−22	−71	−19	−691	−165
2002	−137	−30	−357	−86	−54	−12	−81	−27	−76	−21	−704	−175
2003	−161	−36	−427	−105	−58	−13	−103	−35	−71	−19	−821	−209
2004	−209	−49	−553	−121	−61	−14	−122	−42	−71	−20	−1,016	−245
2005	−249	−59	−641	−160	−62	−15	−133	−46	−71	−20	−1,156	−300
2006	−291	−73	−684	−175	−68	−17	−151	−54	−76	−22	−1,270	−341
2007	−339	−86	−769	−198	−71	−18	−176	−64	−96	−29	−1,451	−395
2008	−484	−126	−882	−230	−74	−19	−193	−72	−123	−38	−1,756	−485
2009	−372	−90	−700	−176	−73	−17	−179	−64	−99	−29	−1,423	−376
2010	−469	−118	−749	−194	−82	−19	−208	−76	−109	−32	−1,616	−440
2011	−579	−149	−848	−225	−92	−22	−177	−65	−104	−31	−1,800	−492
2012	−608	−154	−834	−220	−82	−19	−163	−59	−104	−30	−1,791	−484
2013	−675	−171	−892	−231	−78	−18	−160	−59	−118	−35	−1,923	−514
2014	−688	−172	−1,023	−211	−99	−23	−161	−59	−135	−40	−2,105	−505
2015	−559	−134	−889	−185	−107	−21	−171	−63	−134	−38	−1,861	−442
2016	−577	−142	−892	−190	−140	−33	−185	−69	−159	−46	−1,953	−480
2017	−573	−138	−969	−253	−172	−40	−226	−82	−139	−40	−2,078	−553
2018	−613	−225	−1,064	−307	−205	−53	−204	−75	−137	−44	−2,222	−704
2019	−632	−225	−1,068	−301	−214	−54	−205	−75	−146	−46	−2,265	−701

Source: Own elaborations on UNCTAD-EORA, IMF, WB, and ILO data.

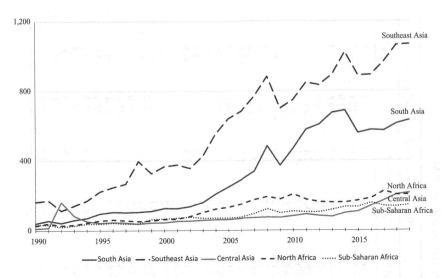

Figure 6.10 Poor Periphery regions: Outflow total value transfers. Billions of dollars, 1990–2019. (*Source*: Own elaborations on UNCTAD-EORA, IMF, WB, and ILO data.)

in the region, such as Bangladesh, experienced an increase in their role within global supply chains, partially replacing the reorientation of the Chinese economy towards positions of greater national economic autonomy. In the other regions of the Poor Periphery, what stands out is the great burden of unequal exchange on the North African economies, further increased after the political crises of the Arab Spring in the second half of the last decade, and the growth in outward value transfers from Central Asian countries, particularly Turkey, in recent years. Finally, the relatively low outflow of value from Sub-Saharan Africa, by far the poorest region, reflects the marginality of this region from the circuit of the global capitalist market, rather than better economic performance.

6.4 The relevance of unequal exchange in the actual global economy

The analysis previously carried out shows that unequal exchange has been a phenomenon of absolute importance in the globalized economy over the last 30 years. The value transfers implicit in the market transactions of goods and services between countries through international trade significantly contribute to the reproduction of the inequalities of income and economic development between the Centre and the Peripheries of the world economy. The data highlighted the continuous reproduction of a stable dualistic global economic structure. It is characterized by a small group of developed countries that capture a higher value than the value domestically produced through international trade to the detriment of a larger group of countries with a lower level of economic development, where the vast majority of the world's population lives,

Table 6.7 Poor Periphery: Outflow value transfers in total and GVC trade in value added. Percentage of GDP, 1990–2019

	South Asia		Southeast Asia		Central Asia		North Africa		Sub-Saharan Africa		Poor Periphery	
	TOT	GVC	TOT	GVC	TOT	GVC	TOT	GVC	TOT	GVC	TOT	GVC
1990	-9.5	-1.8	-44.0	-9.1	-5.5	-1.1	-11.8	-3.7	-8.7	-2.0	-17.1	-3.7
1991	-14.5	-2.8	-41.1	-8.7	-6.9	-1.2	-23.0	-7.1	-8.6	-2.0	-20.1	-4.4
1992	-10.5	-2.0	-23.7	-6.9	-70.2	-10.0	-16.1	-5.1	-5.3	-1.3	-21.9	-4.7
1993	-14.8	-2.9	-26.6	-6.8	-31.0	-5.3	-18.3	-5.5	-7.3	-1.7	-19.5	-4.4
1994	-15.4	-3.1	-28.1	-6.8	-25.1	-4.7	-25.1	-7.8	-10.2	-2.4	-20.6	-4.8
1995	-18.7	-4.0	-31.3	-7.4	-15.6	-3.0	-28.6	-9.3	-8.2	-2.1	-21.1	-5.1
1996	-19.0	-4.1	-31.3	-7.7	-15.3	-3.3	-28.1	-9.2	-8.3	-2.2	-21.1	-5.2
1997	-17.7	-3.7	-35.6	-8.0	-14.0	-2.9	-25.3	-8.2	-7.0	-1.7	-21.1	-4.9
1998	-17.9	-3.8	-78.1	-18.6	-11.3	-2.5	-22.6	-7.4	-7.2	-1.9	-28.7	-6.9
1999	-17.6	-3.7	-54.7	-13.2	-14.2	-3.0	-22.8	-7.4	-16.2	-4.1	-27.7	-6.7
2000	-19.9	-4.4	-57.6	-13.4	-13.9	-3.0	-24.9	-8.3	-16.7	-4.5	-29.7	-7.2
2001	-19.2	-4.2	-61.5	-13.7	-20.6	-4.6	-25.9	-8.6	-18.4	-5.0	-32.0	-7.6
2002	-19.9	-4.4	-52.1	-12.6	-18.0	-3.9	-34.6	-11.4	-18.2	-4.9	-30.3	-7.5
2003	-20.1	-4.6	-55.2	-13.6	-15.0	-3.3	-39.9	-13.3	-13.5	-3.7	-29.9	-7.6
2004	-22.5	-5.2	-63.5	-13.9	-12.1	-2.8	-41.9	-14.3	-10.9	-3.0	-31.3	-7.6
2005	-23.5	-5.6	-66.0	-16.5	-9.9	-2.3	-39.1	-13.5	-9.2	-2.6	-30.7	-8.0
2006	-24.1	-6.0	-58.7	-15.0	-9.4	-2.3	-39.0	-14.0	-8.5	-2.5	-29.0	-7.8
2007	-22.2	-5.6	-55.2	-14.2	-7.9	-2.0	-38.4	-14.1	-9.2	-2.8	-27.3	-7.4
2008	-31.1	-8.1	-54.3	-14.2	-7.1	-1.8	-34.9	-13.0	-10.2	-3.2	-29.4	-8.1
2009	-21.8	-5.3	-43.7	-11.0	-8.0	-1.9	-34.3	-12.2	-8.7	-2.5	-24.2	-6.4
2010	-22.5	-5.7	-37.7	-9.8	-7.5	-1.8	-34.8	-12.8	-8.1	-2.3	-22.7	-6.2
2011	-25.7	-6.6	-36.8	-9.8	-7.4	-1.8	-28.2	-10.3	-6.7	-2.0	-22.6	-6.2
2012	-26.6	-6.8	-34.2	-9.0	-6.3	-1.5	-22.9	-8.4	-6.5	-1.9	-21.4	-5.8
2013	-28.7	-7.3	-35.4	-9.2	-5.4	-1.3	-22.8	-8.4	-6.9	-2.0	-22.1	-5.9
2014	-26.8	-6.7	-40.3	-8.3	-7.0	-1.6	-22.9	-8.4	-7.5	-2.2	-23.4	-5.6
2015	-20.8	-5.0	-36.2	-7.5	-8.5	-1.6	-25.9	-9.6	-8.3	-2.4	-21.4	-5.1
2016	-19.9	-4.9	-34.7	-7.4	-11.6	-2.7	-28.2	-10.5	-10.6	-3.1	-22.1	-5.4
2017	-17.4	-4.2	-35.1	-9.2	-14.2	-3.3	-28.2	-14.0	-8.7	-2.5	-22.0	-5.9
2018	-17.8	-6.5	-41.2	-11.9	-17.7	-4.6	-38.6	-12.0	-8.2	-2.6	-23.4	-7.4
2019	-17.3	-6.1	-38.8	-11.0	-18.7	-4.7	-30.8	-11.2	-8.4	-2.7	-22.8	-7.0

Source: Own elaborations on UNCTAD-EORA, IMF, WB, and ILO data.

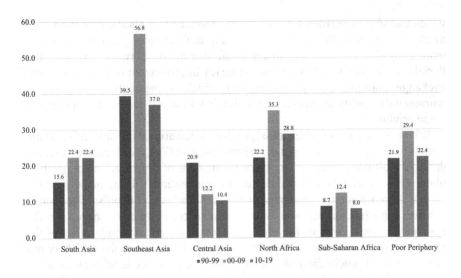

Figure 6.11 Poor Periphery regions: Outflow total value transfers. Percentage of GDP, ten-year average, 1990–2019. (*Source*: Own elaborations on UNCTAD-EORA, IMF, WB, and ILO data.)

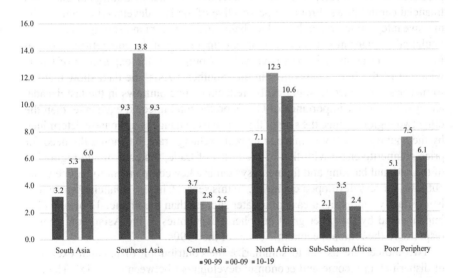

Figure 6.12 Poor Periphery regions: Outflow GVC value transfers. Percentage of GDP, ten-year average, 1990–2019. (*Source*: own elaborations on UNCTAD-EORA, IMF, WB, and ILO data.)

which transfer a considerable part of the produced value abroad. Within each of the two groups, the situation is largely differentiated both spatially and temporally. Particularly significant is the distinction between an Emerging Periphery, characterized by a slow but steady improvement of its international exchange relations, and a Poor Periphery, which, on the contrary, has steadily worsened the ability to capture and maintain within the domestic economy the value produced.

With regard to the channels through which international transfers of value are achieved, we have observed that the relative share of GVCs has steadily increased during the 30 years in question. The new methods of organization and international division of labour implemented by multinational firms, made possible by new information and communication technologies and neoliberal economic policies, constitute an increasingly important source of value drainage from the Periphery to the Centre of the global economic system. The relocation of the more labour-intensive stages of production from the Centre to the Periphery has provided a dual benefit for multinational capital. On the one hand, it has reduced the bargaining power of workers in capitalistically developed countries through increased unemployment and the precariousness of labour contracts. On the other hand, it has provided multinational capital with a new tool to capture the value produced in less developed countries, additional to that of traditional trade and financial capital flows. From the perspective of the less developed countries, the massive integration into global value chains does not seem in itself to produce particular advantages in terms of the strategic upgrading of the competitive position in the appropriation of international value. Comparing the experience of China with that of the Indian subcontinent and Southeast Asia, the data show that the former has succeeded in significantly reducing value outflows in the last decade, along with a lower importance of GVCs on the total unequal exchange, than the other two regions. Since the size of the unequal exchange is ultimately determined by the country's ability to manage its real exchange rate, balancing the need for price competitiveness with that of the terms of trade, the control and regulation of the national banking and financial system is a key complement to reduce value outflows for less developed countries. In this sense, Chinese financial protectionism certainly represents a case of greater success than the financial liberalization implemented by the other great peripheral economies of the Asian continent in response to the regional economic crises of the 1990s.

Two indices are useful to summarize the contribution of unequal exchange of disparities in income and economic development between countries. The first index displays annual per capita value transfers expressed in current dollars, as Table 6.8 shows for the year 2019. It is possible to look at these transfers of value as a tribute that every inhabitant of the Periphery pays on average to the Centre, and in parallel as a monetary benefit that every inhabitant of the Centre receives on average from the Periphery.

As can be seen from Table 6.8, in absolute terms, the value transfers resulting from the unequal exchange are substantial and contribute decisively to determine

Table 6.8 Per capita value transfers in total, GVC, and domestic net exports in current dollars, 2019

Geographic areas		Value transfer per capita		
Groups	Regions	UE total	UE in GVC	UE in domestic net exports
Centre	North America	2,679	760	1,919
	Western Europe	6,920	1,871	5,049
	Oceania	3,635	915	2,720
	EMU	4,837	1,296	3,541
	East Asia	2,537	1,459	1,078
	Total	**3,810**	**1,174**	**2,636**
Emerging Periphery	Eastern Europe	−1,309	−507	−803
	China	−426	−128	−298
	Russia and CSI	−1,850	−563	−1,288
	Middle East	−950	−297	−652
	Central America	−454	−118	−336
	South America	−490	−140	−350
	Total	**−634**	**−194**	**−440**
Poor Periphery	Central Asia	−994	−251	−743
	Southeast Asia	−1,631	−460	−1,171
	North Africa	−1,033	−378	−655
	South Asia	−352	−125	−226
	Sub-Saharan Africa	−133	−42	−91
	Total	**−571**	**−177**	**−394**

the national per capita income, upwards for the regions of the Centre and downwards for those of the Periphery. On average, a citizen living in one of the richest countries in the world received the considerable sum of $3,810 from the poorest countries in 2019, in the form of transfers of value implicit in foreign trade relations, of which $1,174 was through GVCs. For the two central European regions, this figure is very impressive, amounting to more than $400 per capita per month for EMU citizens and an astonishing $576 per capita per month for Western European citizens. The same impression, in the opposite direction, is generated by the hundreds and thousands of dollars per year transferred on average by each citizen of the poorest regions of the world to the richest regions. It should be noted, anyway, that these data refer to the aggregate average of the per capita value transfers received or made by each individual region, and from them nothing can be deduced about their distribution between labour or capital income within the receiving countries. What can be said, however, without forcing the meaning of the data, is that the wage-bargaining process between capital and labour in the Centre's countries is made less conflictual by the existence of a rent stemming from the unequal exchange with the Periphery.

The second index, which I define as the unequal exchange (UE) dependency index, is inspired by the concept of economic surplus developed by Paul Baran (1957), who identified the withdrawal of resources from the process of capital accumulation of the less developed countries as the main effect of unequal economic relations at the international level. The dependency index is defined by the following formula:

$$UE \text{ Dependency index} = \frac{T^{UE}}{\left|T^{UE}\right| + GKF}$$

where:

T^{UE} = value transfers in international trade;
GKF = gross capital formation.

For peripheral countries, which experience value outflows through unequal exchange, the denominator represents the total economic surplus potentially available within the domestic economy, and the dependency index, ranging between the values of 0 and −1, indicates the share of potentially available economic surplus transferred abroad. For central countries, the index ranges from 0 to 1 and indicates the contribution of value inflows from abroad to the capital accumulation process. When the index is below 0.5, capital accumulation is partly supported by the contribution of unequal exchange and, for the difference between 0.5 and the index value, partly by domestic resources, while when it exceeds 0.5, value inflows from abroad fully cover capital accumulation and in addition support domestic levels of private and public consumption. Table 6.9 shows the dependency ratio calculated for 2018.

In 2018, for seven peripheral regions, the outflow of value abroad through unequal exchange was more than a quarter of the potentially available economic

Table 6.9 Unequal Exchange Dependency Index, 2018

Groups	Regions	UE Dependency Index
Centre	North America	0.16
	Western Europe	0.41
	Oceania	0.27
	EMU	0.37
	East Asia	0.20
Emerging Periphery	Eastern Europe	−0.28
	China	−0.09
	Russia and CSI	−0.49
	Middle East	−0.22
	Central America	−0.22
	South America	−0.12
Poor Periphery	Central Asia	−0.39
	Southeast Asia	−0.59
	North Africa	−0.57
	South Asia	−0.39
	Sub-Saharan Africa	−0.28

surplus, and for three of them (Russia, Southeast Asia, and North Africa), it was equal to or more than half. Conversely, the central regions of Europe are significantly more dependent on foreign value inflows for the capital accumulation process than the other central regions. As can be seen, the usefulness of this indicator lies in the possibility of capturing in a concise form the position of economic dependence from abroad of a crucial variable in the economic development of a country such as domestic capital accumulation. Therefore, the monitoring over time of this index could provide interesting indications on the hierarchical position of the different countries within the global economic structure.

Notes

1 See Amin (1976), Gibson (1980), Joseph and Tomlinson (1991), Marelli (1983), Nakajima and Izumi (1995), Webber and Foot (1984), and Williams (1985).

2 The measure of value transfers based on the unequal exchange model of Chapter 5, presented by Ricci (2019a), was made using gross export data derived from the WIOD database.

3 The issue of GVCs was introduced in the literature in the early 1990s, see Gereffi and Korzeniewicz (1994). Since then, a large number of publications have been dedicated to the spatial organization of firm activities on a global scale, which adopted different terminologies to define the phenomenon, depending on the approaches and intellectual traditions, e.g. commodity chains, supply chains, value networks, global production networks. For a sympathetic detailed review of the literature, see Hernández and Pedersen (2017). For critical discussions of this approach from a Marxist perspective, see Starosta (2010) and Selwyn (2012, 2015).

4 On the spatial, social, and political effects of the new international division of labour, see Taylor (2008) and Charnock and Starosta (2016).

5 See Madumbi (2008) and also Kraemer, Linden, and Dedrick (2011) on Apple's case. Lauesen and Cope (2015) oppose the "sour smiley" of Marxist value to the happy "smiley curve" of the market price.

6 On the current relevance of the category of aristocracy of labour, see the debate between Post (2014) and Cope (2013, 2014).

7 See Milanovic (2016).

8 On the negative impact of GVCs on labour share on income in the US, see Milberg and Winkler (2013, chap. 5).

9 See World Bank (2020).

10 On the "upgrading" strategies of development for peripheral countries, see Cattaneo, Gereffi, and Staritz (2010) and van Dijk and Trienekens (2012).

11 On this line of research, see Heintz (2006), Smith (2016), Roy (2017), and Suwandi (2019).

12 When international trade is totally liberalized in a fully integrated single market, this phenomenon can give rise to monetary dumping, with massive relocations of traditional manufacturing industries to less developed countries of the area, as happened within the European Union, see Ricci (2015, 2019b).

13 The net product corresponds to the national income as showed by Sraffa (1960, chap. 2, p. 11): "The national income of a system in a self-replacing state consists in the set of commodities which are left over when from the national gross product we have removed item by item the articles which go to replace the means of production used up in all the industries. The value of this set of commodities, or 'composite commodity'... forms the national income".

14 The UNCTAD-EORA Global Value Chain (GVC) database offers global coverage (189 countries and a "Rest of World" region) and a time series from 1990 to 2019 of the key GVC indicators, see https://worldmrio.com/unctadgvc/. The data used for our calculations refer to the country-by-country breakdown set. On the methodological aspects of the dataset, see Casella, Bolwijn, Moran, and Kanemoto (2019).

15 On the features of U.S.'s "Rentier Economy" in the world economy see Baiman (2014).

Bibliography

Amin, S. (1976). *Unequal development: An essay on the social formations of peripheral capitalism.* New York: Monthly Review Press.

Baiman, R. (2014). Unequal exchange and the rentier economy. *Review of Radical Political Economics 46*(4), 536–557.

Baran, P. (1957). *The political economy of growth.* New York: Monthly Review Press.

Casella, B., Bolwijn, Moran, D., and Kanemoto, K. (2019). Improving the analysis of global value chains: the UNCTAD-Eora Database. *Transnational Corporations, 26*(3). United Nations, 115–142.

Cattaneo, O., Gereffi, G., and Staritz, C. (Eds.). (2010). *Global value chains in a postcrisis world: A development perspective.* Washington, DC: The World Bank.

Charnock, G., and Starosta, G. (Eds.). (2016). *The new international division of labour global transformation and uneven development.* London: Palgrave Macmillan.

Cope, Z. (2013). Global wage scaling and left ideology: A critique of Charles post on the 'labour aristocracy'. *Research in Political Economy, 28,* 89–129.

Cope, Z. (2014). Final Comments on Charles Post's Critique of the Theory of the Labour Aristocracy. *Research in Political Economy, 29,* 275–286.

Gereffi, G., and Korzeniewicz, M. (Eds.). (1994). *Commodity chains and global capitalism.* Santa Barbara, CA: ABC-CLIO.

Gibson, B. (1980). Unequal exchange: Theoretical issues and empirical findings. *Review of Radical Political Economics, 12*(3), 15–35.

Heintz, J. (2006). Low-wage manufacturing and global commodity chains: A model in the unequal exchange tradition. *Cambridge Journal of Economics, 30*(4), 507–520.

Hernández, V., and Pedersen, T. (2017). Global value chain configuration: A review and research agenda. *BRQ Business Research Quarterly, 20*(2), 137–150.

Joseph, G. G., and Tomlinson, M. (1991). Testing the existence and measuring the magnitude of unequal exchange resulting from international trade: A Marxian approach. *Indian Economic Review, 26*(2), 123–48.

Kraemer, K. L., Linden, G., and Dedrick, J. (2011). *Capturing value in global networks: Apple's iPad and iPhone.* Alfred P. Sloan Foundation and the US National Science Foundation (CISE/IIS).

Lauesen, T., and Cope, Z. (2015). Imperialism and the transformation of values into prices. *Monthly Review, 67*(3), 54–67.

Marelli, E. (1983). Empirical estimation of intersectoral and interregional transfers of surplus value: The case of Italy. *Journal of Regional Science, 23*(1), 49–70.

Milanovic, B. (2016). *Global inequality: A new approach for the age of globalization.* Cambridge, MA: Harvard University Press.

Milberg, W., and Winkler, D. (2013). *Outsourcing economics: global value chains in capitalist development.* Cambridge: Cambridge University Press.

Mudambi, R. (2008). Location, control and innovation in knowledge-intensive industries. *Journal of Economic Geography, 8*(5), 699–725.

Nakajima, A., and Izumi, H. (1995). Economic development and unequal exchange among nations: Analysis of the U.S., Japan, and South Korea. *Review of Radical Political Economics, 27*(3), 86–94.

Post, C. (2014). The roots of working class reformism and conservatism: A response to Zak Cope's defense of the "labor aristocracy" thesis. *Research in Political Economy, 29*, 241–260.

Ricci, A. (2015). La competitività industriale nell'Unione Europea: un confronto tra l'Italia e i Paesi dell'Europa orientale. *Argomenti, 1*, 91–113.

Ricci, A. (2019a). Unequal exchange in the age of globalization. *Review of Radical Political Economics, 51*(2), 225–245.

Ricci, A. (2019b). Is there social or monetary dumping in the European Union? Manufacturing competitiveness in Central and Eastern Europe. *Entrepreneurial Business and Economics Review, 7*(1), 159–180.

Roy, S. (2017). Rent and surplus in the Global Production Network: Identifying 'value capture' from the South. *Agrarian South: Journal of Political Economy, 6*(1), 32–52.

Selwyn, B. (2012). Beyond firm-centrism: Re-integrating labour and capitalism into global commodity chain analysis. *Journal of Economic Geography, 12*(1), 205–226.

Selwyn, B. (2015). Commodity chains, creative destruction and global inequality: a class analysis. *Journal of Economic Geography, 15*(2), 253–274.

Smith, J. (2016). *Imperialism in the twenty-first century: Globalization, super exploitation and capitalism's final crisis*. New York: Monthly Review Press.

Sraffa, P. (1960). *Production of commodities by means of commodities: Prelude to a critique of economic theory*. Cambridge: Cambridge University Press.

Starosta, G. (2010). Global commodity chains and the Marxian law of value. *Antipode, 42*(2), 433–465.

Suwandi, I. (2019). *Value chains: The new economic imperialism*. Monthly Review Press.

Taylor, M. (Ed.) (2008). *Global economy contested. Power and conflict across the international division of labour*. London: Routledge.

van Dijk, M. P., and Trienekens, J. (Eds.). (2012). *Global Value Chains. Linking local producers from developing countries to international markets*. Amsterdam: Amsterdam University Press.

Webber, M. J., and Foot, S. P. H. (1984). The measurement of unequal exchange. *Environment and Planning A, 16*(7), 927–947.

Williams, K. M. (1985). Is "unequal exchange" a mechanism for perpetuating inequality in the modern world system? *Studies in Comparative International Development (SCID), 20*(3), 47–73.

World Bank. (2020). *Trading for development in the age of global value chains. World Development Report 2020*. Washington, DC: The World Bank.

Appendix 6.1 Country classification in geographical regions

North Africa: Algeria, Egypt, Libya, Morocco, Tunisia.

Sub-Saharan Africa: Angola, Benin, Botswana, Burkina Faso, Burundi, Cameroon, Cape Verde, Central African, Chad, Congo Dem., Congo Republic of, Côte d'Ivoire, Djibouti, Eritrea, Ethiopia, Gabon, Gambia,

Ghana, Guinea, Kenya, Lesotho, Liberia, Madagascar, Malawi, Mali, Mauritania, Mauritius, Mozambique, Namibia, Niger, Nigeria, Rwanda, São Tomé, Senegal, Seychelles, Sierra Leone, Somalia, South Africa, South Sudan, Sudan, Swaziland, Tanzania, Togo, Uganda, Zambia, Zimbabwe.

Oceania: Australia, Fiji, New Zealand, Papua New Guinea, Samoa, Vanuatu.

China: China, Hong Kong SAR, Macao SAR, Taiwan.

East Asia: Japan, South Korea, Singapore.

South Asia: Bangladesh, Bhutan, India, Maldives, Nepal, Pakistan, Sri Lanka.

Southeast Asia: Brunei Darussalam, Cambodia, Indonesia, Lao People's, Malaysia, Myanmar, Philippines, Thailand, Vietnam.

Central Asia and the Caucasus: Afghanistan, Azerbaijan, Armenia, Georgia, Kazakhstan, Kyrgyz Republic, Tajikistan, Turkmenistan, Turkey, Uzbekistan, Mongolia.

Western Europe: Denmark, Iceland, Norway, San Marino, Sweden, Switzerland, United Kingdom.

Eastern Europe: Albania, Bosnia, Bulgaria, Croatia, Czech Republic, Hungary, Macedonia, Montenegro, Poland, Romania, Serbia.

Russia and CSI: Moldova, Russia, Ukraine, Belarus.

EMU: Austria, Belgium, Cyprus, Finland, France, Germany, Greece, Ireland, Italy, Luxembourg, Malta, Netherlands, Portugal, Spain, Latvia, Lithuania, Estonia, Slovak Republic, Slovenia.

Middle East: Bahrain, Iran, Iraq, Israel, Jordan, Kuwait, Lebanon, Oman, Qatar, Saudi Arabia, Syrian Arab, United Arab, Yemen.

Central America and Caribbean: Bahamas, Antigua, Aruba, Barbados, Belize, Costa Rica, Dominican Rep., El Salvador, Guatemala, Haiti, Honduras, Jamaica, Mexico, Nicaragua, Panama, Trinidad and Tobago.

North America: Canada, United States.

South America: Argentina, Bolivia, Brazil, Chile, Colombia, Ecuador, Guyana, Paraguay, Peru, Suriname, Uruguay, Venezuela.

INDEX

223